Royal Academy Illustrated 2000

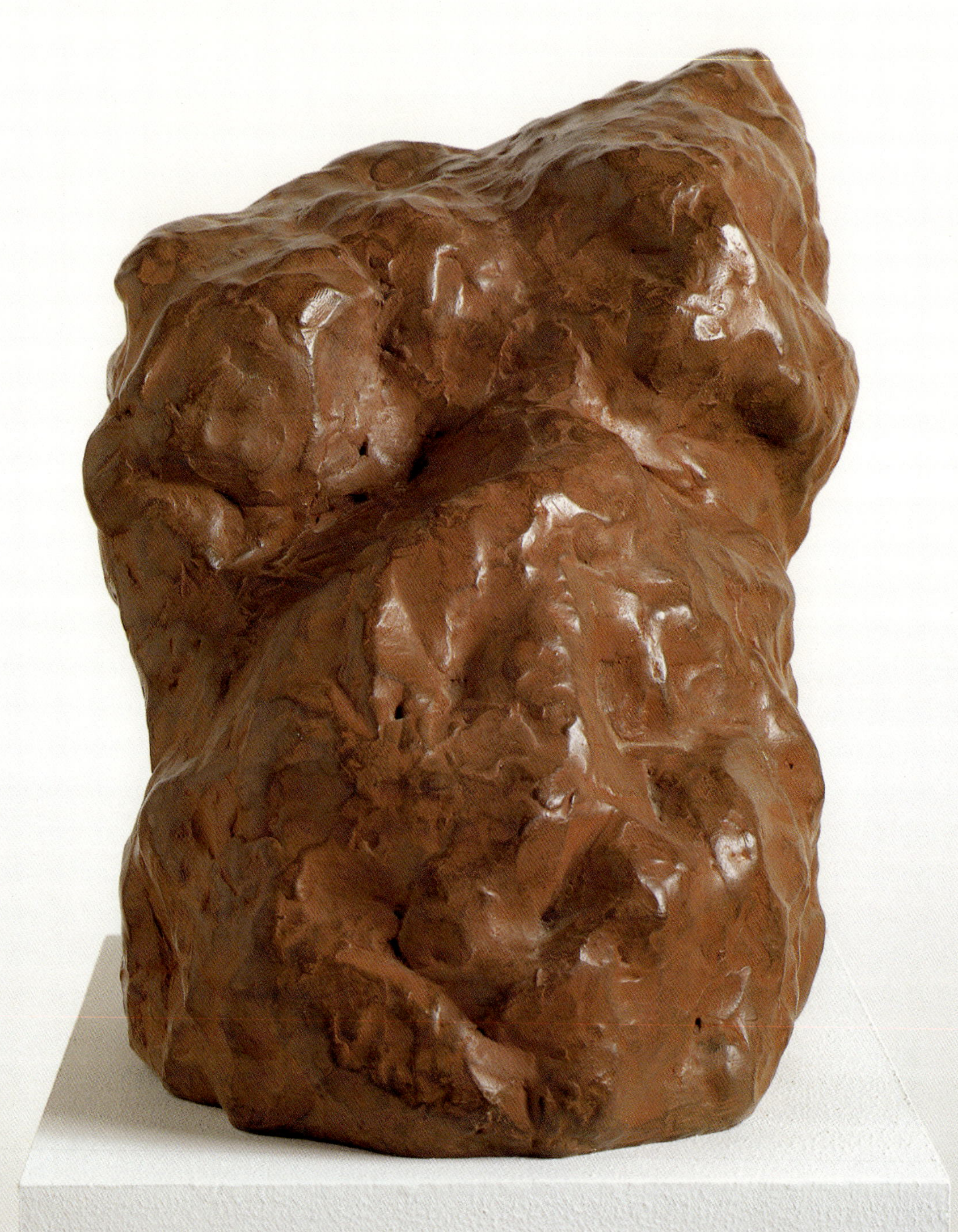

We shall not cease from exploration
And the end of all our exploring
Will be to arrive where we started
And know the place for the first time.

T.S. Eliot. *Four Quartets – Little Gidding*

Royal Academy Illustrated 2000

A Selection from the 232nd Summer Exhibition

Edited by Paul Huxley RA

Sponsored by

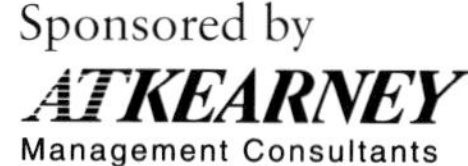

ROYAL ACADEMY OF ARTS

Contents

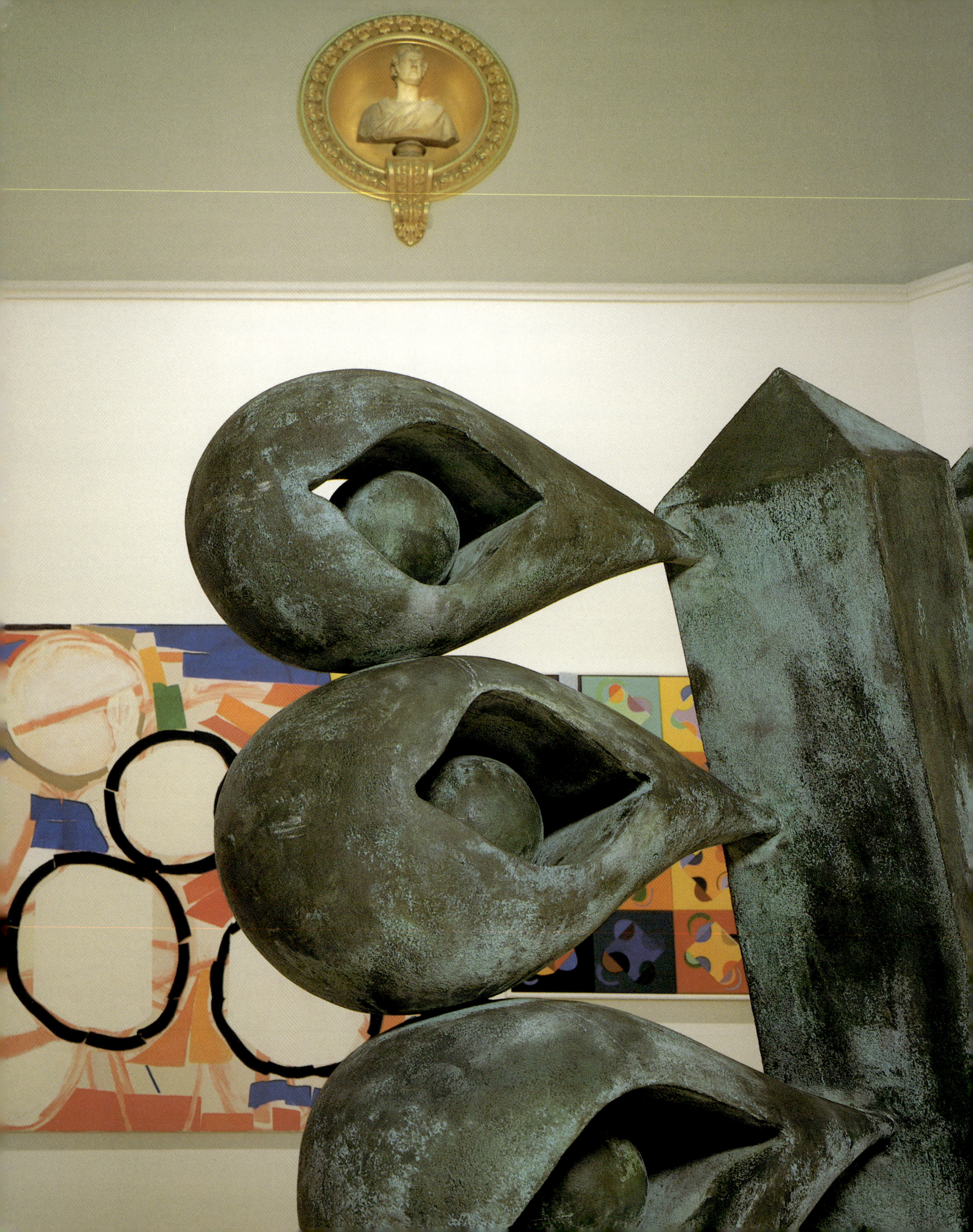

SPONSOR'S PREFACE

A.T. Kearney celebrates more than seventy years of service to global business, the arts and charitable organisations around the world. Once again we are pleased to sponsor the Summer Exhibition.

This year we continued to explore ideas with the Royal Academy to show the links between arts and business. Four Royal Academicians were asked to give their impressions of the business of four of our clients, which we called 'Portraits of Business'. We hope that these works, hanging in the vestibule, will inspire dialogue between arts and business.

A.T. Kearney is one of the leading management consulting firms in the world. We assist organisations to develop practical plans for growth in new and existing markets and business sectors. We help businesses develop world class operations that serve customers in a superior and competitively differentiated manner. We are known for our collaborative style and for working at every level in client organisations.

In the same way an artist presents the viewer with a new perspective of a familiar object or issue, we seek to help our clients see their business issues in a different light. We believe we are ambitious, pragmatic and imaginative, all qualities required to be an 'artist in business'.

We believe strongly in the power of art and artists. We believe that in business, as in art, creativity, inspiration and communication can be used as a means to expand the vision and perspectives of people.

We have enjoyed our relationship with the Royal Academy in sponsoring this year's exhibition. We hope that visitors will be equally enthused about this year's display of variety and innovation.

Jan-Willem Broekhuysen
Managing Director
A.T. Kearney Limited

INTRODUCTION

Anyone with the slightest affection for cinema will know the final scene of the great Orson Welles epic, Citizen Kane, where the camera gradually tracks back across the vast basement of Kane's palace, Xanadu, to reveal acre upon acre of hoarded exotic objects. Eventually the screen is filled to the far horizon with a sea of treasures, both precious and trivial, which would make the Antique Road Show look like your local corner shop. There are times each year when the Royal Academy's galleries resemble this scene, as the 'Hanging' Committee sets about its task to select and hang the annual Summer Exhibition.

In the large central gallery a human chain of helpers pass a continuous stream of art-works along the line for scrutiny and decision by the committee. At this stage typically about 10,000 works are viewed: some receive the dreaded chalked 'X' on the back to denote rejection, some the hopeful 'D' for doubtful and join a pool of submissions (some 5 per cent) for further consideration. It is from this bank that the Academicians draw the pieces for their individual rooms.

There are approximately one hundred Academicians or 'members', each of whom has the privilege to exhibit up to six works in the show. But being an Academician is not all privileges; membership brings with it duties and responsibilities. The Royal Academy is the only institution of its kind with postgraduate schools, an extensive permanent collection and a major exhibition programme which is wholly governed by its artist membership. Members are obliged to take their turn sitting on Council which not only meets every month to debate and decide on matters of policy but selects and hangs the Summer Exhibition. The system guarantees that no consecutive year has the same committee and thus maintains a state of change and renewal.

Artists are not usually professional curators (though there are some exceptions). This is particularly evident in their eccentric approach to hanging the Summer Exhibition. For better or worse this is the character of the show. It is hung by leading artists who are brave enough to allow their own work to be included in a democratic mix, who have contributed their own time and effort and who are willing to pit their own taste and beliefs against those of their colleagues. Although backed by a highly professional team at every level from senior officers to picture handlers, the task is extremely demanding. There is not a single member who does not end each day of selection with the bittersweet mix of feelings which include frustration, affection, respect, empathy, anger, pity, humility and guilt, coupled with sheer physical and ocular exhaustion.

This is the result of the day to day experience. In the background is the much wider responsibility of the Summer Exhibition as a whole. In this context we continue to discuss daily the direction of the show, what we are doing wrong, where we might be going and where the exhibition should be steered next. This debate shapes each year's Summer Exhibition. It is within these discussions that the various points of view become apparent. Some Academicians believe in preserving the recent tradition which has evolved and dominated during our lifetimes: a pluralist and populist inclusion of works at all levels and arranged much in the grand manner of a nineteenth-century salon. Opposed is the thought many of us hold that the exhibition must be returned to its original rather purist purpose: to show the best new works by leading artists of our time. Over the last few years, change has come about, though the progress has been slowed by conflicting opinions which in some cases are passionately held.

The Academy's Summer Exhibition has long been an institution in its own right; one to which a wide church of artists and art followers turn to see who is exhibiting and what is new. However, as familiar and popular as the event is, we have realised that very few visitors know about the process which brings it to fruition. We are thus pulling back the curtain to reveal something of the buzz of activity which consumes the galleries for the weeks prior to the opening. To this end I have provided these background notes and the art critic Andrew Lambirth has interviewed each member of the Hanging Committee on the subject of their own designated gallery. He boldly arrived like Coleridge's person from Porlock to interrupt their work and rouse them from their reveries of Xanadu. Extracts of their discussions follow under each gallery section prefaced by an interview with Anthony Green, the Senior Hanger – the Academician responsible for the overall look of the exhibition.

The Senior Hanger is the most senior member by election of the Hanging Committee. As well as overseeing the hang Green drew up the list of who was to hang which gallery, and was responsible for several galleries himself. 'Some of the Academicians are out of fashion and they have to be honoured. It's only fair. You have to be very diplomatic, you don't want to hurt people. The Academy's changing very very fast. The so-called conservative vote within the Academy is now in a minority, no longer the majority it was until a few years ago.

'It may well be that the Academy's Summer Exhibition is going to see radical changes that would not have been envisaged ten years ago. I would back this. I feel we have to service the needs of the nation artistically and if the young professionals are not sending in their work we have to reach out a helping hand. That's something for the future: we will have it on our agenda in the autumn, because I will put it there. Possibly we should be going out to the studios in the East End of London and saying "We like that picture, why don't you send it in to next year's Summer Exhibition?"

'We could guarantee the picture not the person. That's the key. In the past we've guaranteed the person and not the picture and we've ended up with egg all over our bosom. It may be that the Membership won't want that, but it will be my recommendation in October that we investigate all possibilities to upgrade the send-in. I feel that at the moment we're only addressing a limited section of the community. The send-in this year was weak even by last year's standard which was poor. This exhibition is primarily an exhibition of Academicians, it's not attracting the younger professional artists. This place seems to them to be dyed-in-the-wool and they don't think they've got a chance. We've got to change that. We have to point out that it's actually desirable.

My association with the Academy started in the 1960s when it was very unfashionable. I've never regretted it: every moment has been one of great happiness. And I want to share that with the next generation.'

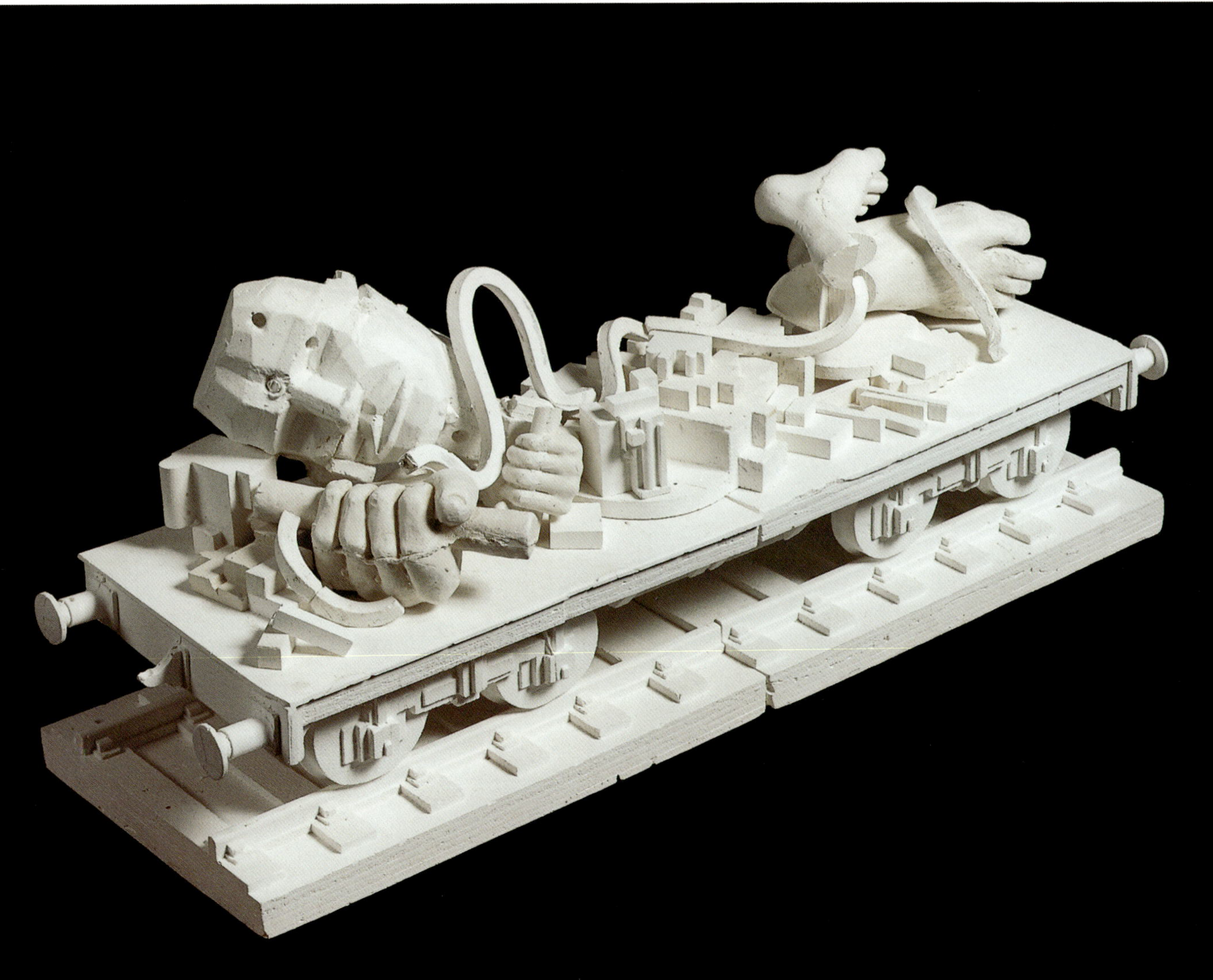

THE ANNENBERG COURTYARD

This spring the Annenberg Courtyard has undergone a major transformation. When completed, it will be an attractive car-free zone of cobbles, granite pavement and fountains: a remarkable outdoor venue for exhibiting sculpture in the heart of London. Eduardo Paolozzi has been chosen as the featured courtyard artist, with a massive railway truck sculpture. The President, Phillip King, explains how this particular work came to be here. 'Eduardo had the idea of having a bronze there in the first place, so when it was decided that the piece should be in wood, we were a bit worried that this was an *ersatz* version. But when I saw the design for the wooden piece I liked it better for our courtyard than the bronze. I think it's more human, somehow. It's certainly not a cheaper version of the original idea. It's been very well made by professional woodworkers costing almost as much as bronze. I'm looking forward to it very much as an extraordinary piece of wood craftsmanship. It'll be quite something to see there will be more variation in colour and texture than if it had been a straightforward cast bronze.'

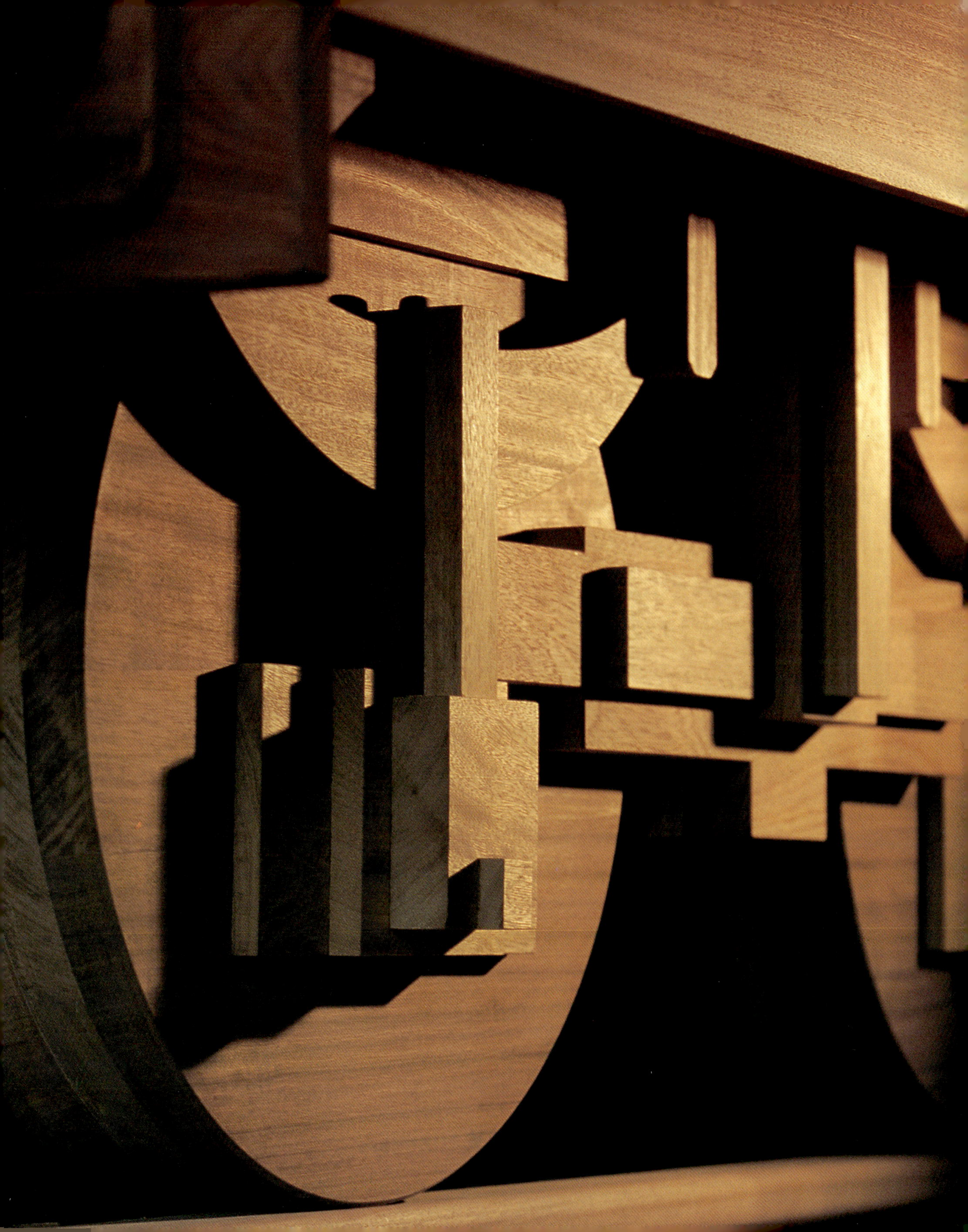

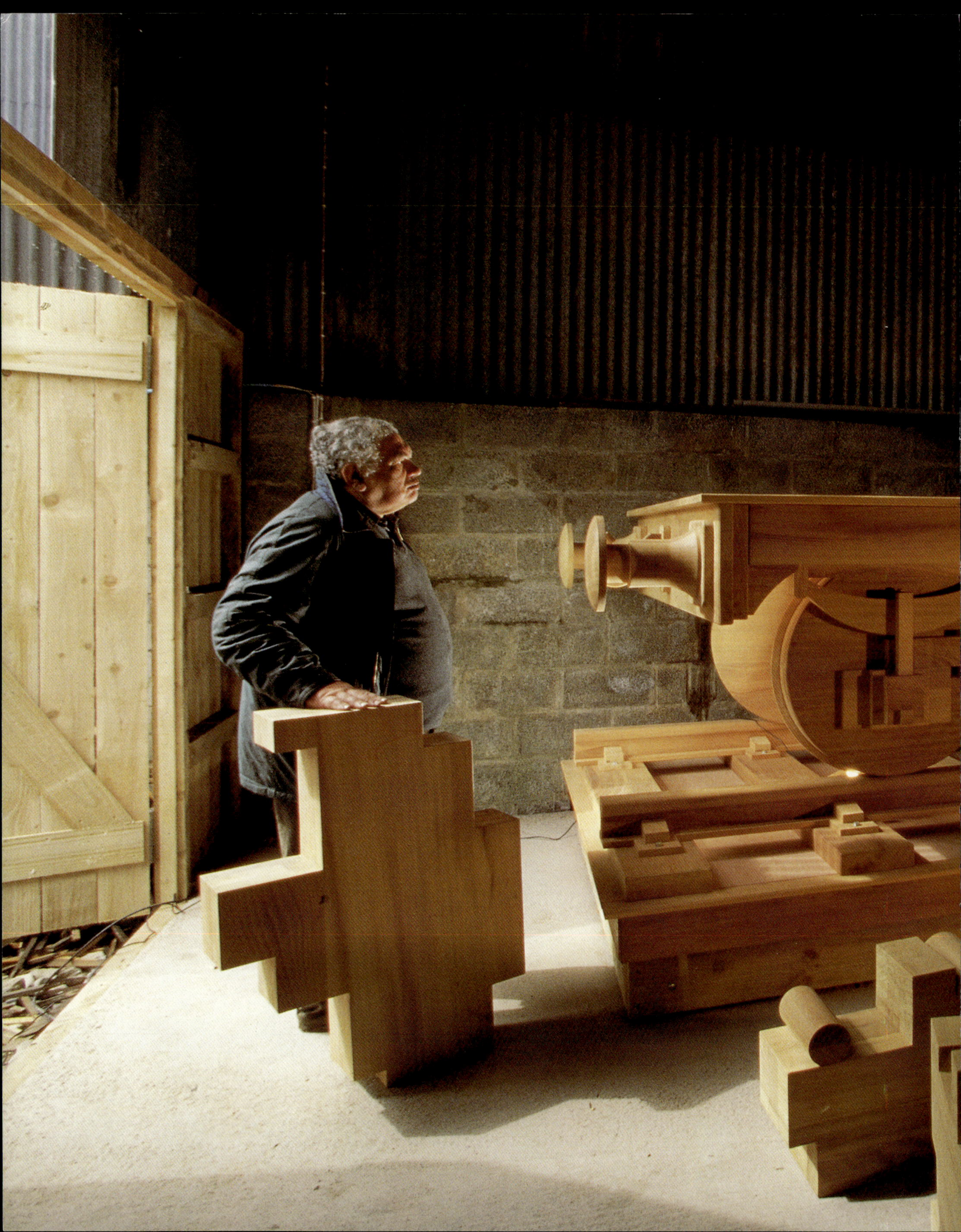

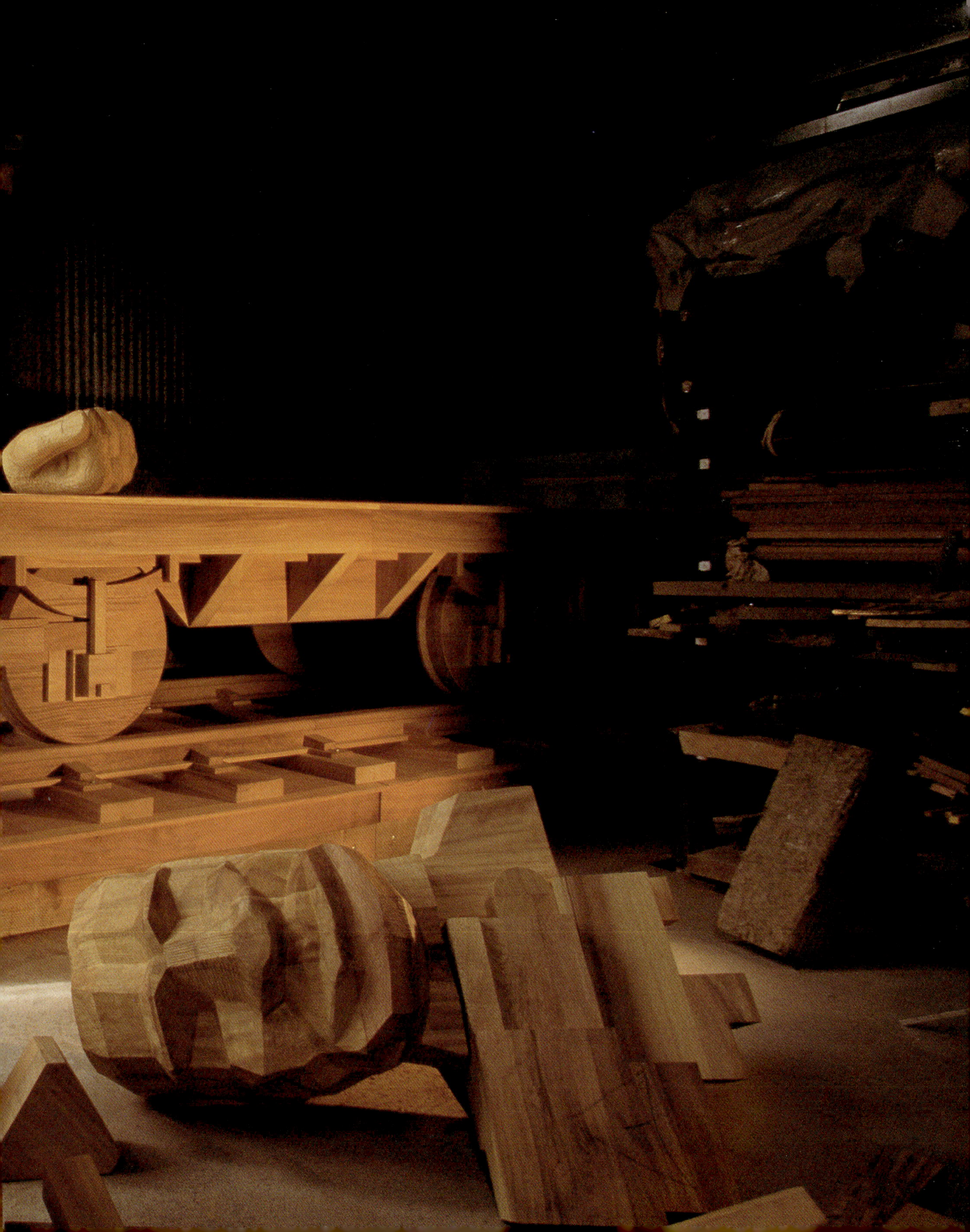

GALLERY I

Traditionally this is the room hung by the President in which the internationally known Honorary RAs are placed. Phillip King has opted to continue this practice. 'They make their presence felt within the exhibition', he says. 'We'll have a Paladino and a Baselitz, a Twombly and a Kiefer. And alongside the Honorary Academicians' work I have placed the senior sculptors of the Academy, including myself, William Tucker, Bryan Kneale and Eduardo Paolozzi. Works of high quality but modest in feel and fairly cool. Paolozzi is represented by maquettes and variations of the sculpture in the courtyard, making a useful connection between inside and outside. Also particularly important in this gallery is the tribute to the late Michael Kenny, who I think is a very important sculptor of his generation.'

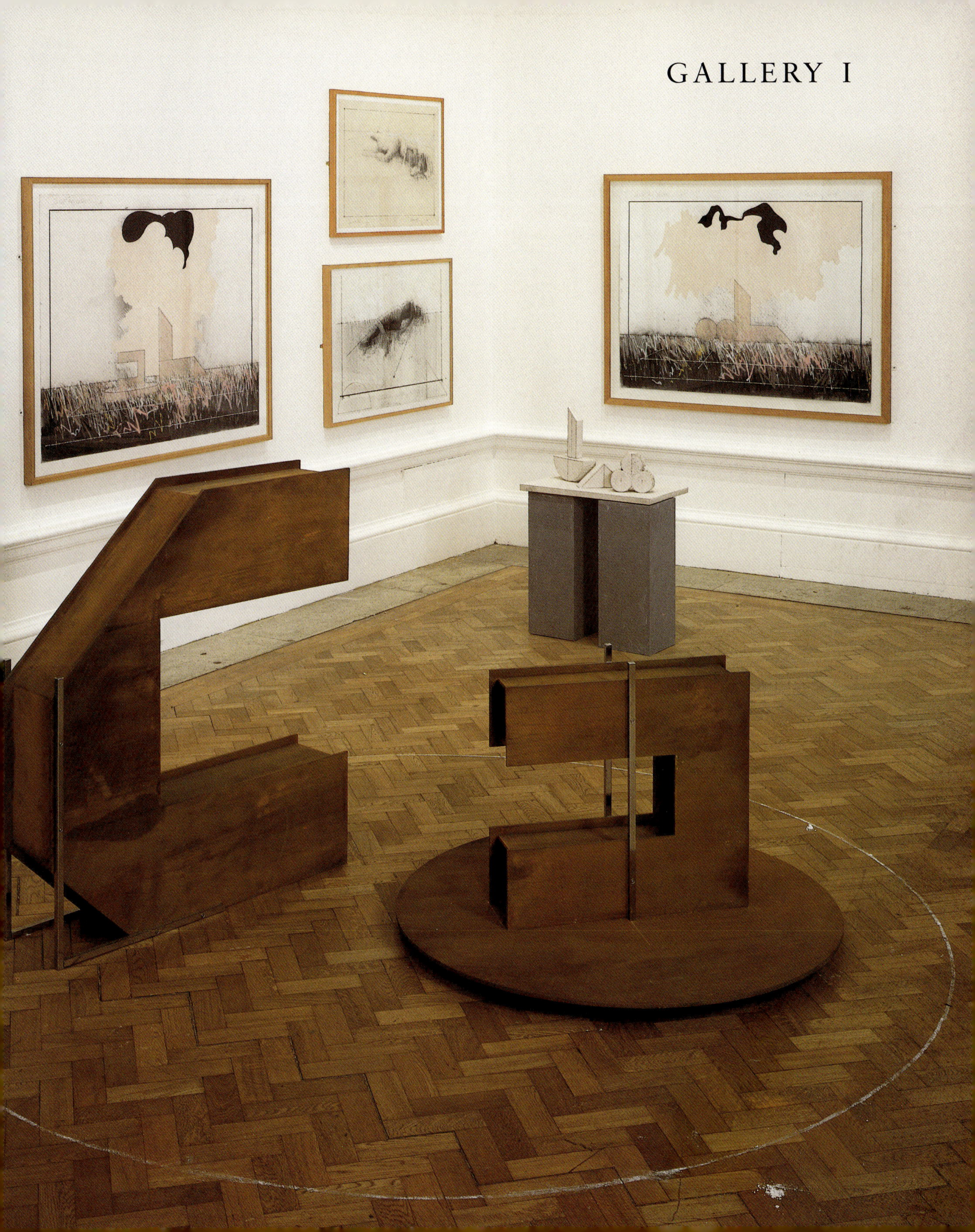

GALLERY I

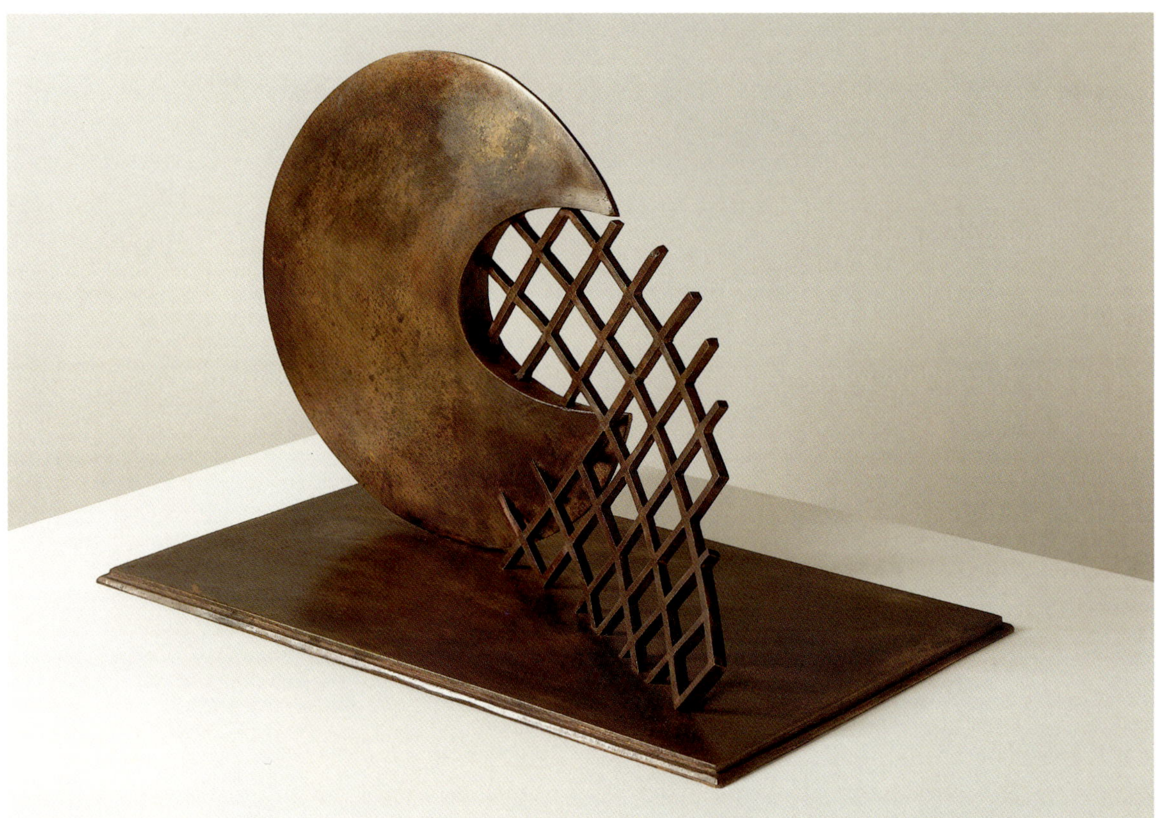

Prof. Phillip King CBE, PRA
Sun Roots
Bronze
h 40 cm

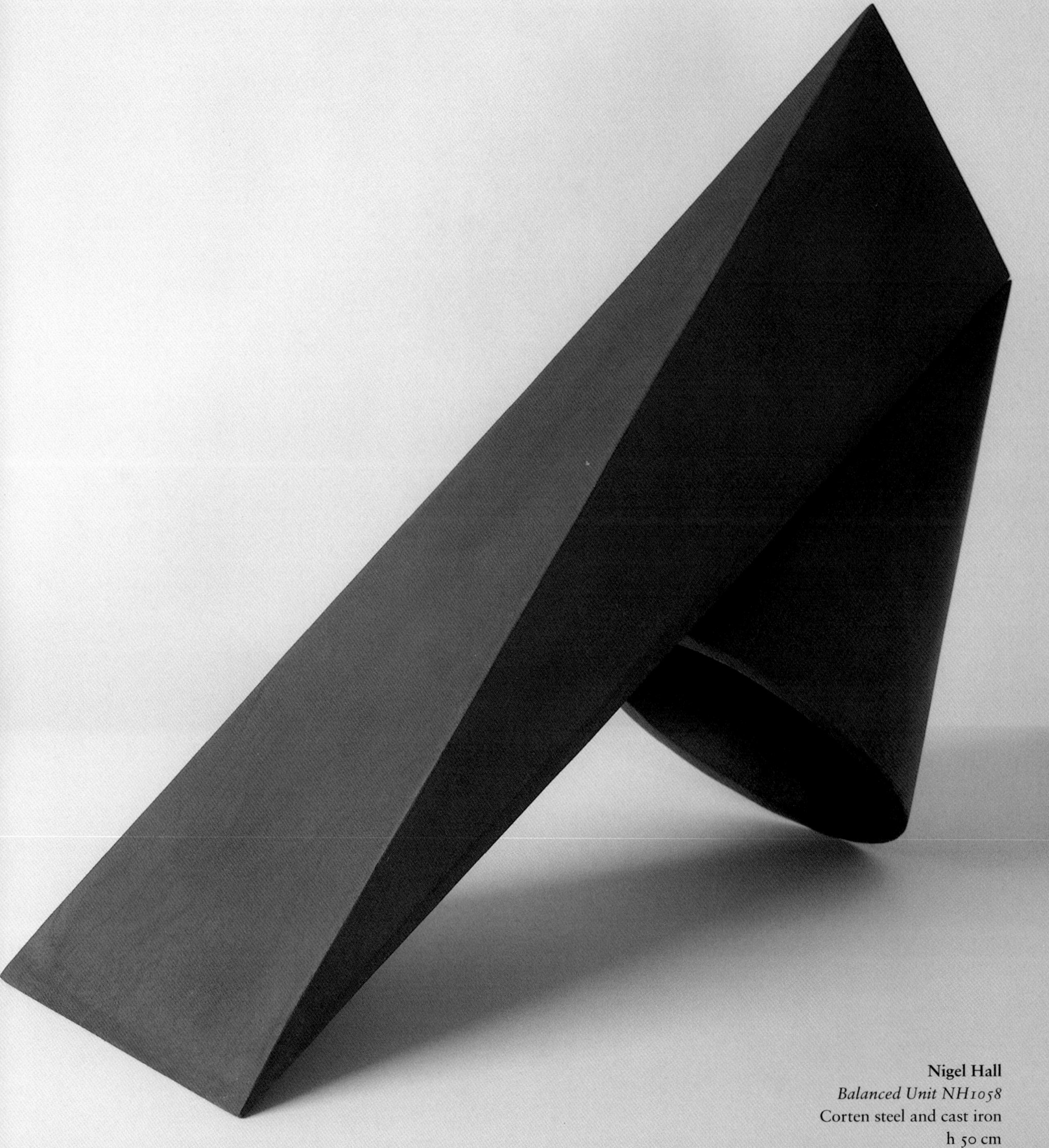

Nigel Hall
Balanced Unit NH1058
Corten steel and cast iron
h 50 cm

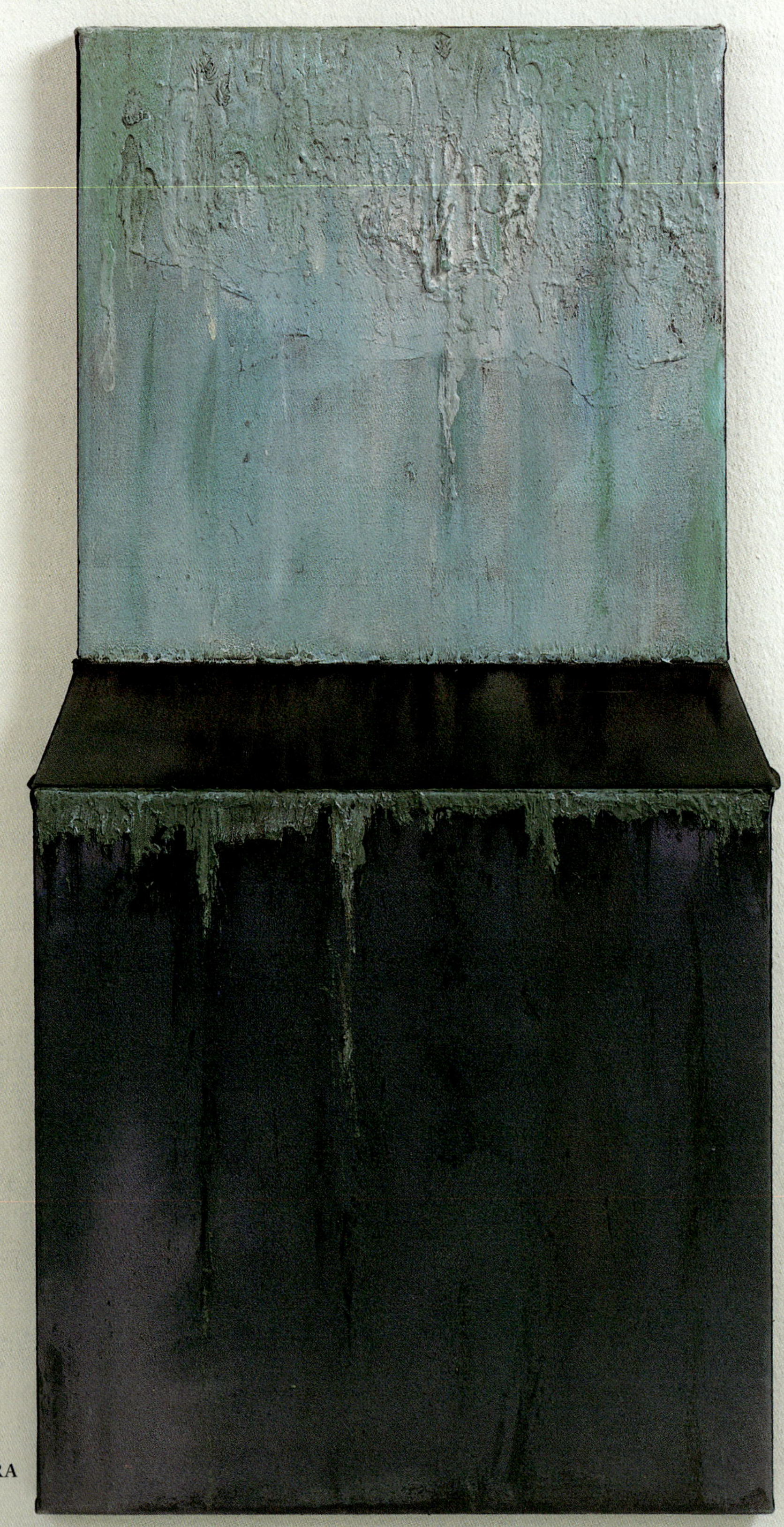

Anthony Whishaw RA
Green Water Weir
Acrylic
83 × 42 cm

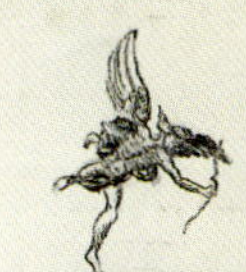

WEST END FINAL

Evening Standard

LONDON MONDAY, 29 MARCH 1999

Incorporating THE EVENING NEWS 35p

Albanians flee Kosovo in their thousands and tell of shootings by Serbs that may have killed hundreds

'BODIES LINE BORDER ROAD'

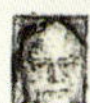

from ROBERT FOX in the Rusulija Pass, Northern Kosovo

THE SECOND city of Kosovo is burning and almost empty of its 80,000 inhabitants. Albanians from the city, Pec, struggling through snowdrifts over the Rusulija Pass into Montenegro, said they were given five minutes to leave their homes or face being shot.

"Half the town was destroyed by the time we left. We saw bodies lying by the road to the border. We counted 13 dead in Novo Selo but we hear there may be hundreds of dead in other villages," said Idres Aslen, 40, who had managed to make it across the mountains in freezing fog and sleet to Rosaje, in Montenegro.

"They came and knocked on our door and told us we had five minutes to get out or we would be shot. Three hundred women and children were led away and locked into the barracks at Pec, where they are hostages in case Nato should bomb. If Nato attacks, they will be killed."

Hundreds of thousands of Kosovar Albanian refugees are on the move, fleeing the rampage of ethnic cleansing by Serbs triggered by Nato's bombing campaign. On the high pass at Rusulija, Šula Sevdia, a 32-year-old mother, sat and wept. She left Klina, seat of fierce bombardment in the Drenica Valley, eight days ago, hoping to meet up with her husband and three children. Now she does not know where they are or even if they are still alive.

New arrivals at the makeshift police post say they are sure

Continued on Page 3 Col 1

OTHER DEVELOPMENTS TODAY:

- Nato aircraft resumed attacks on Serb forces in Kosovo and Serbia, with B-52s taking off again from Fairford and RAF Harriers flying from their base in Italy.
- Russian Prime Minister Yevgeny Primakov is expected to announce that he will fly to Belgrade tomorrow for new talks with President Milosevic.
- Countries bordering Kosovo have appealed for international aid to help them deal with the flood of refugees crossing over to escape the Serb onslaught.
- In a series of BBC World Service interviews, Tony Blair has called for the air war against the Serbs to be stepped up, but reaffirmed that the Government has no plans to send in ground troops, despite growing calls for such intervention.

See Pages 3, 4, 5 and 7. Editorial comment: Page 13

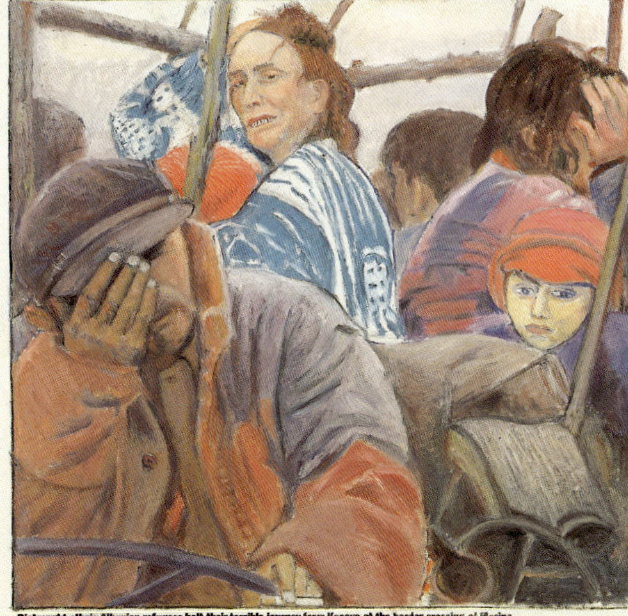

Distraught ethnic Albanian refugees halt their terrible journey from Kosovo at the border crossing of Morina. Hundreds of thousands are being systematically expelled by Serbian forces as Nato continues to mount air strikes

Frederick Gore CBE, RA
The Evening Standard 29 March '99
Oil
183 × 152 cm

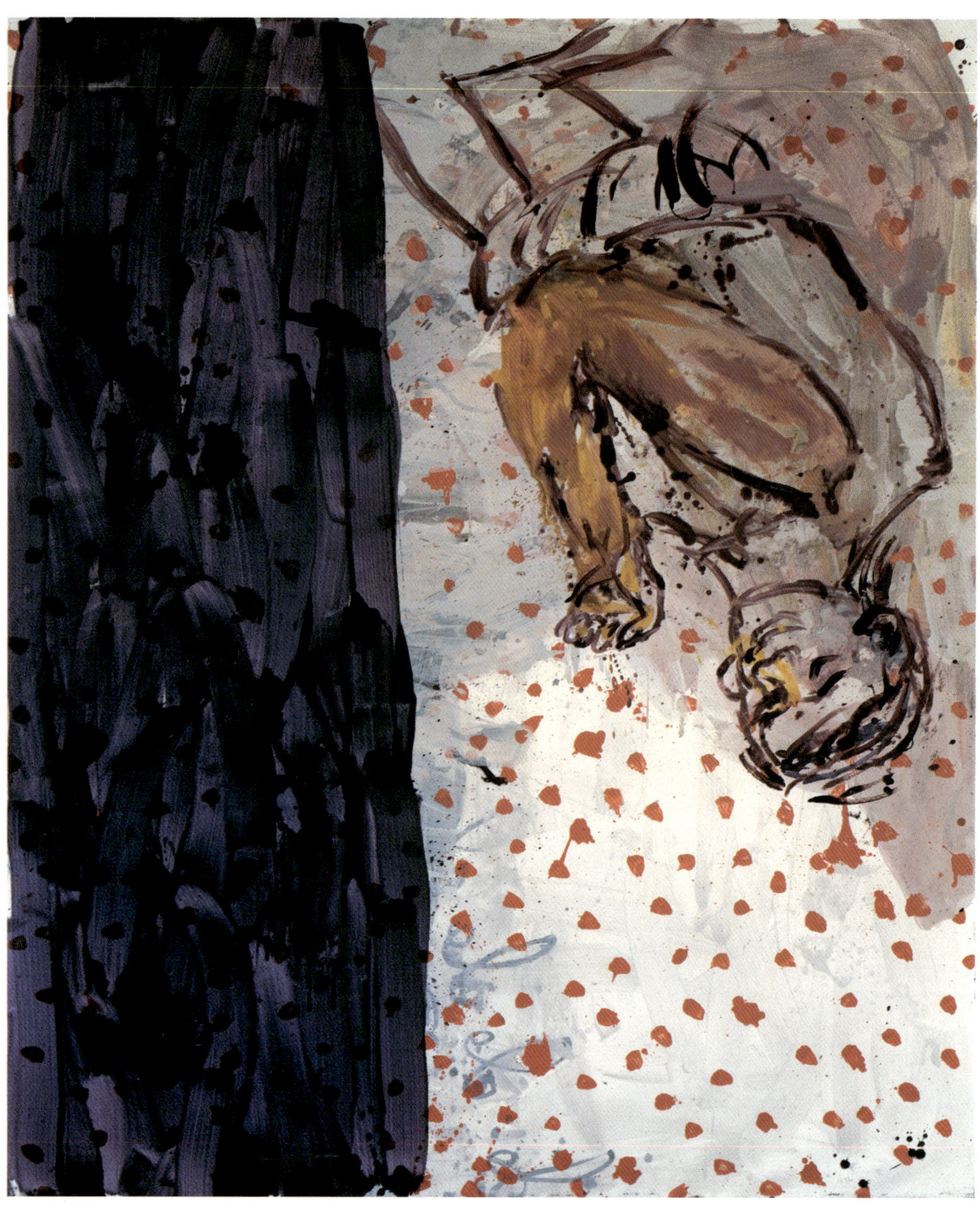

Georg Baselitz Hon RA
Neben Elisabeth (5.IV.98–13.IV.98)
Oil
200× 162 cm

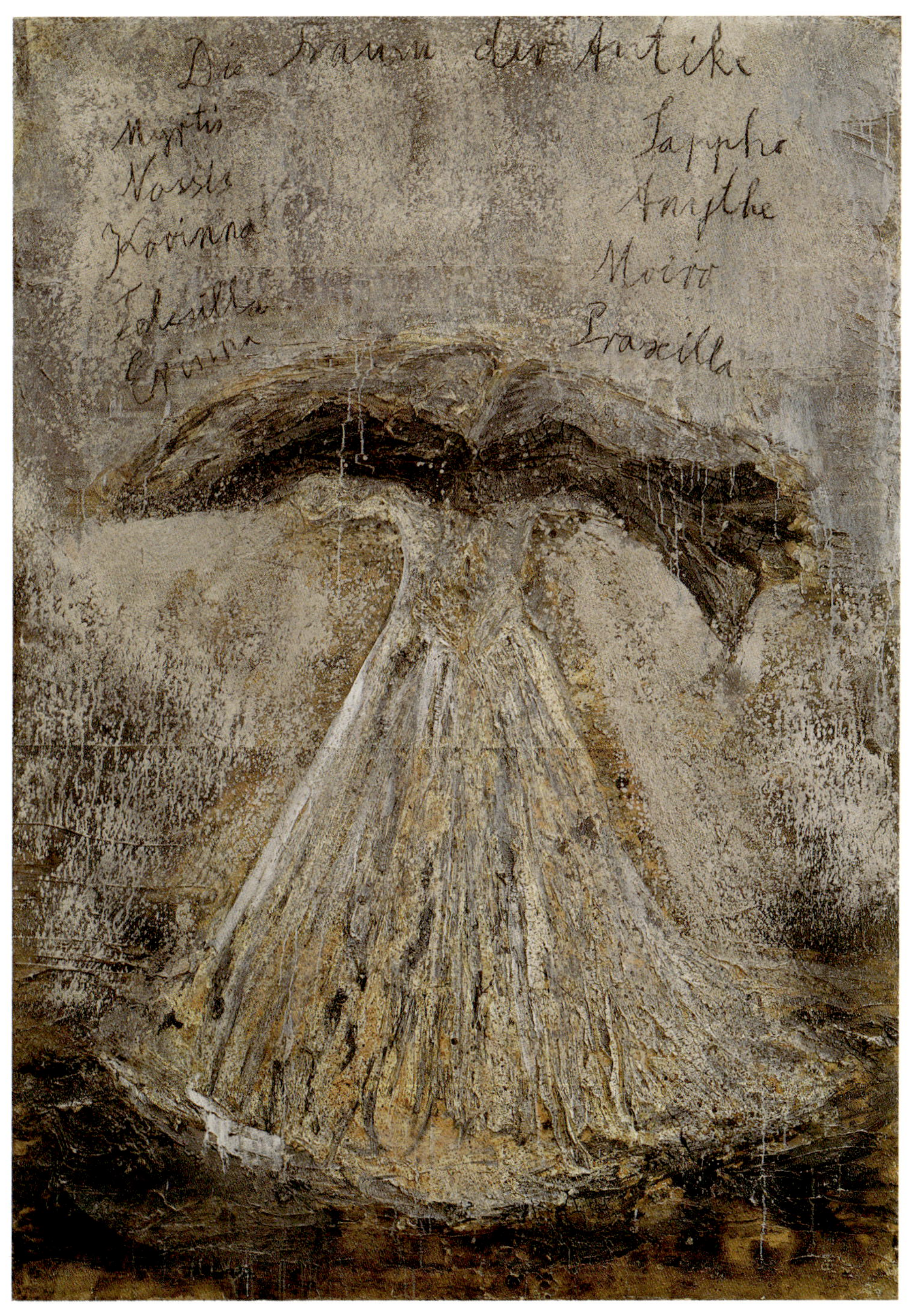

Anselm Kiefer Hon RA
Die Frauen der Antike
Mixed Media
280× 190 cm

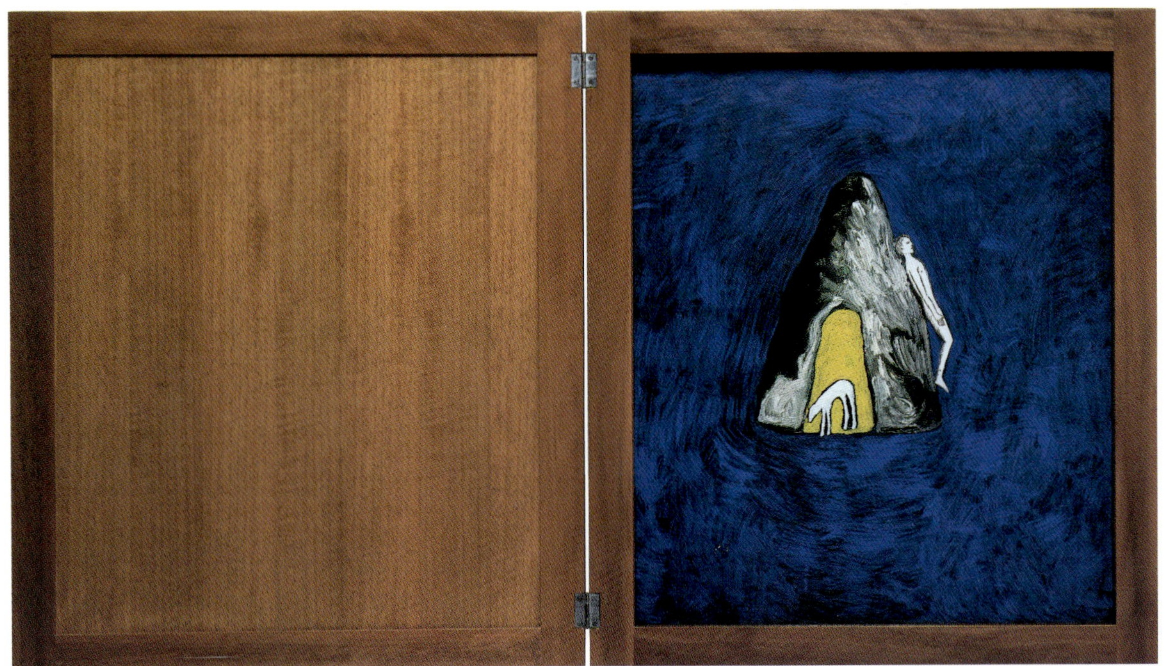

Mimmo Paladino Hon RA
Untitled
Oil
67 × 57 cm

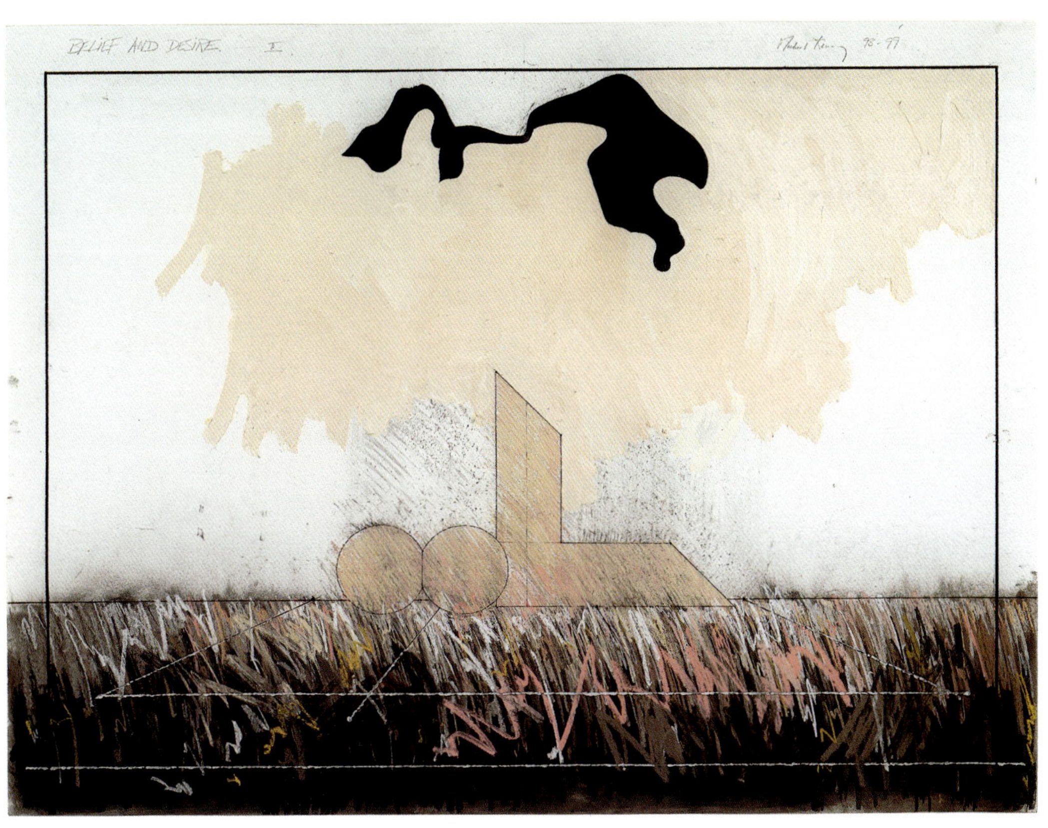

Michael Kenny RA
Belief and Desire II
Drawing
117 × 153 cm

GALLERY II

Brendan Neiland, Keeper of the Academy Schools and currently in charge of Gallery II, has hung an invited artist Hugh O'Donnell in one of the prime positions. This is one of the Summer Exhibition's roles – occasionally to broaden the selection by inviting specific artists to send in work. In hanging the rest of the gallery Neiland has chosen to follow a bold line between abstraction and figuration (his own work here, dealing with the reflections conjured up in car bonnets, exemplifies this), whilst mixing up Academicians with non-members. Neiland singles out one or two artists for special comment. 'Stephen Farthing has always interested me in his exploration of nature, of reality, and the methodology he brings to it. In part it's the play between figuration and abstraction, but there's also a joy, a freshness, a rhythm and a movement, a fluidity that somehow comes out of juxtaposing opposites.' These observations stand as much for Farthing's paintings as they do generally for Neiland's method of arranging the pictures he has chosen. 'It's not opposition so much – I'm looking for that flow – an idea that might exist in all of the works I've selected. This is the first time I've had the opportunity to hang what I would think of as a major room which doesn't have to be densely hung. I'm hoping that my feelings will come through.'

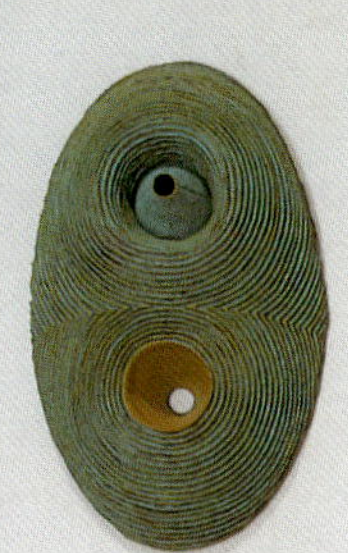

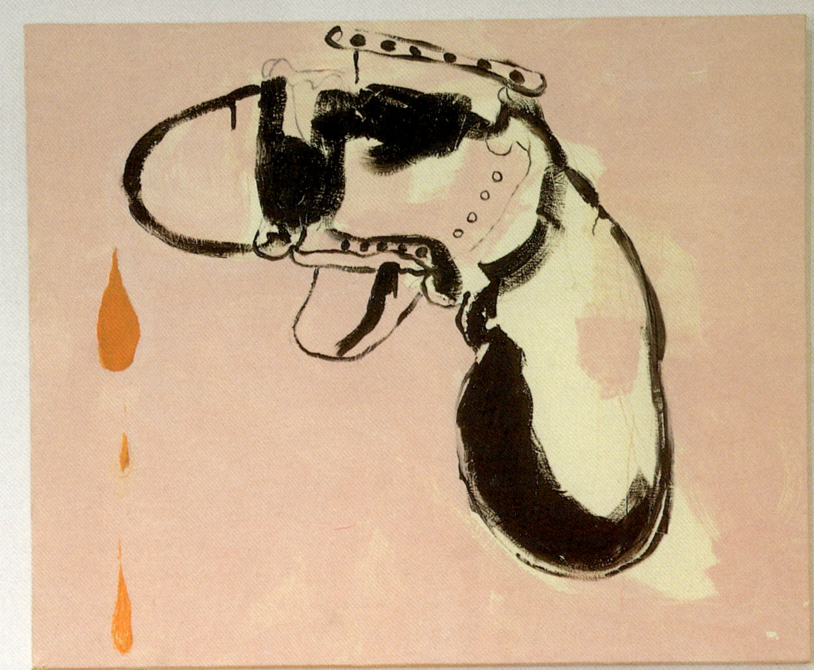

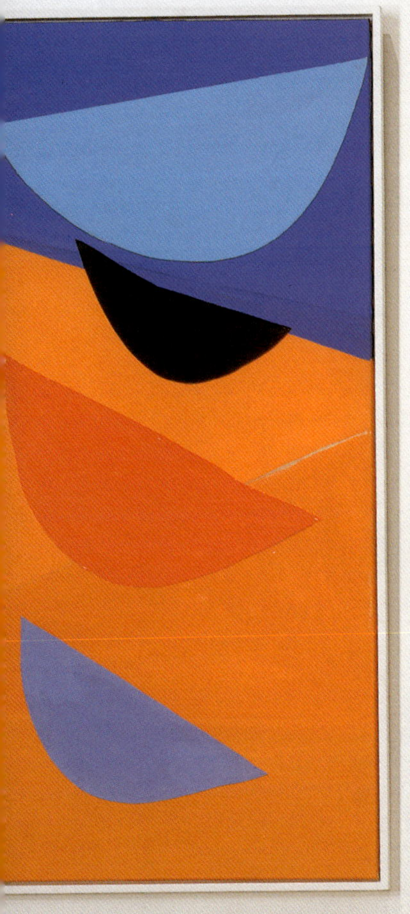

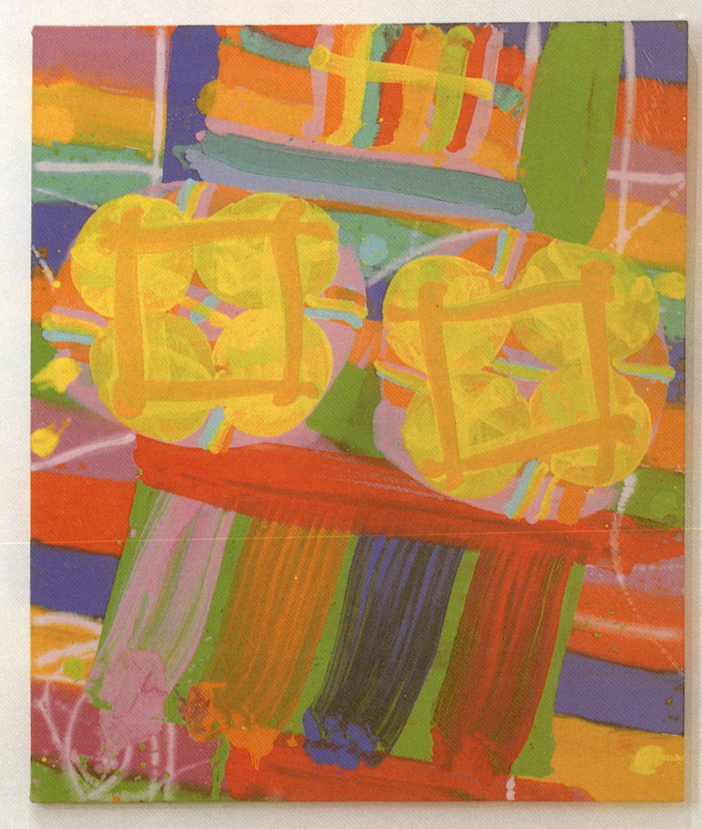

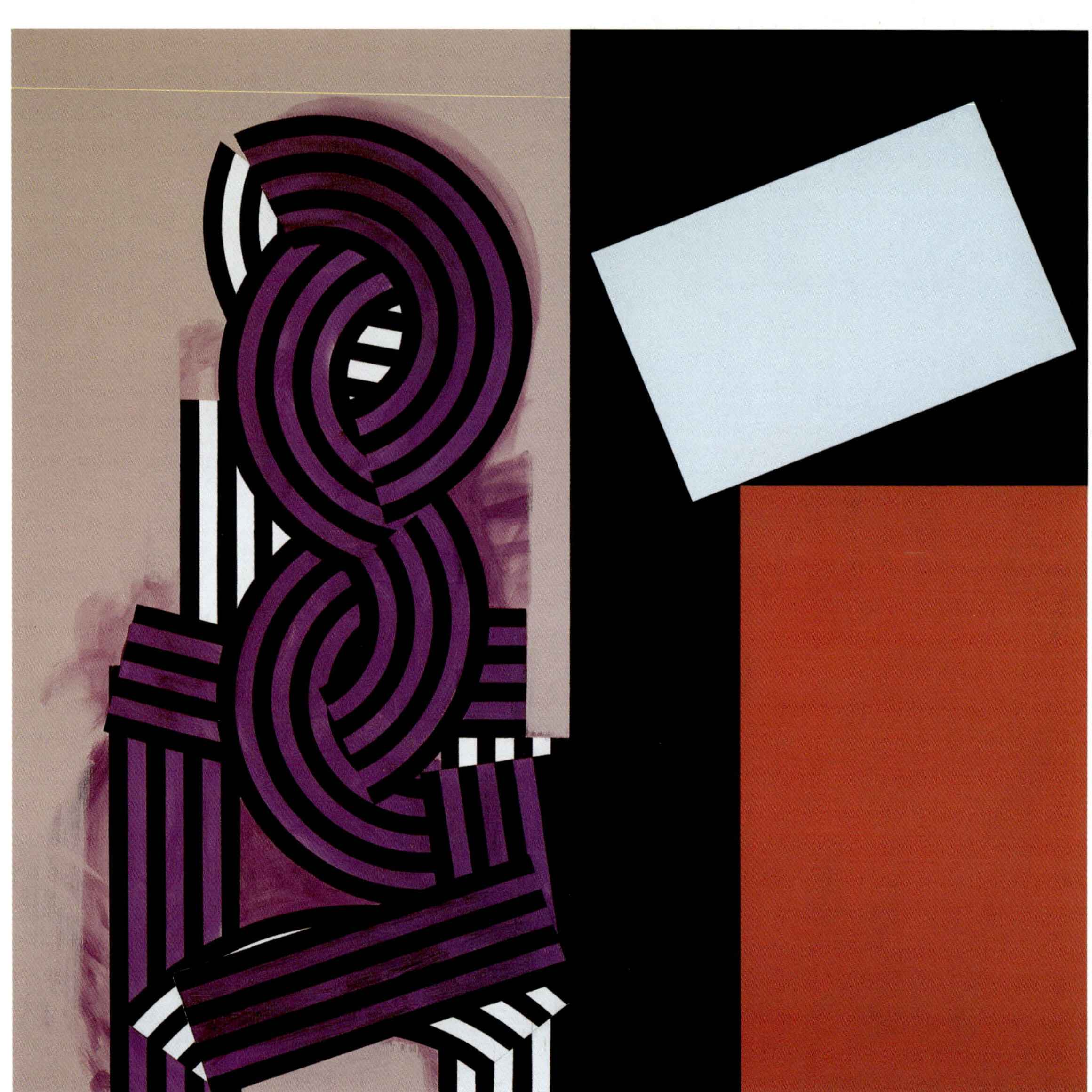

Prof. Paul Huxley RA
Mutatis Mutandis VII
Acrylic
173 × 173 cm

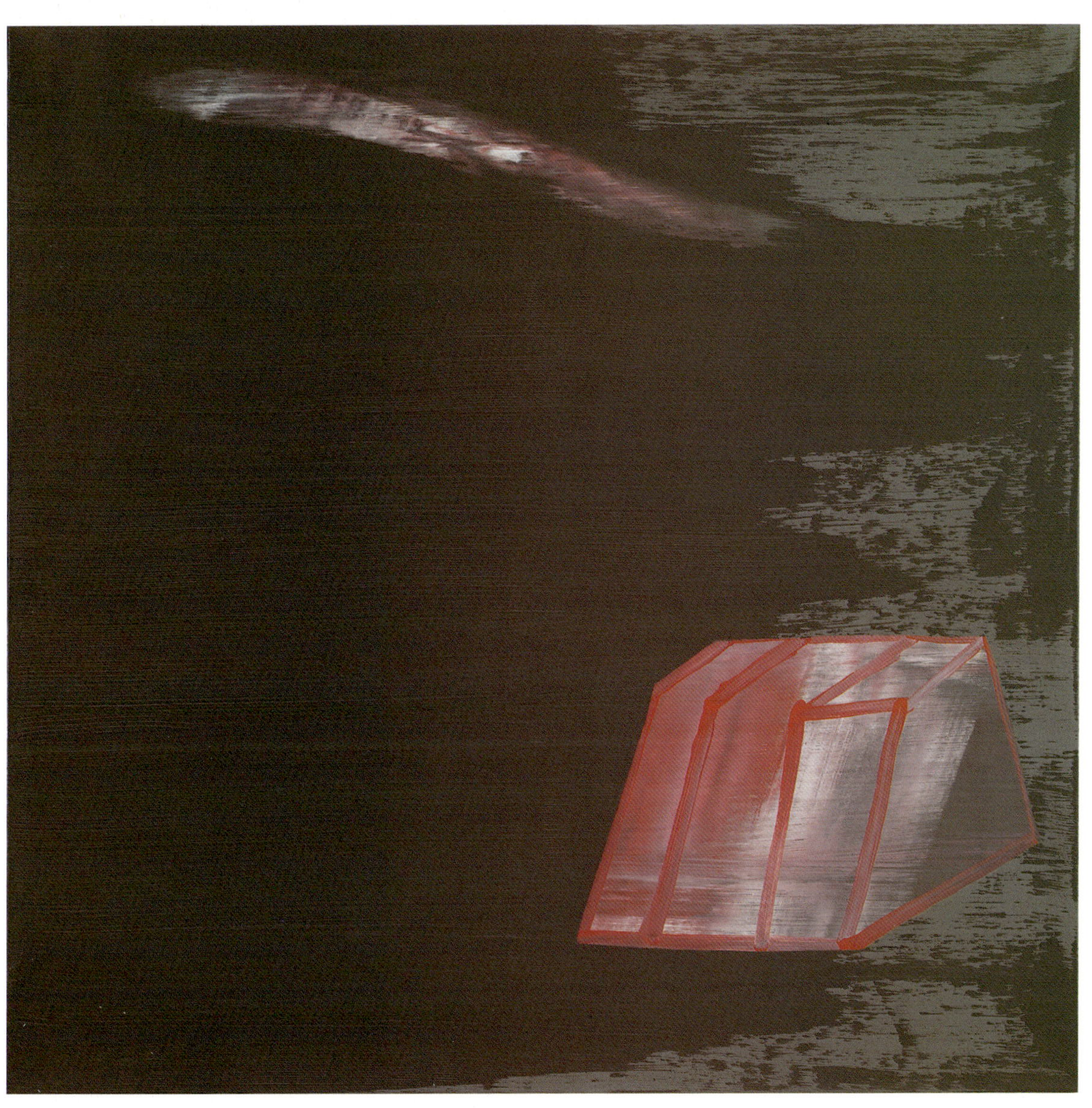

Christina Floyd
Liquid/Solid/Gaseous
Acrylic
150 × 150 cm

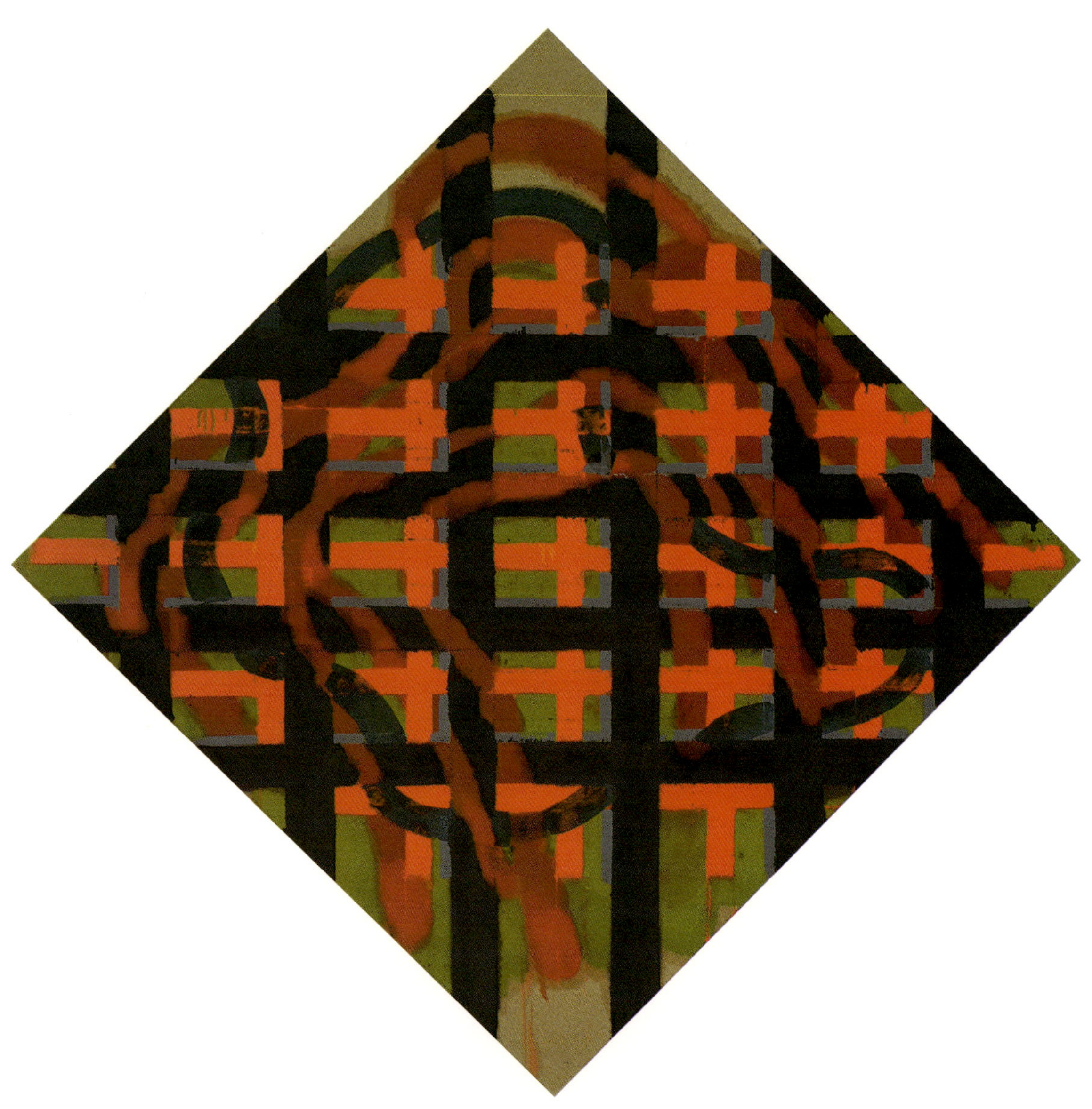

Richard Smith
Diamond 9
Oil
107 × 107 cm

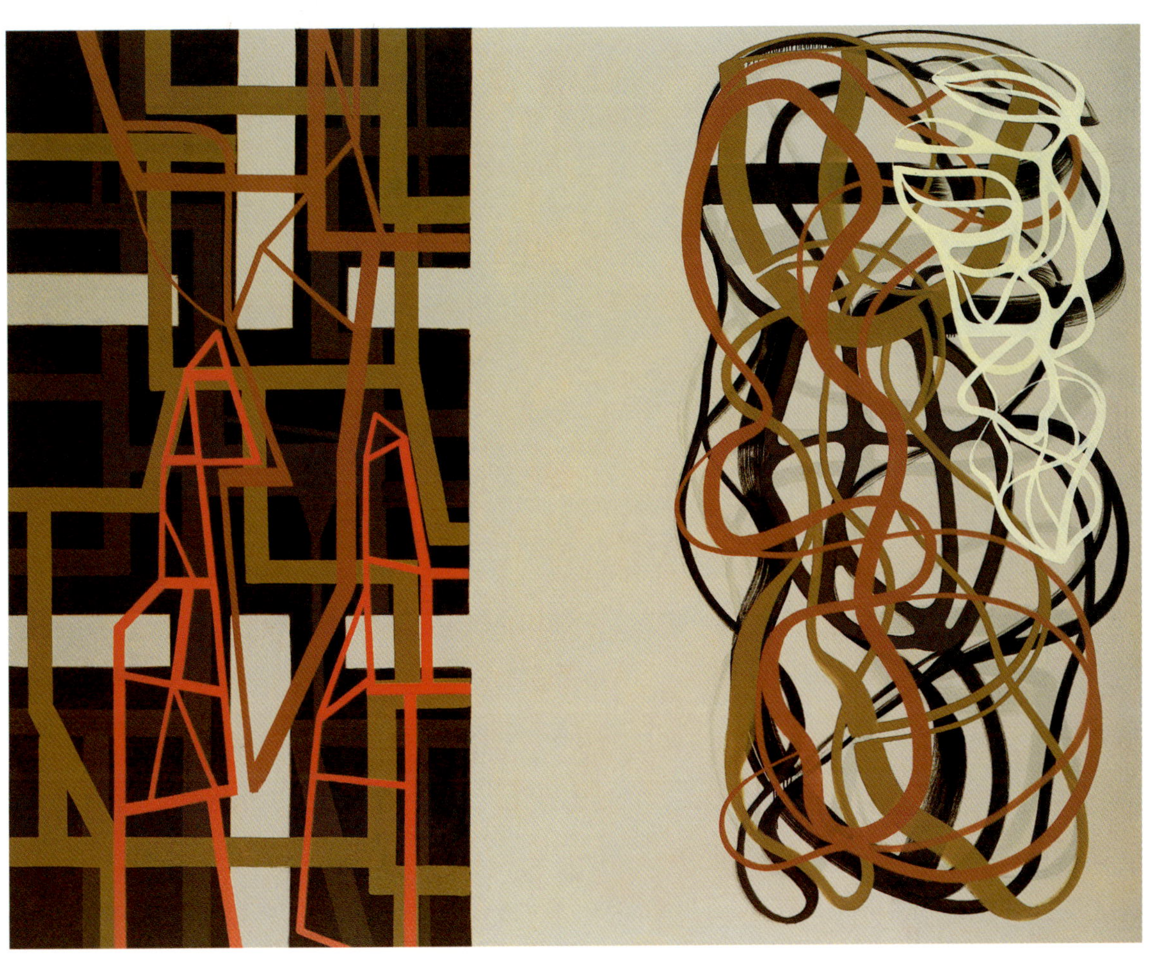

Maurice Cockrill RA
Divided # 84
Oil
244 × 300 cm

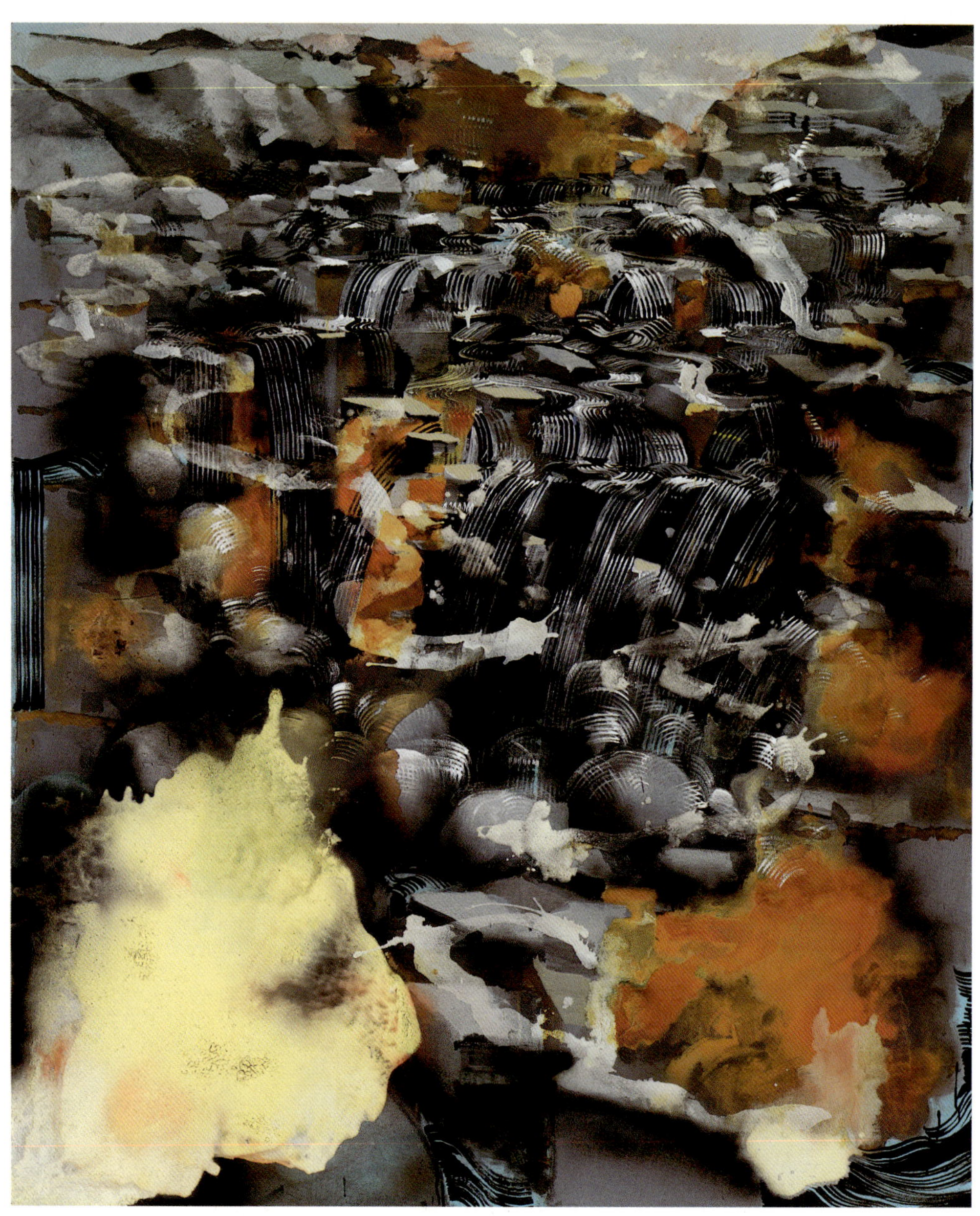

Stephen Farthing RA
The Turnerian Topography # 2
Acrylic
204 × 173 cm

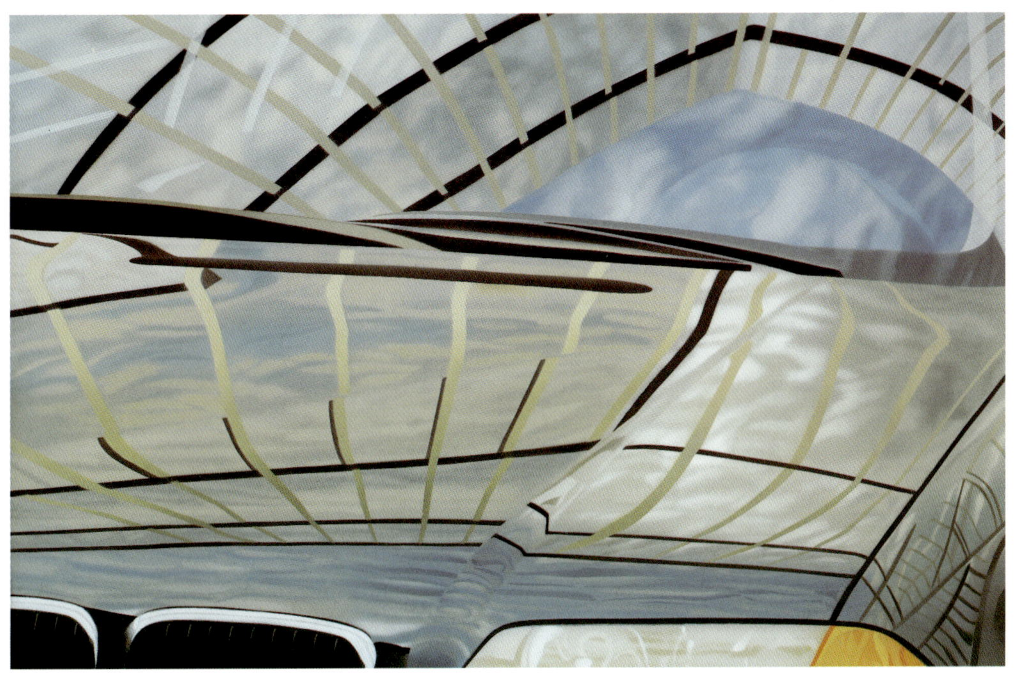

Prof. Brendan Neiland RA
Fiz
Acrylic
121 × 181 cm

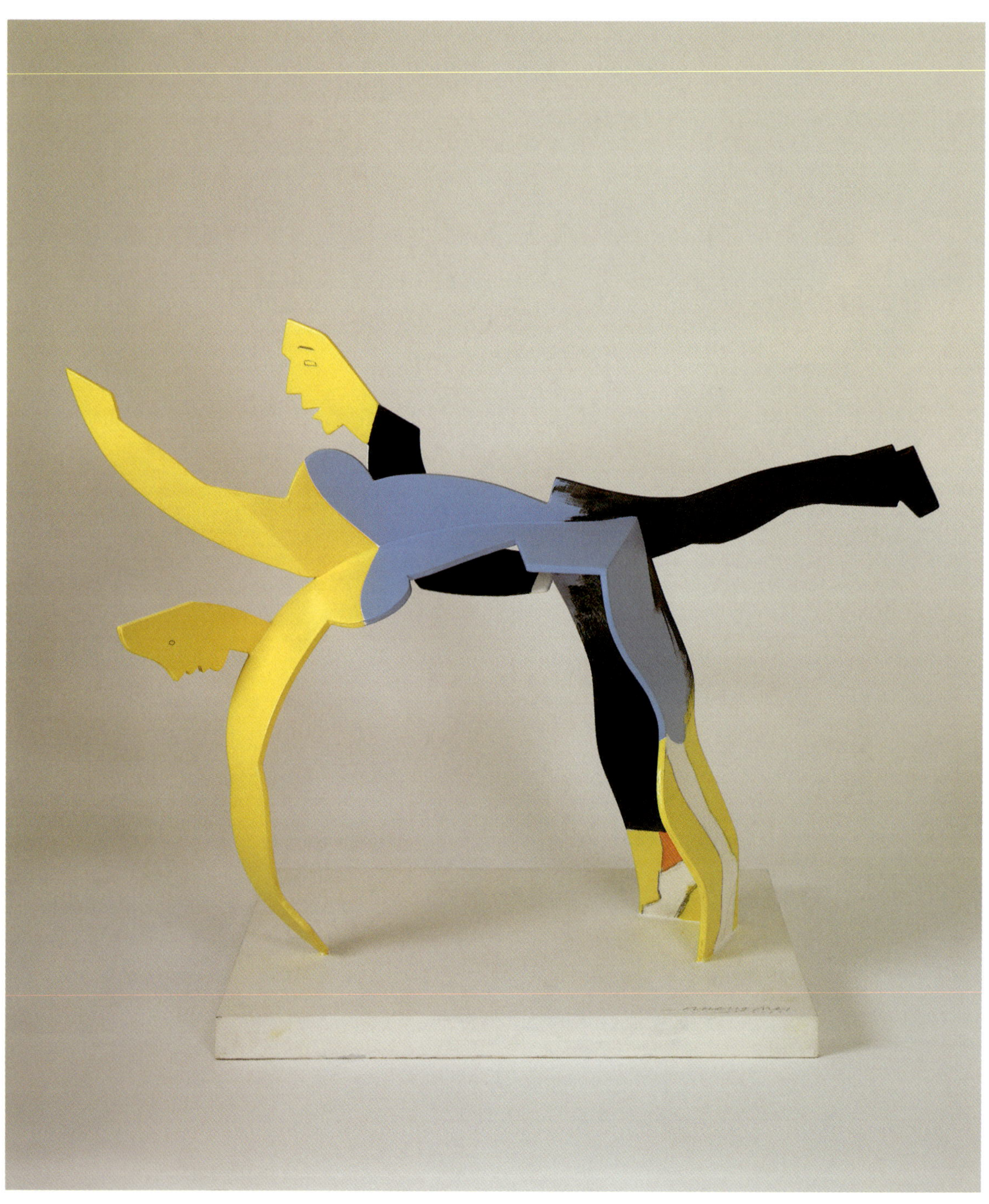

Allen Jones RA
Arabesque
Steel
h 51 cm

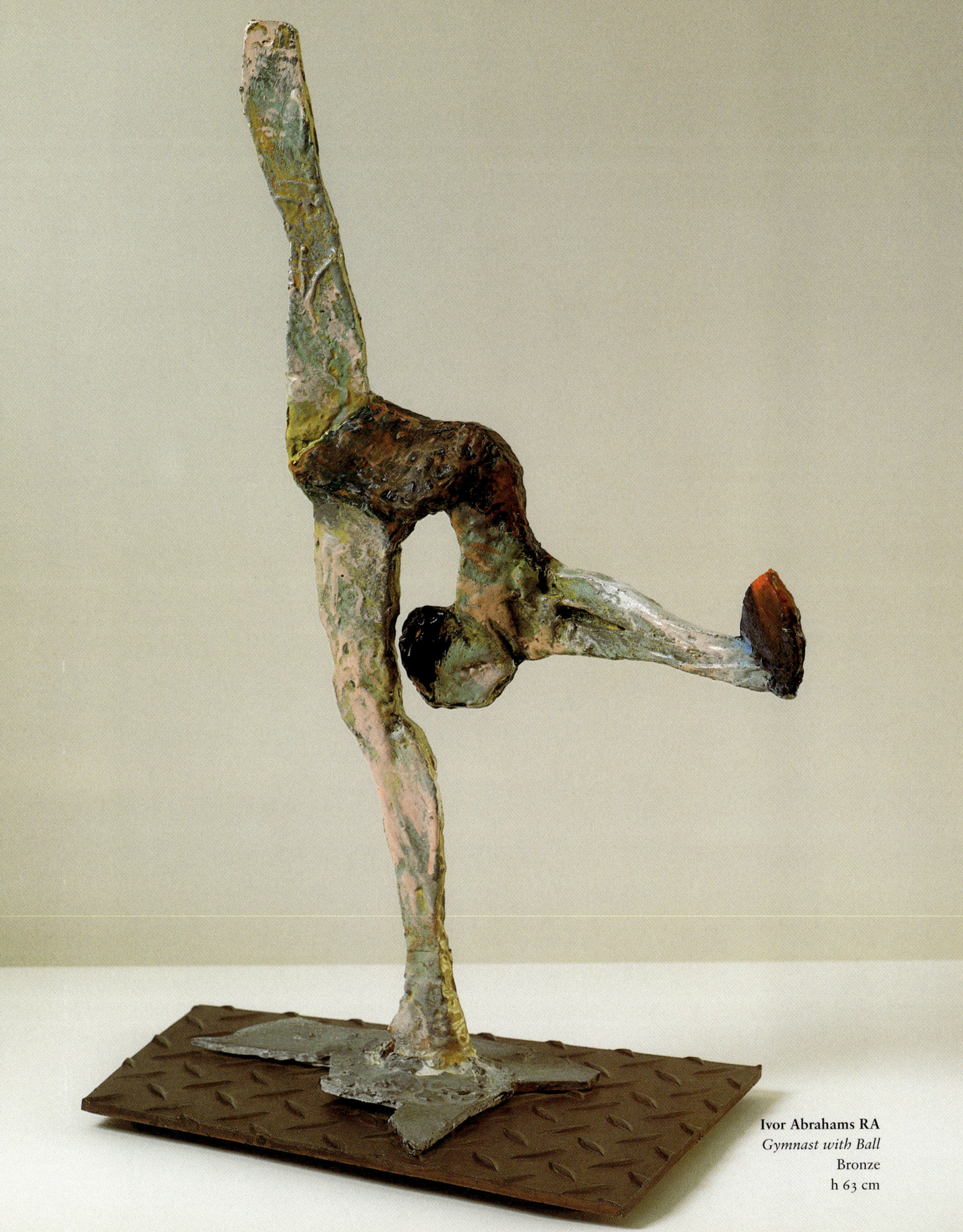

Ivor Abrahams RA
Gymnast with Ball
Bronze
h 63 cm

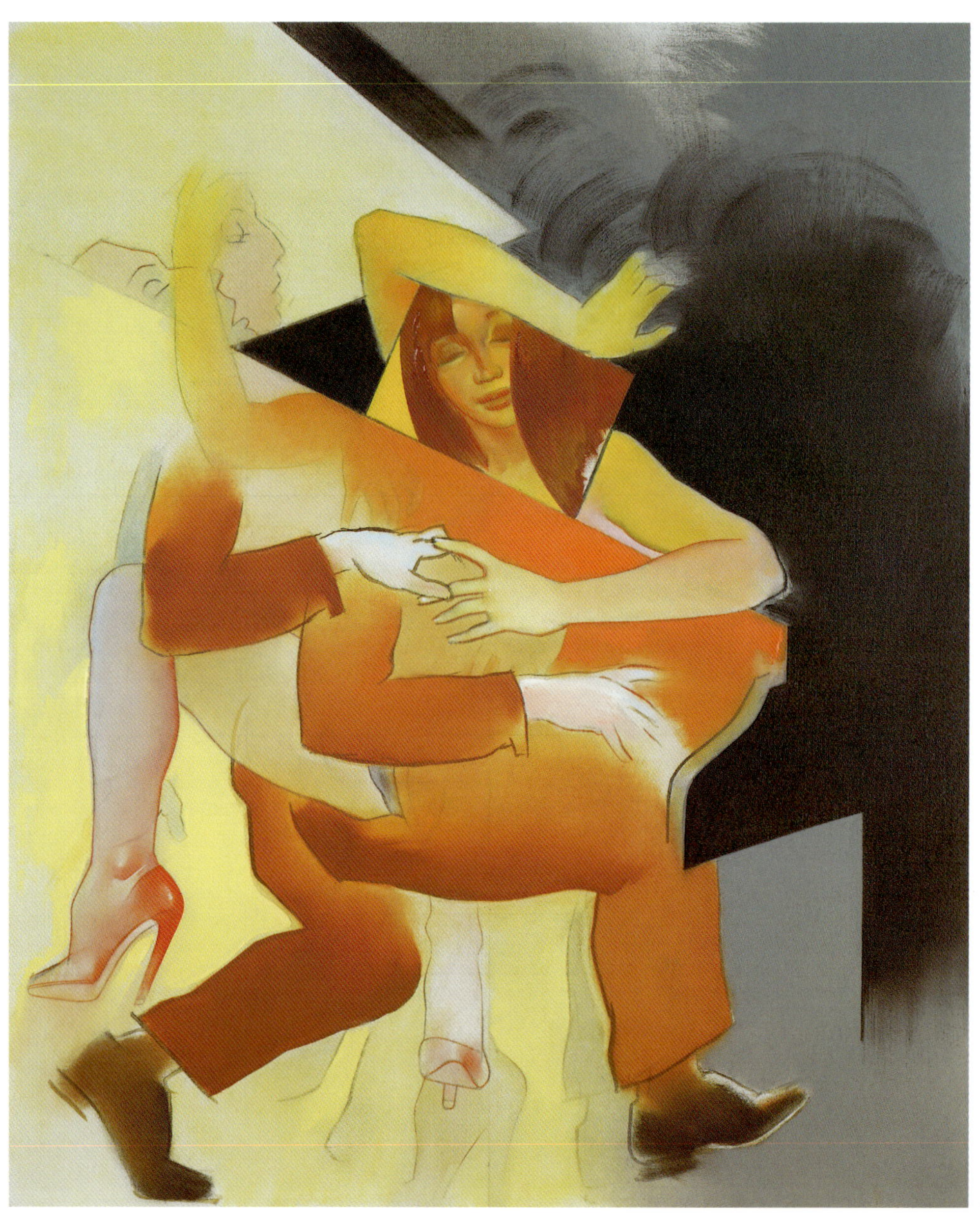

Allen Jones RA
Baby Grand
Oil
127 × 102 cm

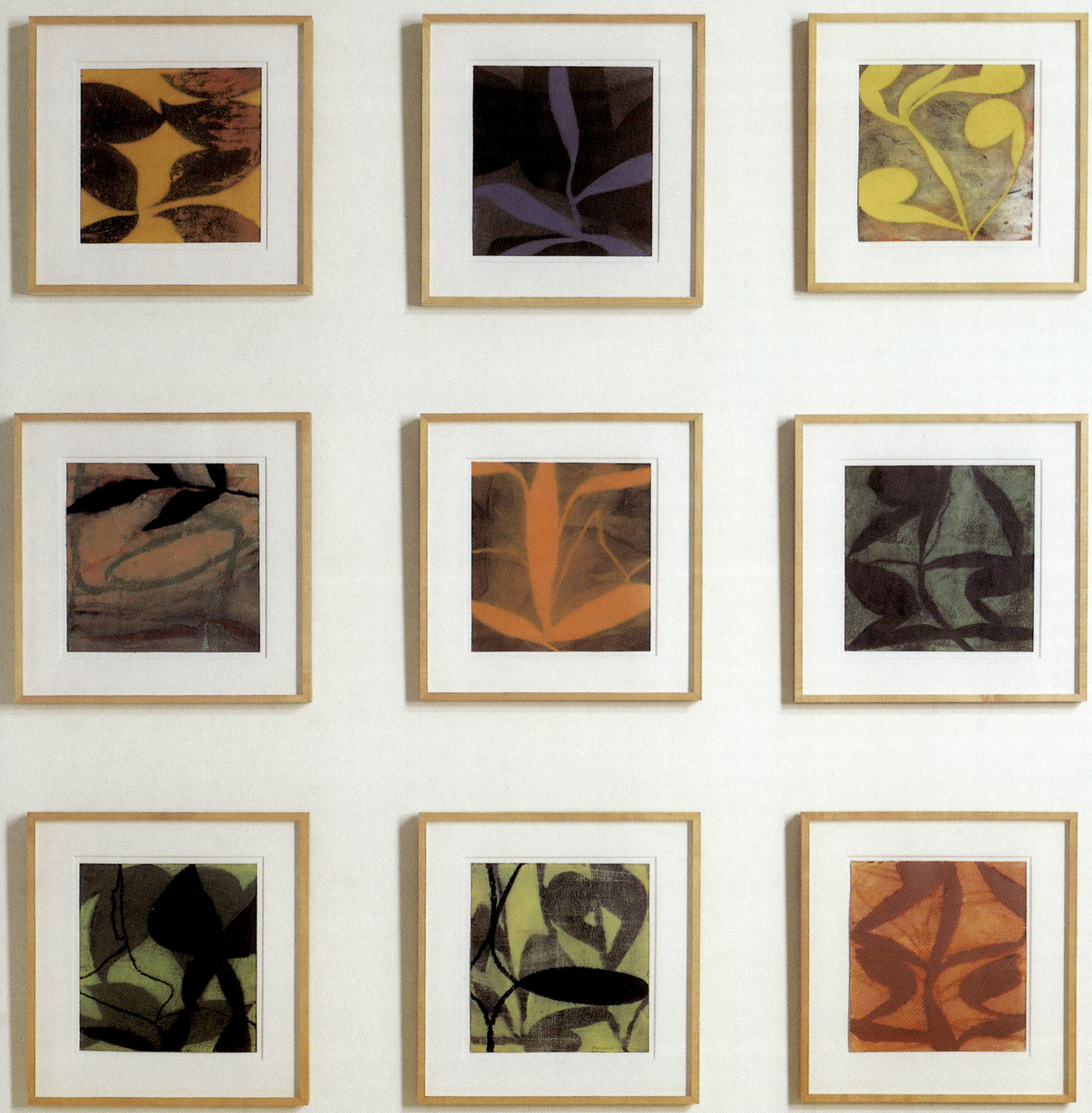

Hugh O'Donnell
Installation of *The Stations of the Breath (for Dylan Thomas)*
Oil

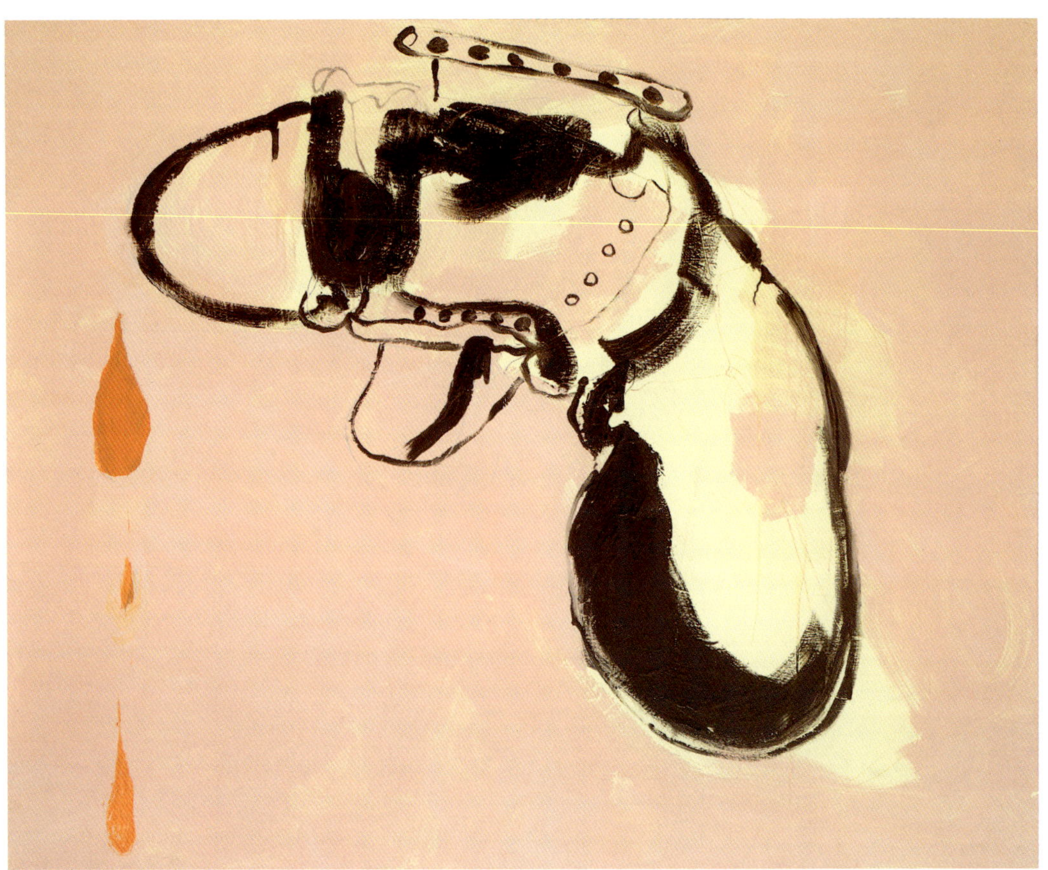

Madeleine Strindberg
No. 14 (limp)
Emulsion paint and gloss
152 × 183 cm

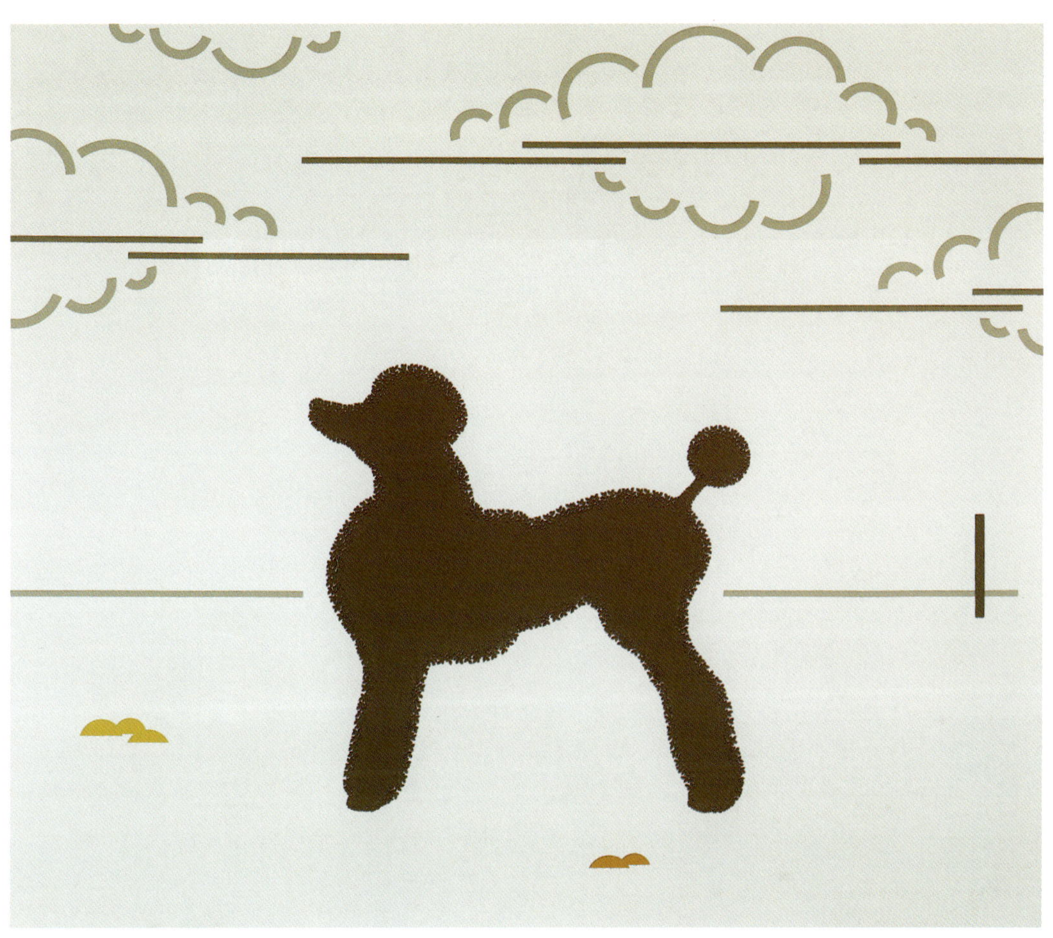

Gerard Hemsworth
Never mind, pourquoi?
Acrylic
43 × 163 cm

LARGE WESTON ROOM

This gallery is given over to printed work and this year is hung by the printmaker Peter Freeth. The task of hanging the Large Weston Room is the perennial one of trying to accommodate and make sense of a very large number of works without succumbing to visual anarchy. Freeth advocates a process of trial and error, of trying different pictures against each other. 'I'm proposing to hang this room as densely as possible because I believe very much in the democratic principle of submission. I am hoping to hang as many unknowns as I can – I think that's part of our remit.'

What kind of work was submitted? 'A lot of prints by painter Academicians. This year there are the beginnings of what certainly will become a tidal wave of computer-generated printed imagery. On the selection it was significant that the proportion of interesting and good work was higher than in painting. This is possibly because prints are generally done in a studio situation with other people commenting on them, so they're not made in isolation. The technique imposes a certain discipline on the artist. And technique-wise we've got a very very wide spread.'

'Each wall has a predominance of Members' work. It's part of the party.' For Freeth, 'juggling' is the word which best describes the hang of this room. 'I shall have as much variety as I possibly can.'

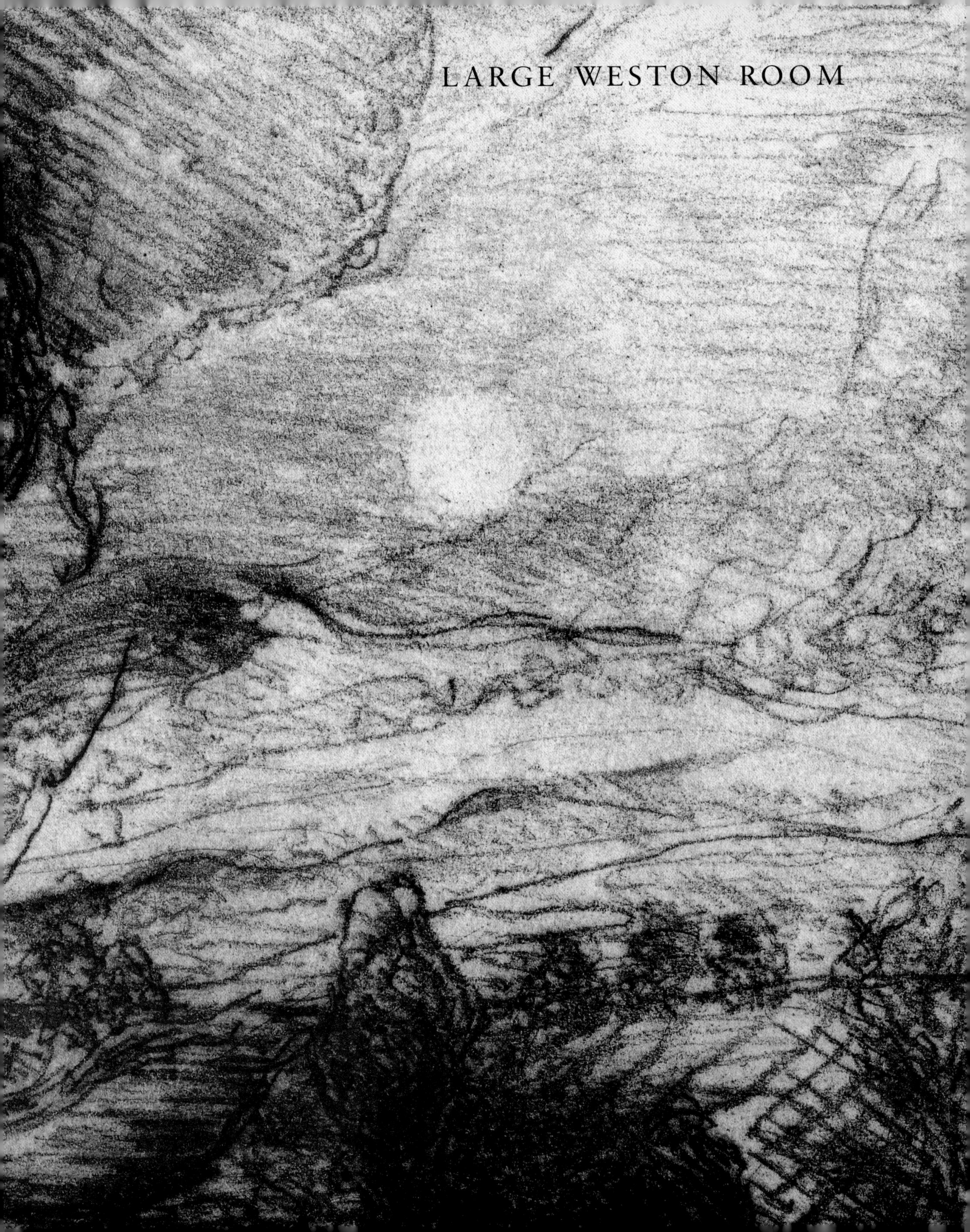

LARGE WESTON ROOM

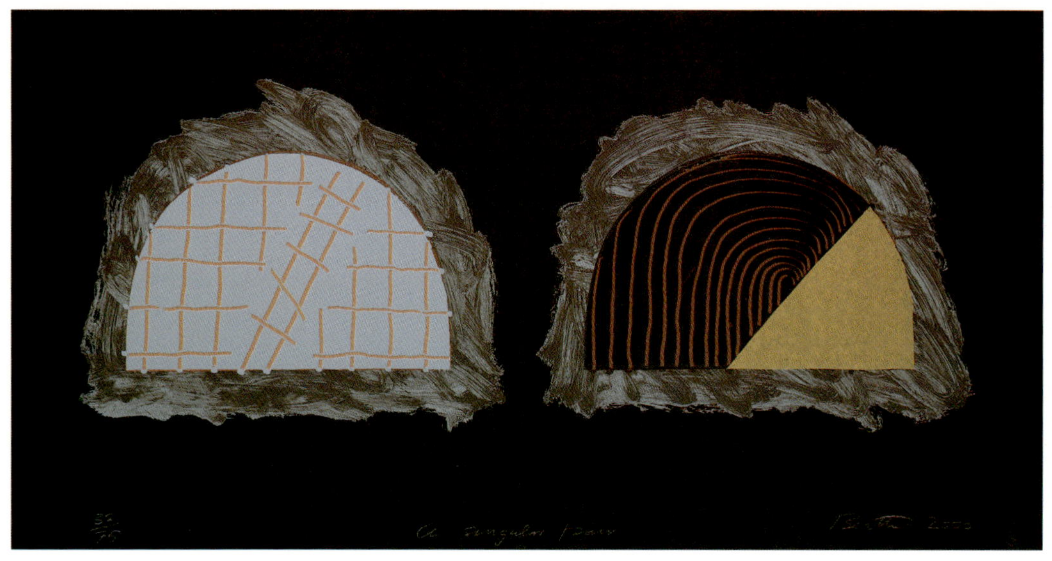

Basil Beattie
A Singular Pair
Screenprint with woodblock
61 × 114 cm

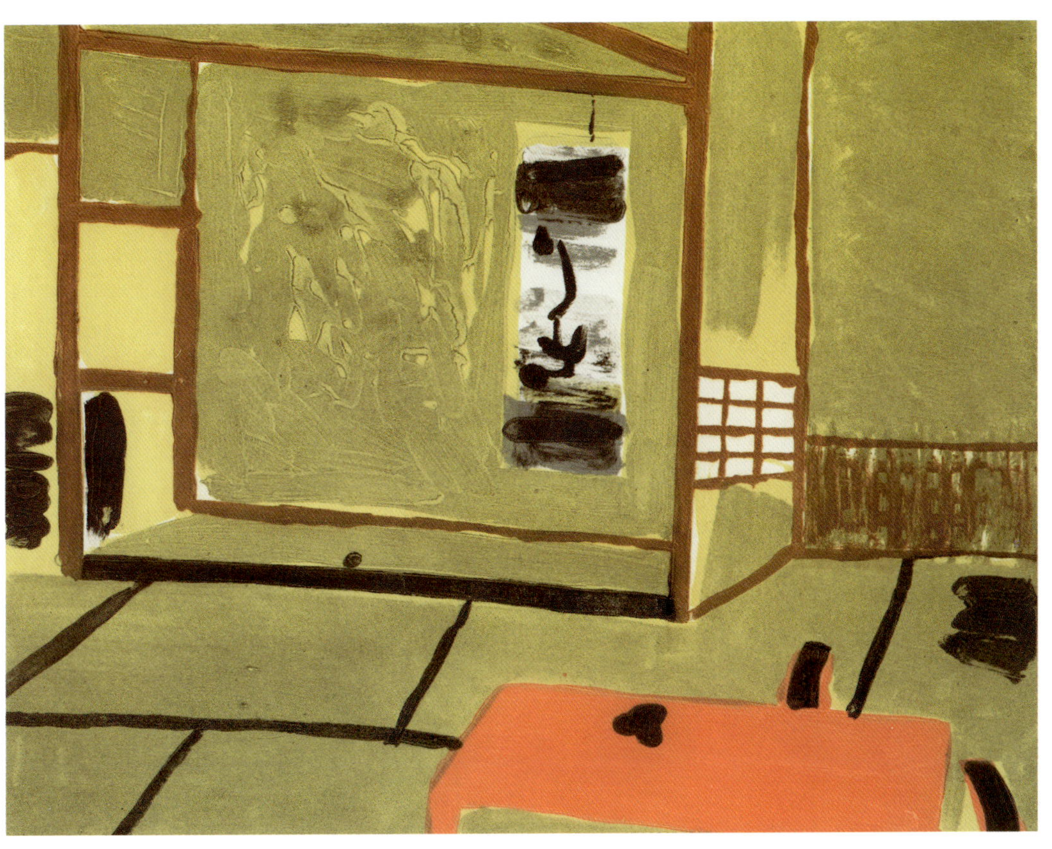

Elizabeth Blackadder OBE, RA
Japanese Interior, Kyoto
Carborundum
43 × 54 cm

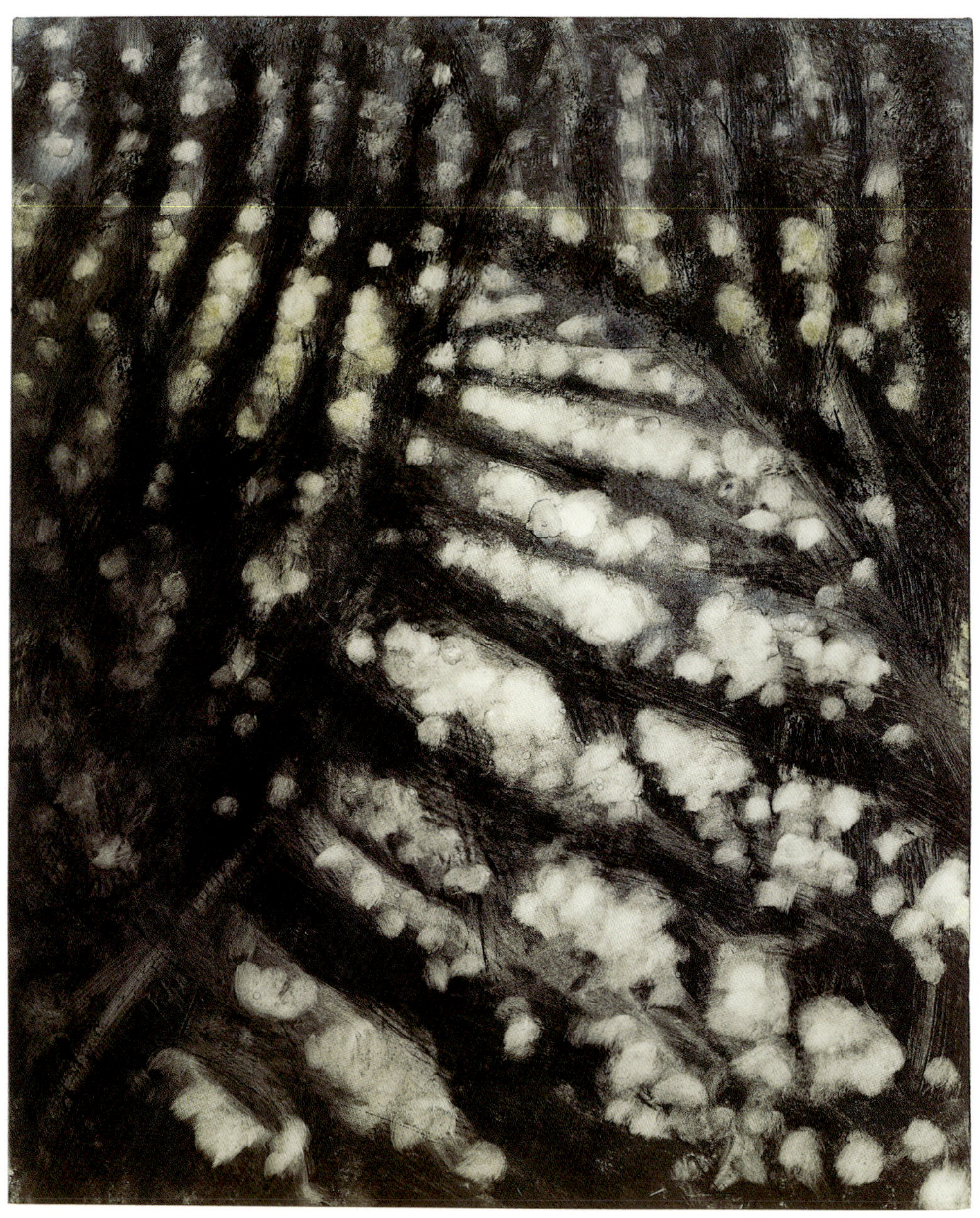

Bill Jacklin RA
Out of the Wood II
Monoprint
50 × 40 cm

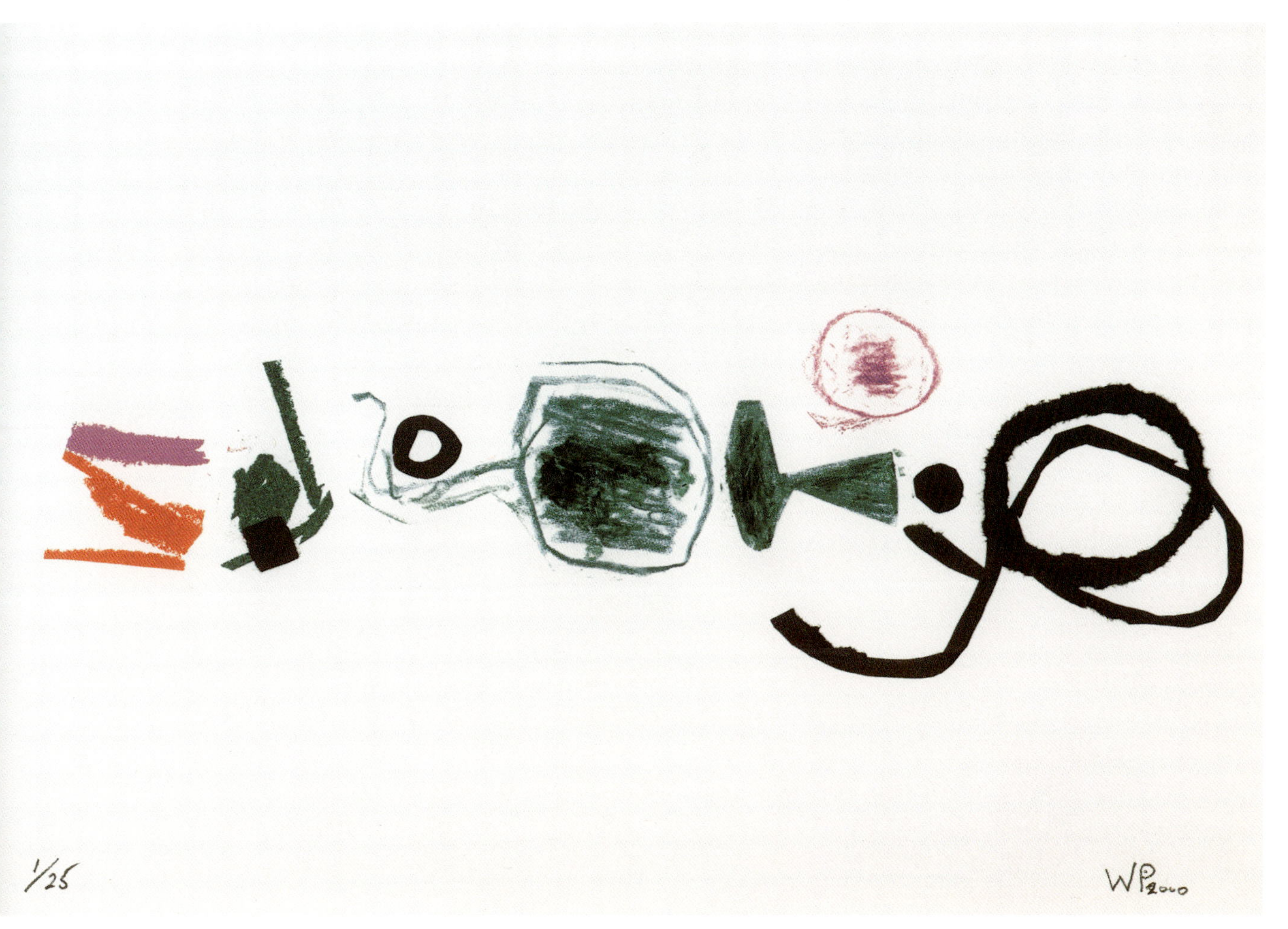

Wendy Pasmore
Odds and Ends No. 2
Silkscreen
23 × 33 cm

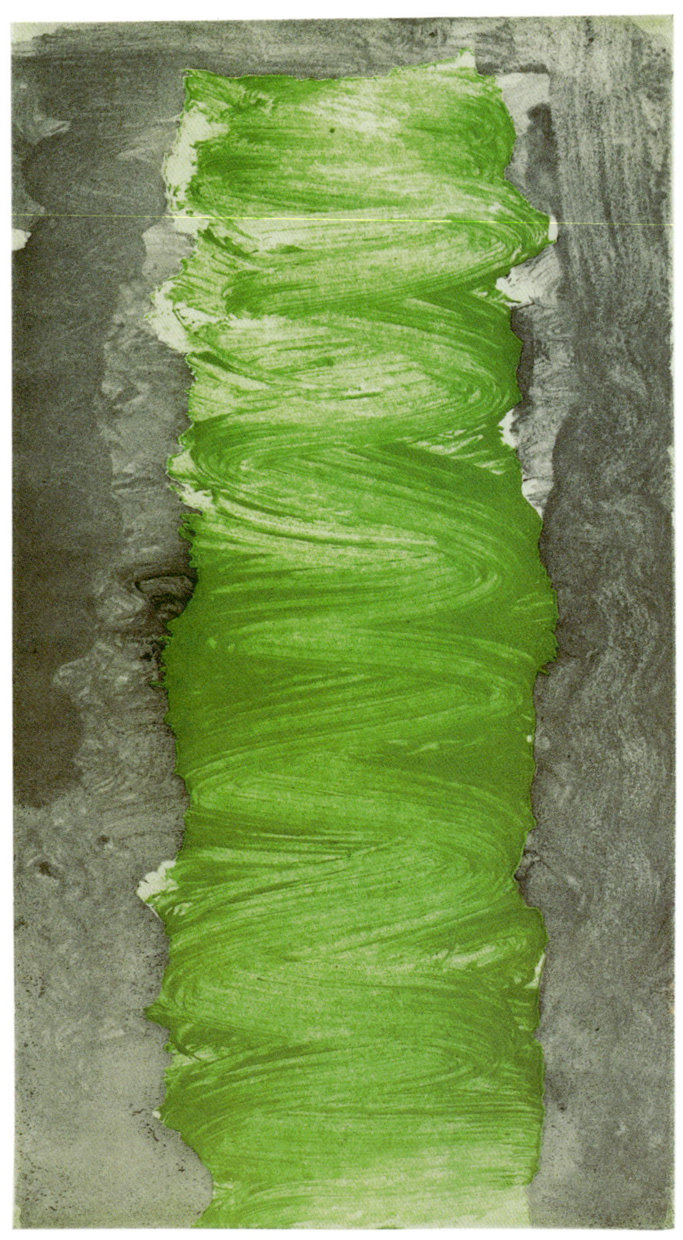

Sir Terry Frost RA
Green Jack
Etching
39 × 21 cm

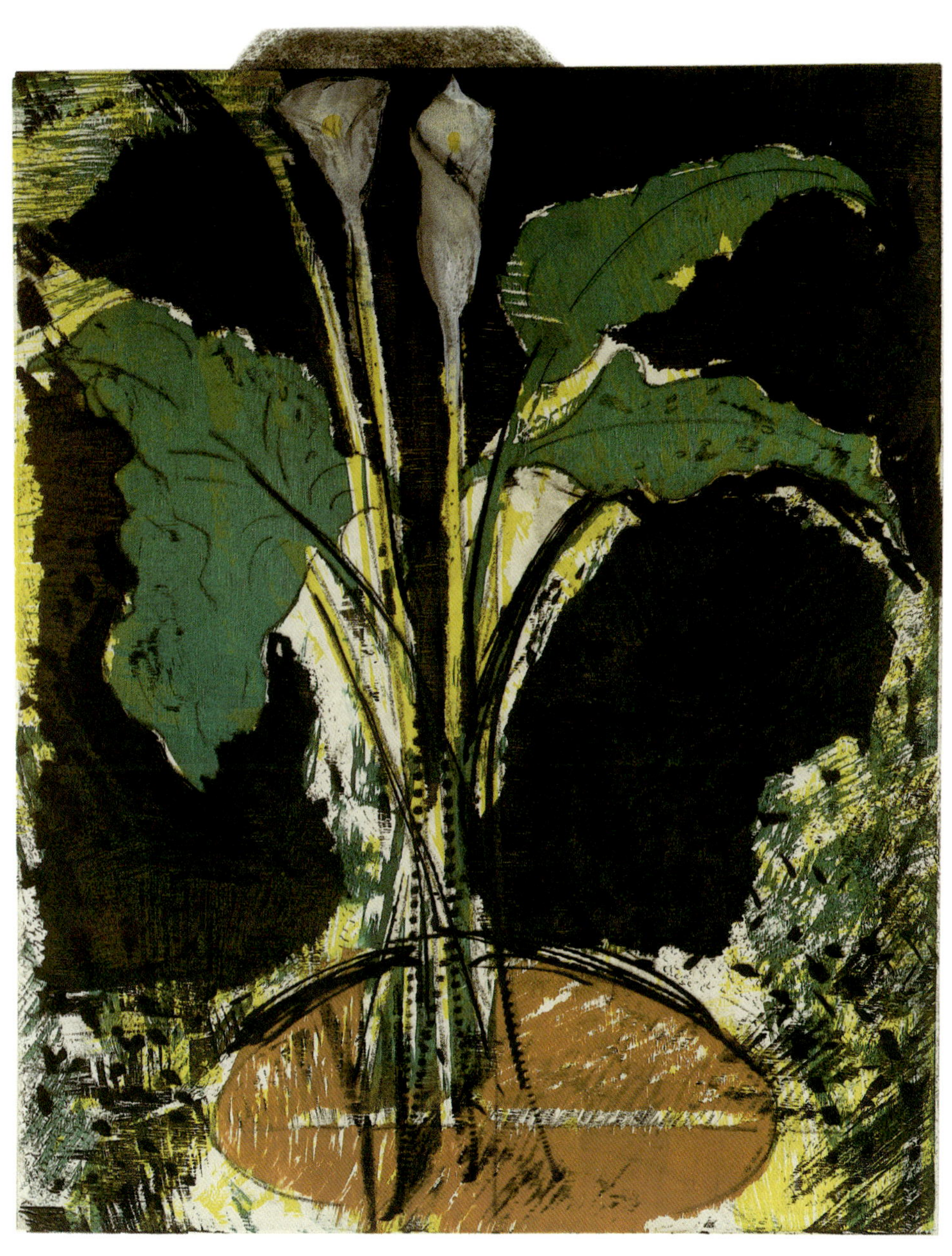

Jim Dine
Calla Lilies, Verona II
Etching and woodblock
70 × 56 cm

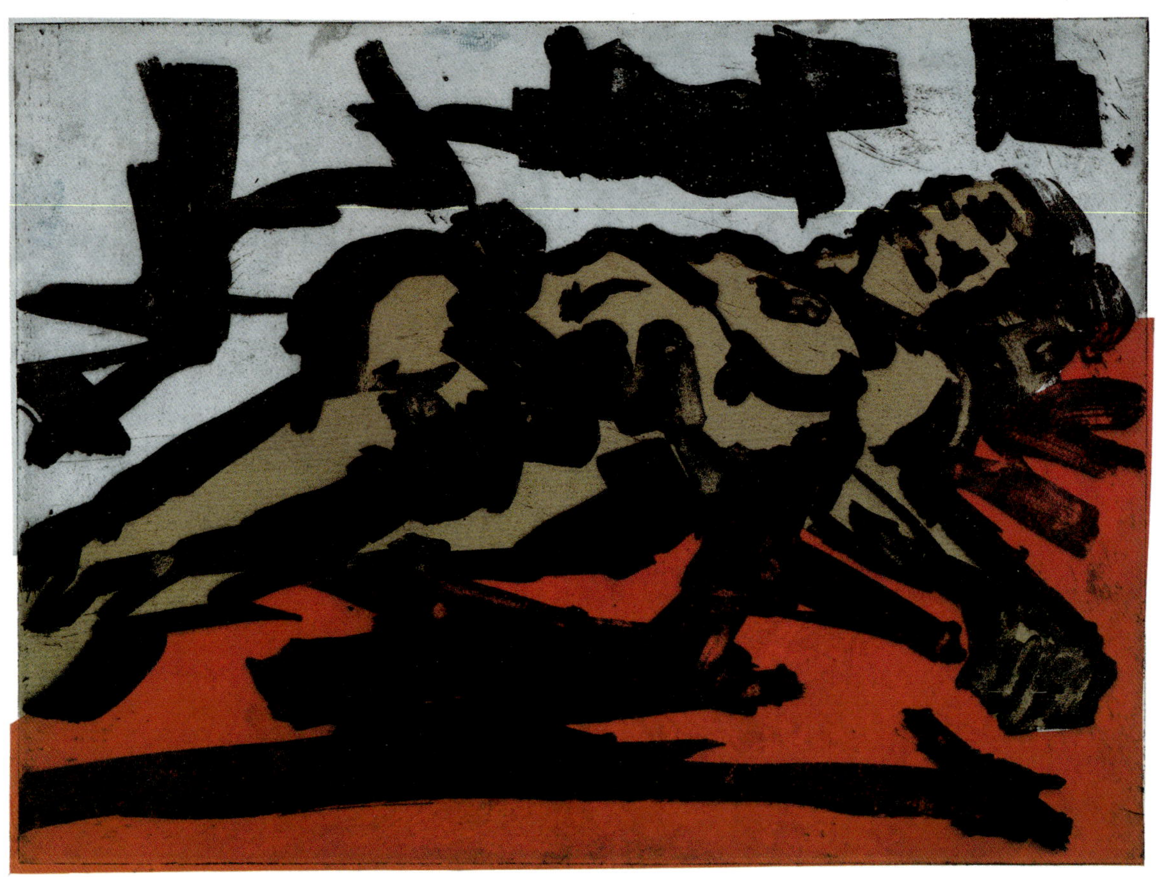

Simon Lawson
Jane Reclining
Sugarlift etching
30× 40 cm

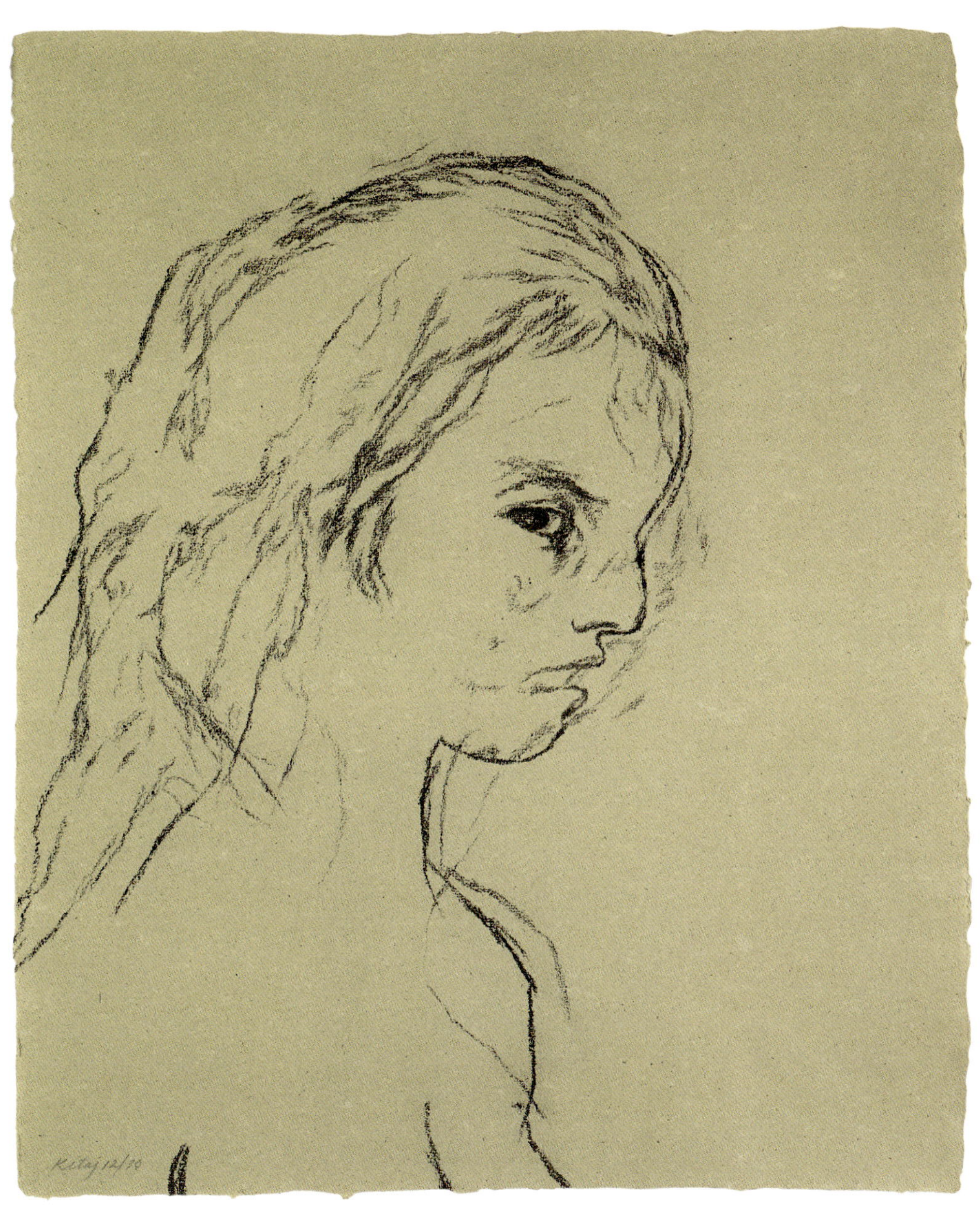

RB Kitaj RA
Eve
Lithograph
64 × 52 cm

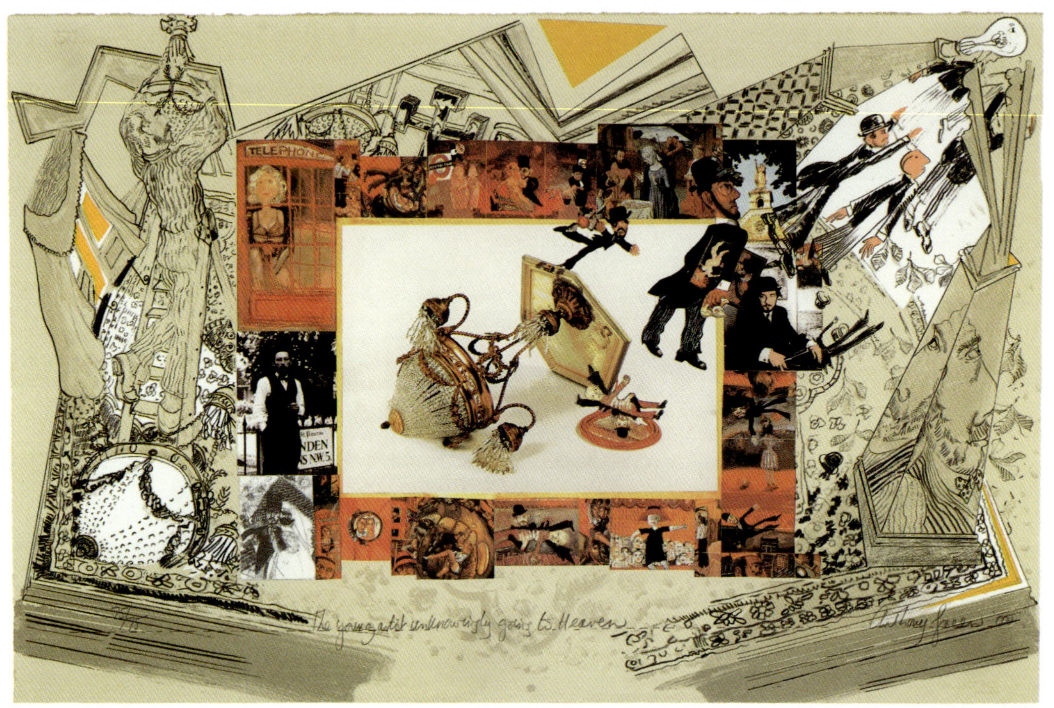

Anthony Green RA
Resurrection/The Young Artist unknowingly going to Heaven!
Silkscreen
75 × 111 cm

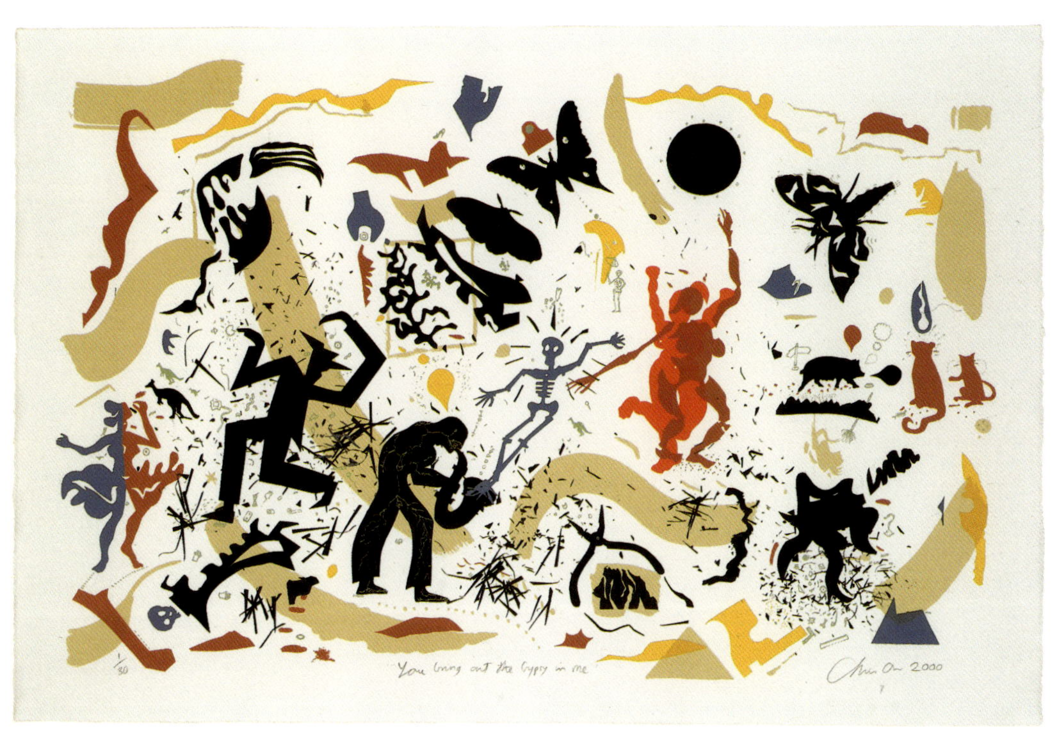

Prof. Chris Orr RA
You bring out the Gypsy in me
Silkscreen
77 × 112 cm

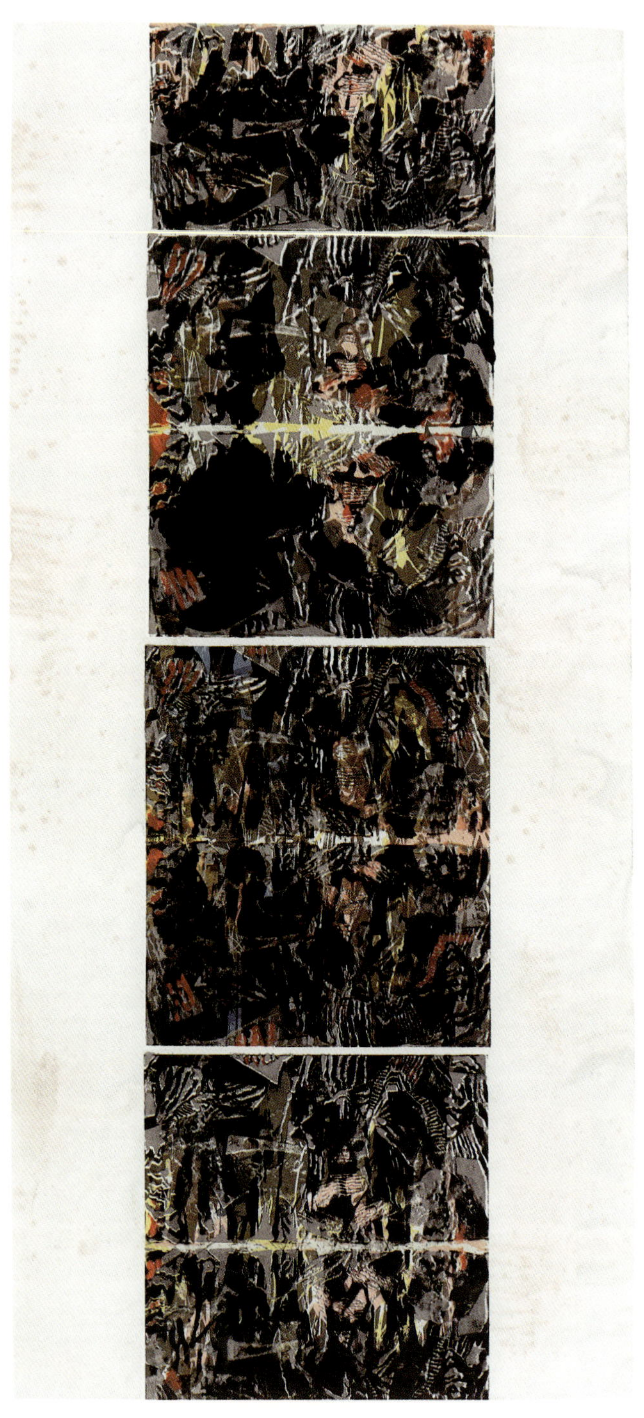

Thérèse Oulton
Untitled (L/8)
Screenprint and monoprint
67 × 30 cm

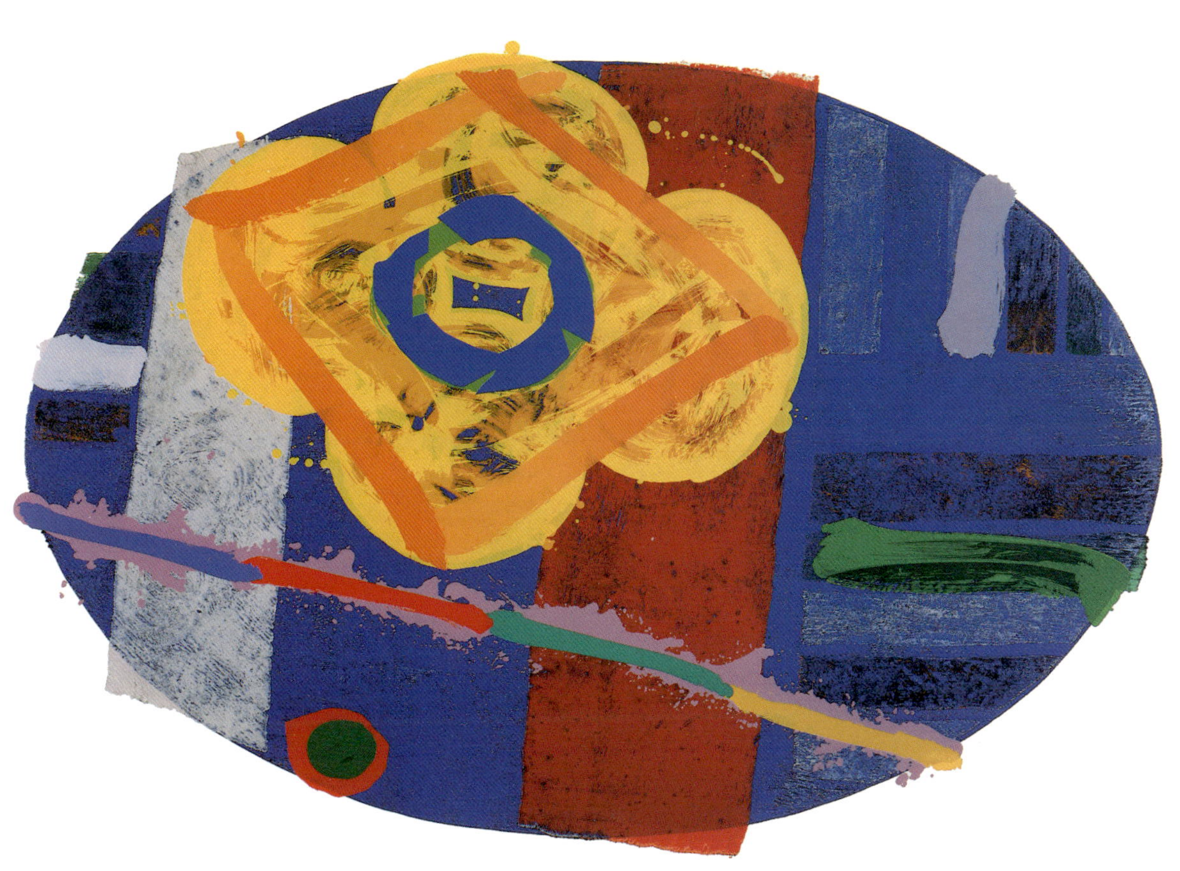

Albert Irvin RA
Oval III
Screenprint with woodblock
115 × 158 cm

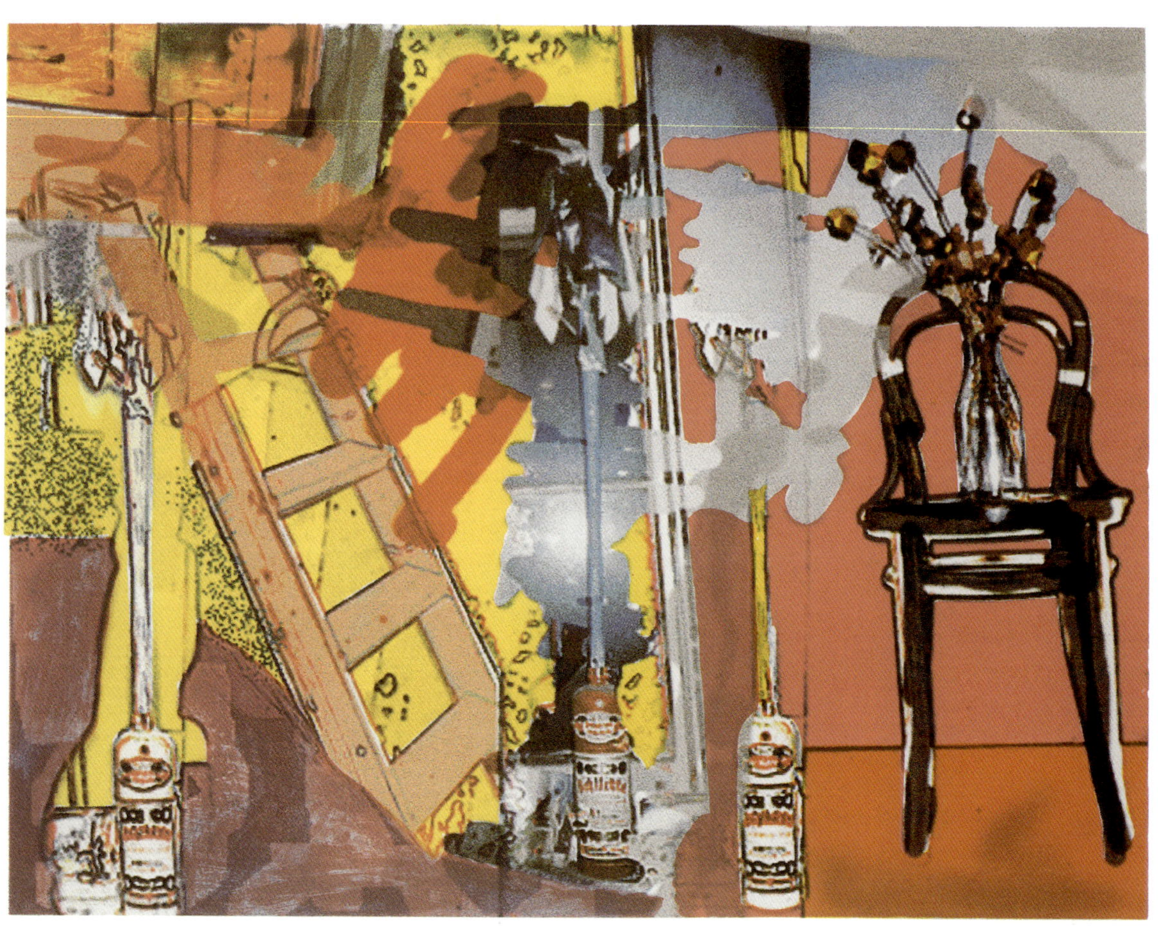

Alan Cox
In the Loft
Lithograph
54 × 68 cm

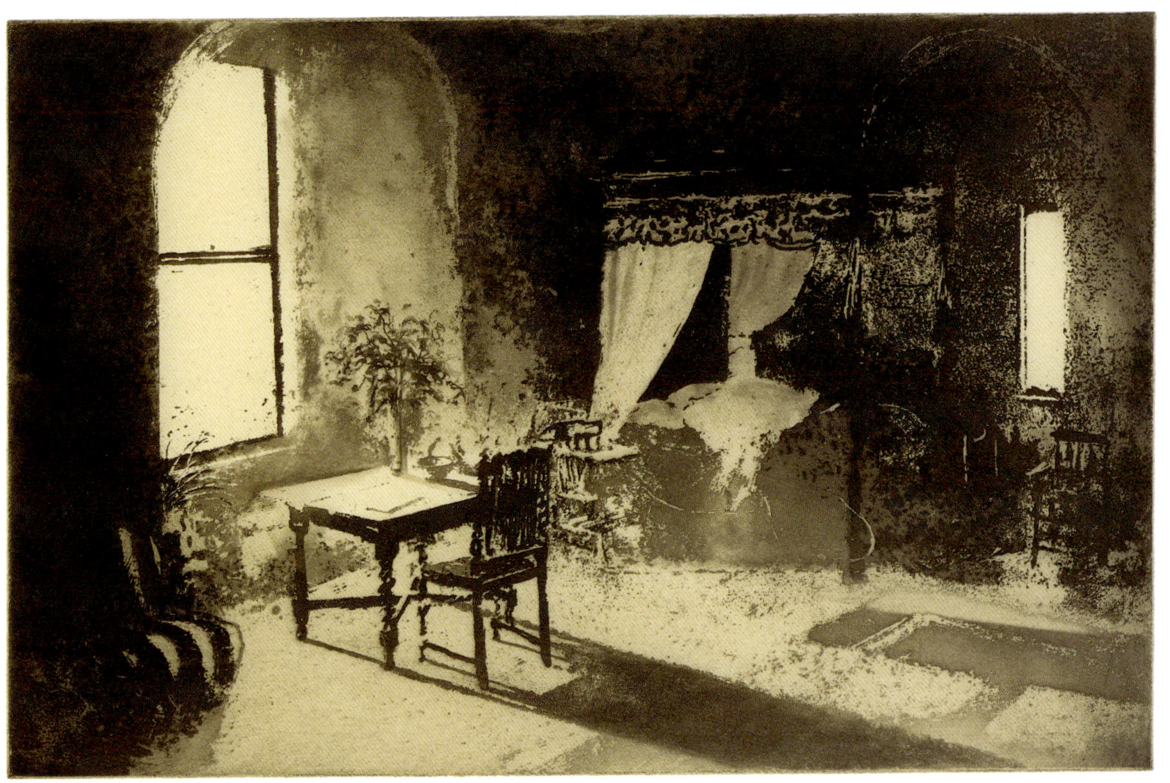

Norman Ackroyd RA
Oranmore Castle – Noon
Etching
37 × 52 cm

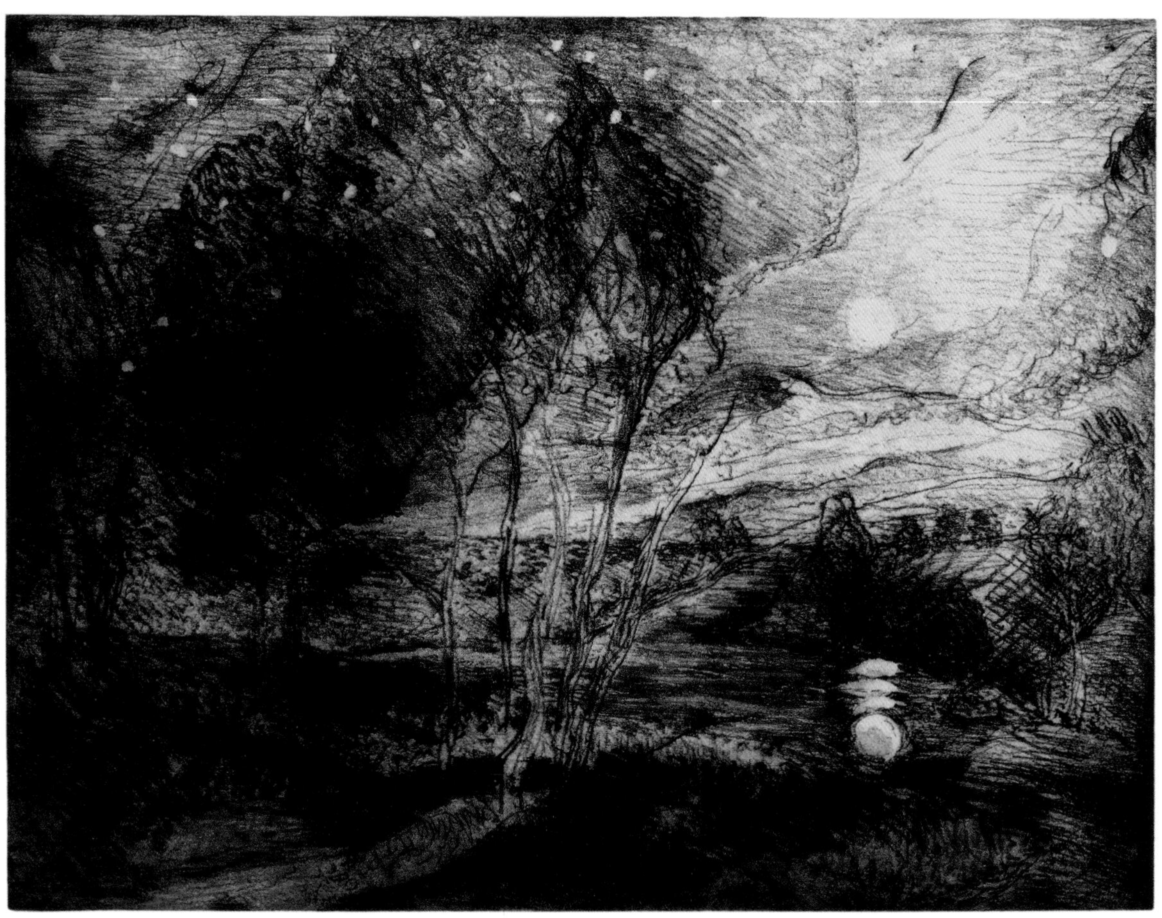

John Hubbard
After Rubens II
Etching
30 × 39 cm

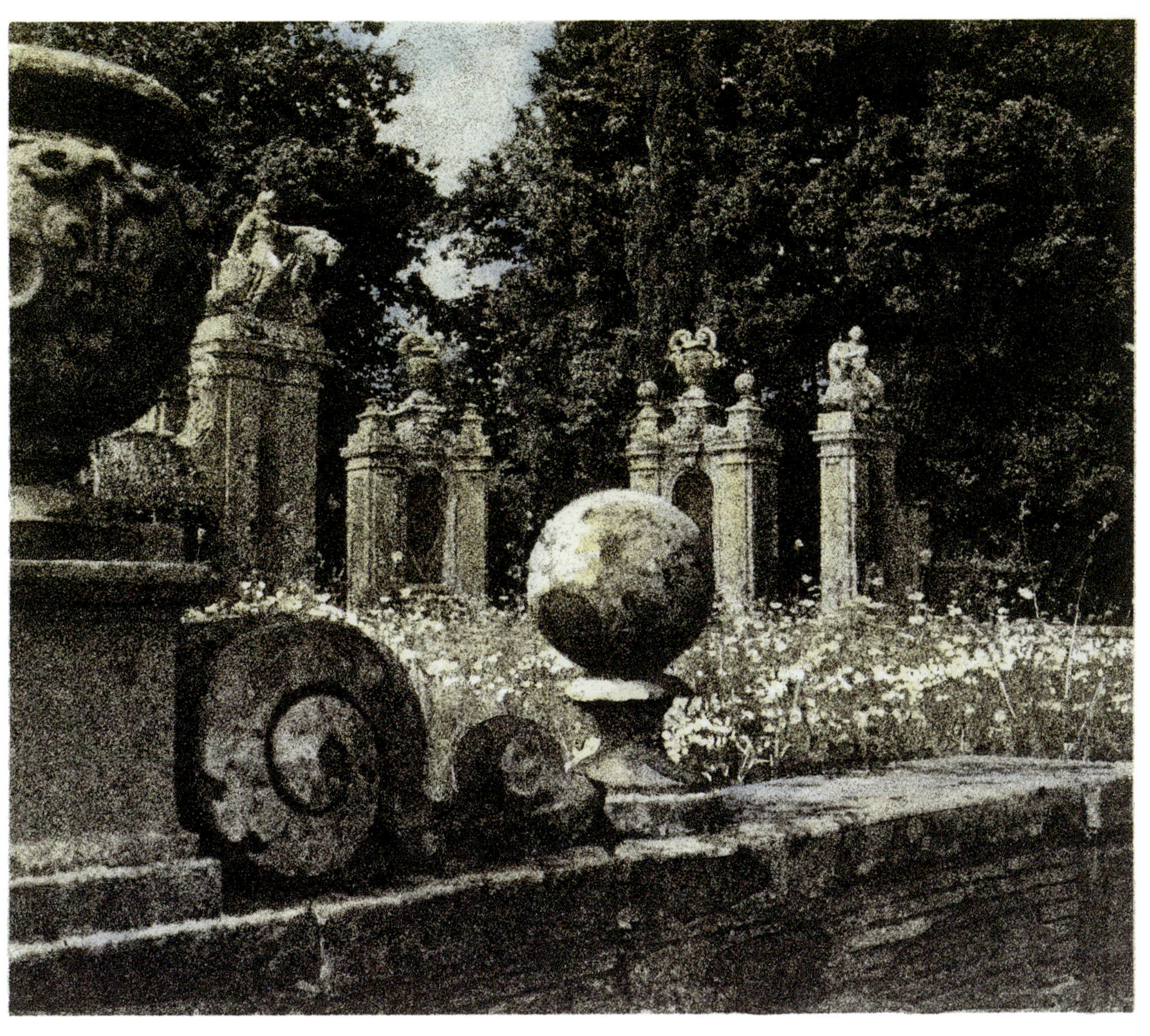

Jennifer Dickson RA
Gateway to Oblivion (Palazzo Farnese, Caprarola)
Etching and watercolour
33 × 37 cm

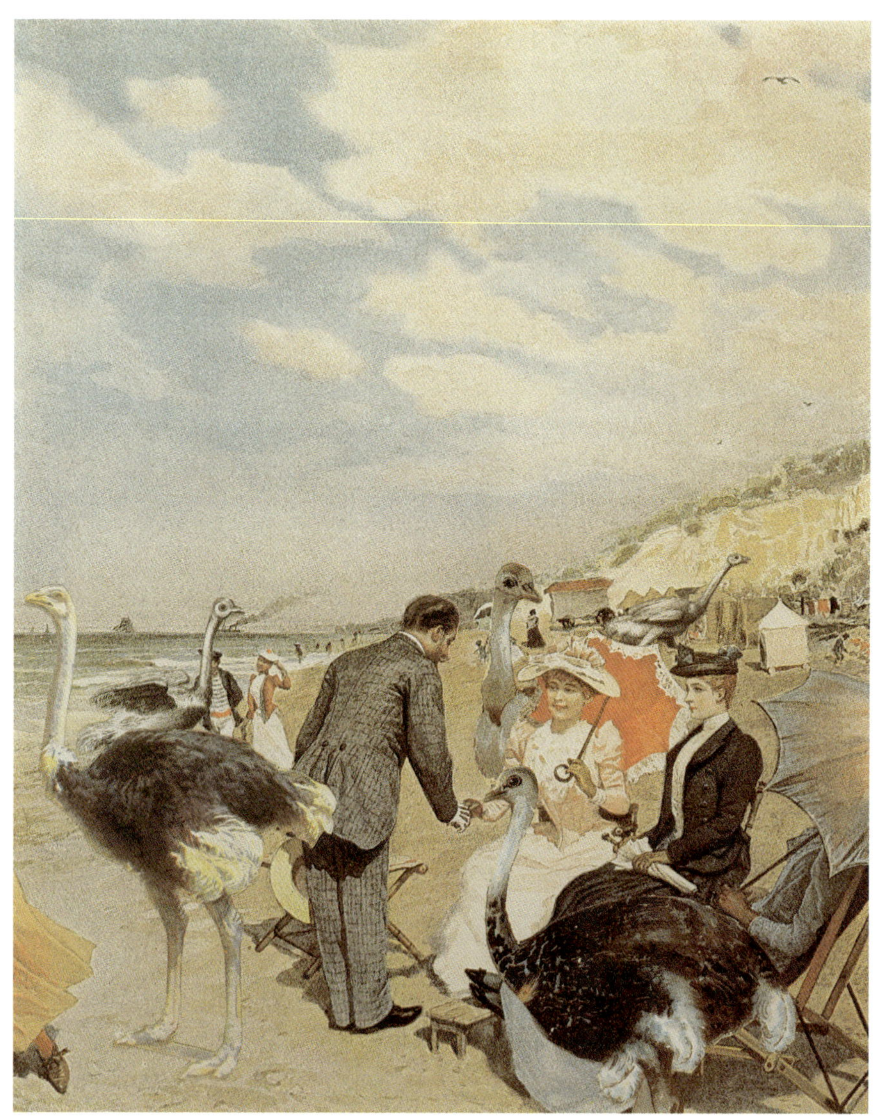

Peter Blake CBE, RA
Ostrich Beach
Silkscreen
32 × 25 cm

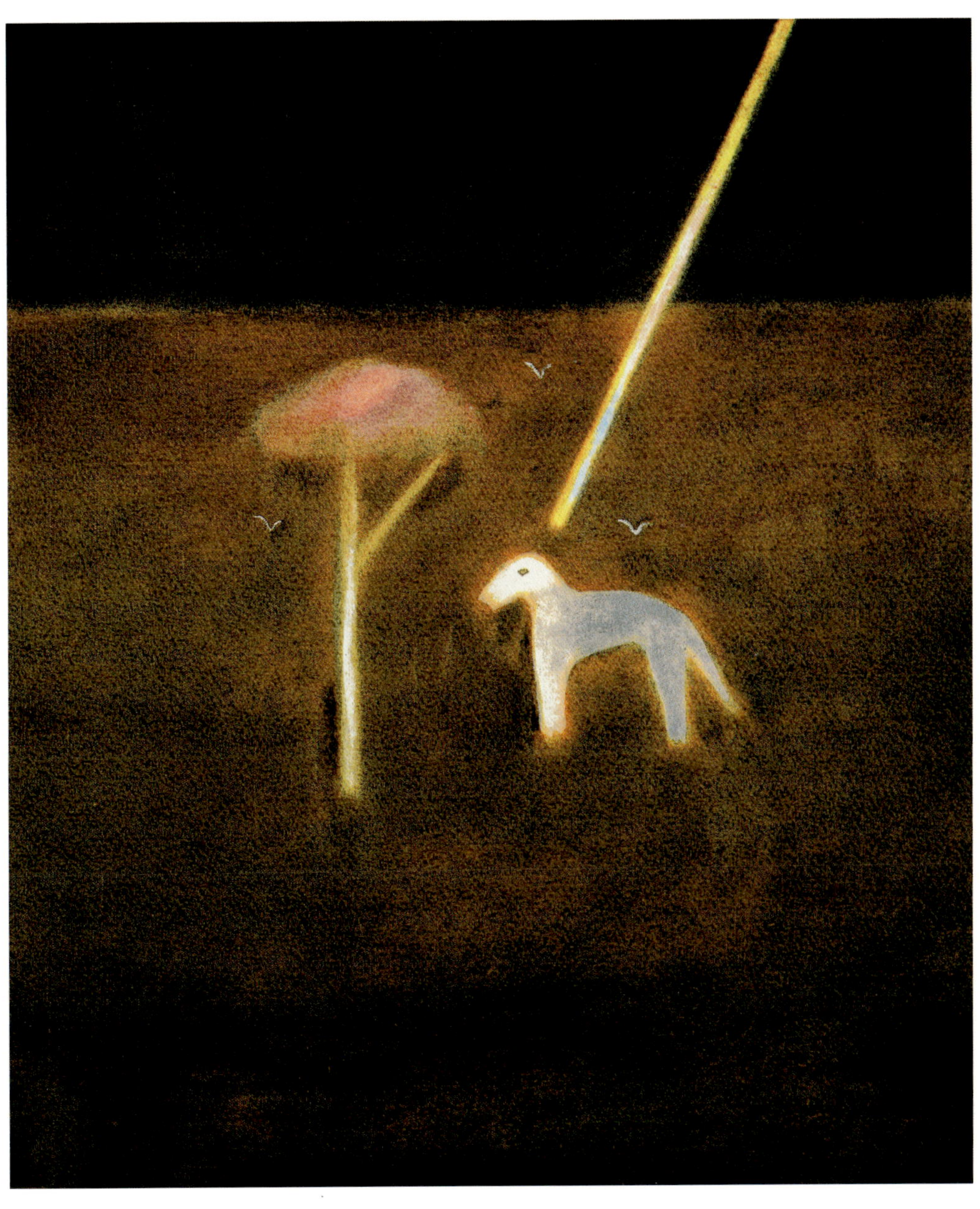

Craigie Aitchison RA
Wayney and the Pink Tree
Screenprint
64 × 54 cm

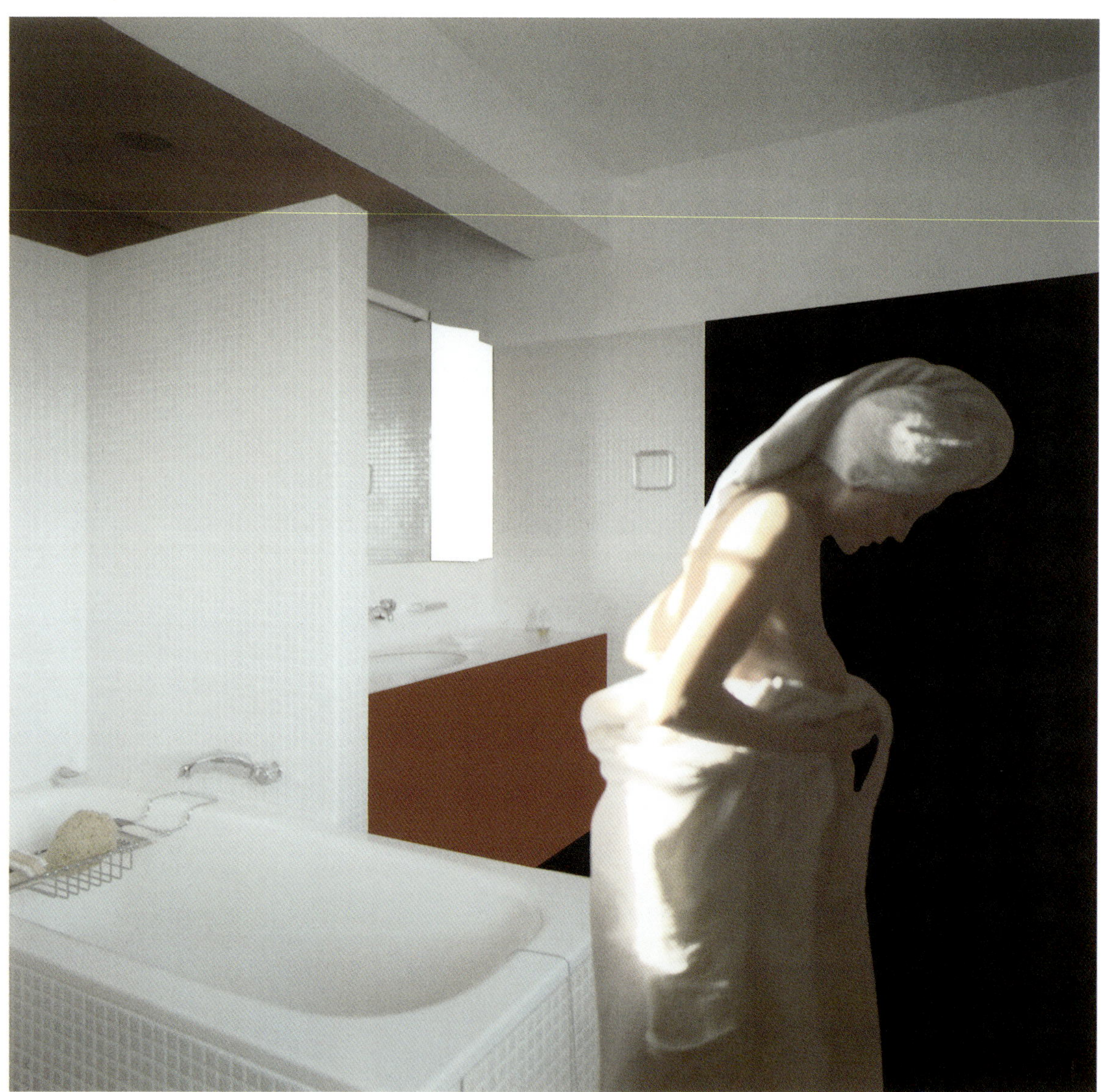

Richard Hamilton
Bathroom, fig. 2
Iris print
40 × 39 cm

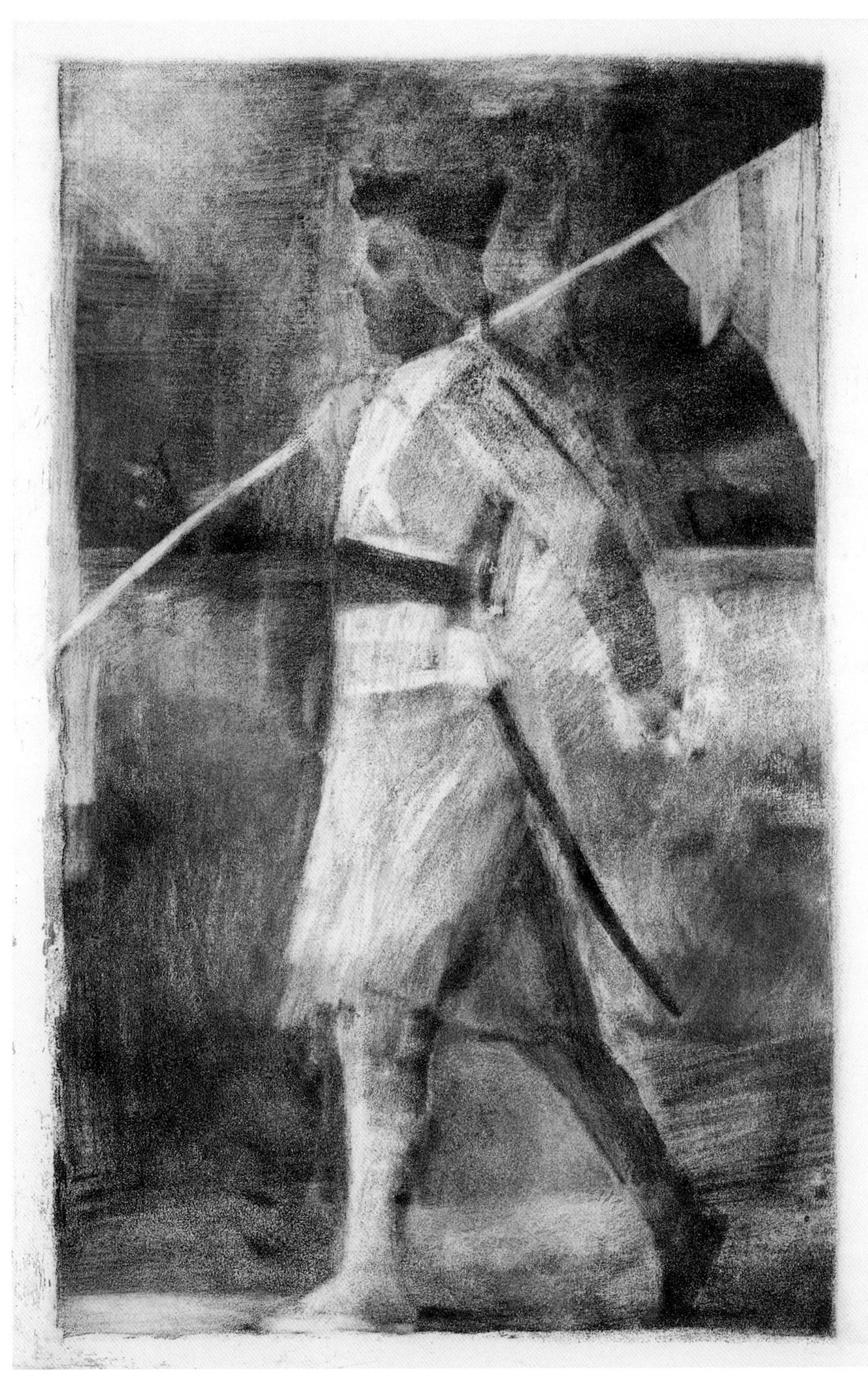

Peter Freeth RA
A Song from Childhood
Aquatint
58 × 36 cm

SMALL WESTON ROOM

As Anthony Green explains it: 'The small south room until last year was packed edge-to-edge with small paintings by both modest professionals and amateur painters, and some distinguished Academicians. Last year because we actually filleted some of our rooms – for instance the David Hockney room only had six works in it – it seemed that this was the time to pare down this room from 300 paintings to 82, which is what I did. This year I'm again going for a similar hang. It will be a mixture of paintings which please me; still revolutionary, although conservative at the edges. Most of the artists that I show here know how to draw, which of course is a lost art nowadays. Artists who are possibly out of fashion – expressionist, figuration, romance – these are not 'going' subjects at the moment but they are timeless. This is what the Academy is at its best doing – it supports these lone voices. This room saves souls.'

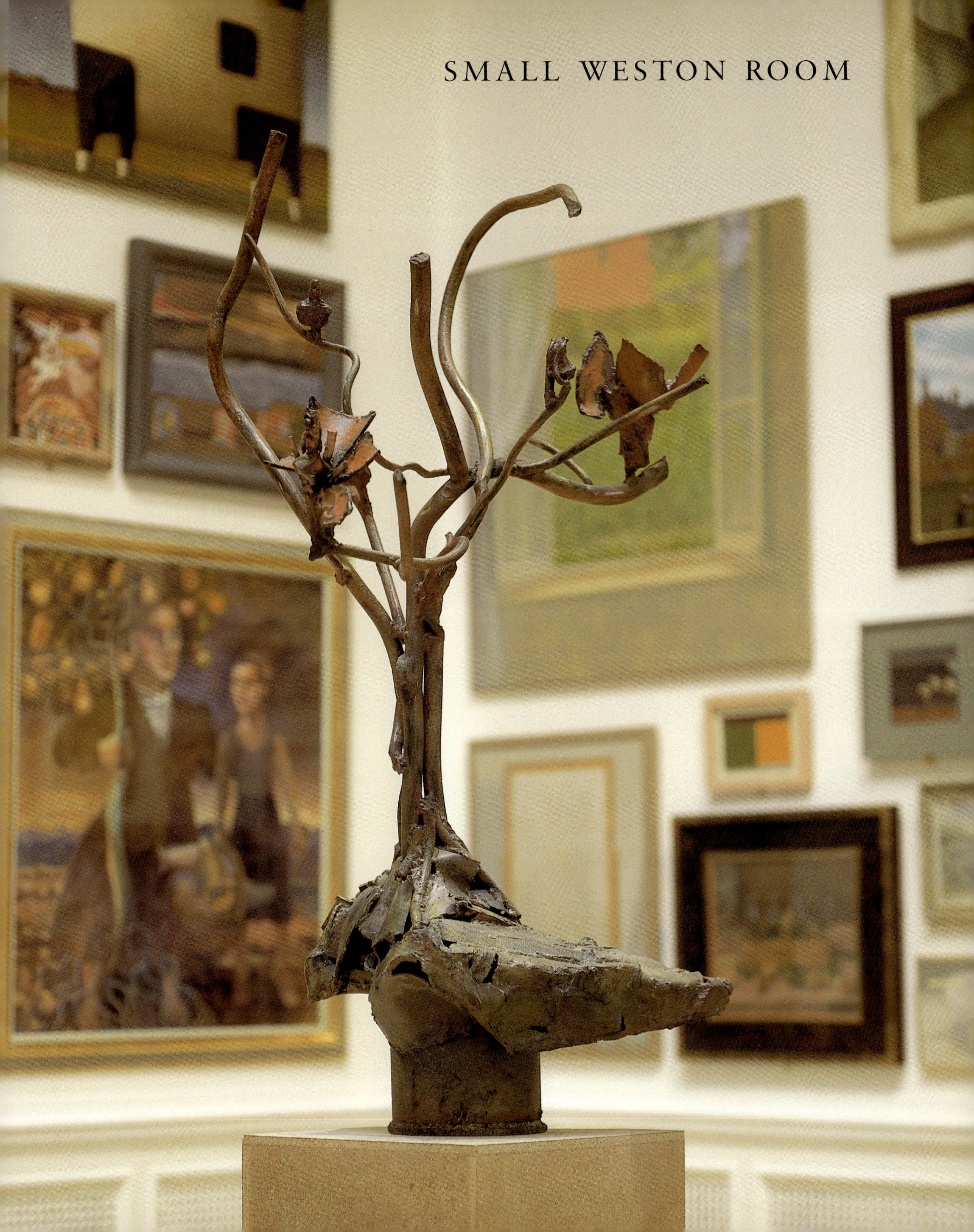

SMALL WESTON ROOM

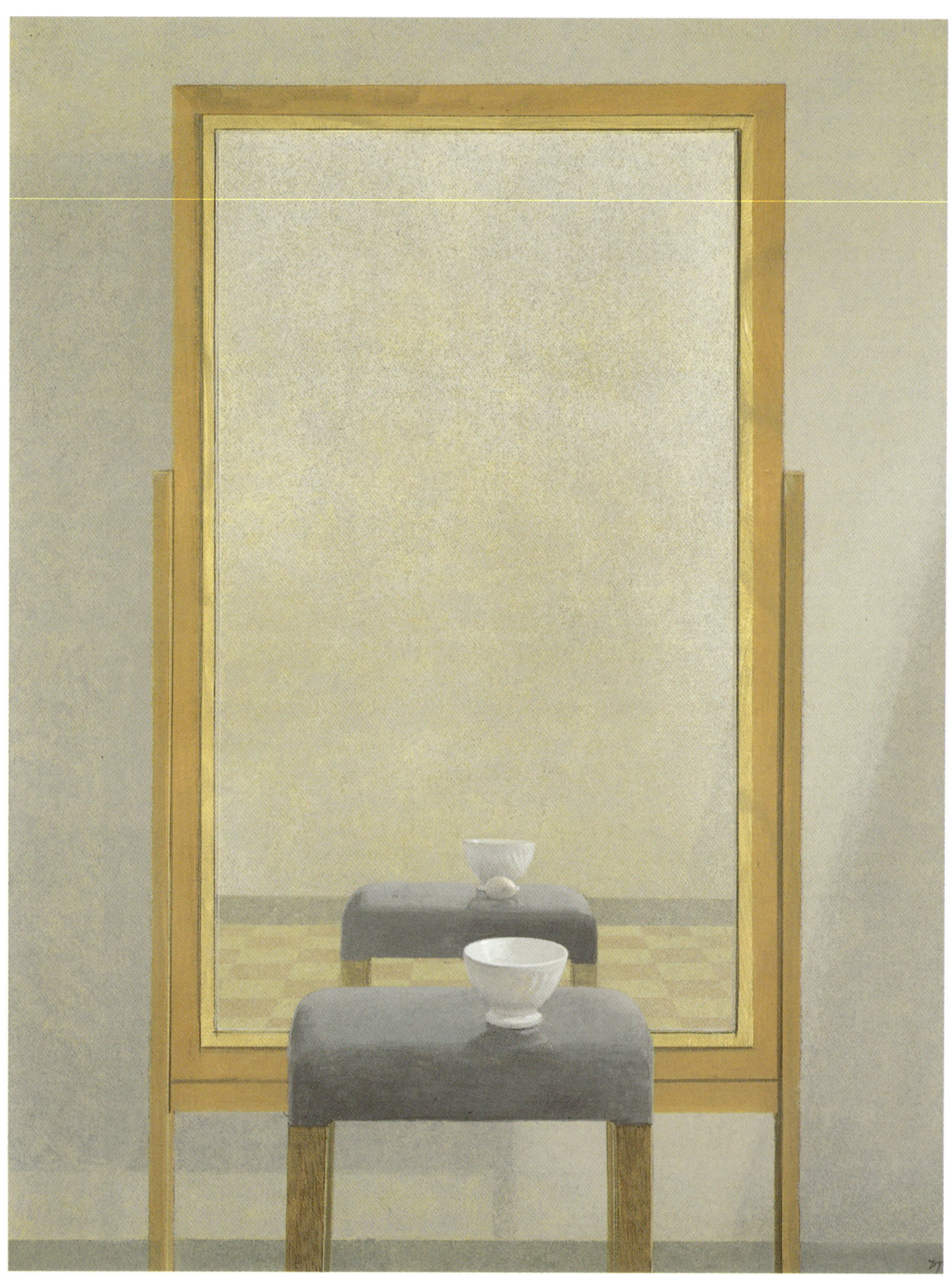

David Tindle RA
The Hidden Egg
Egg tempera
71 × 53 cm

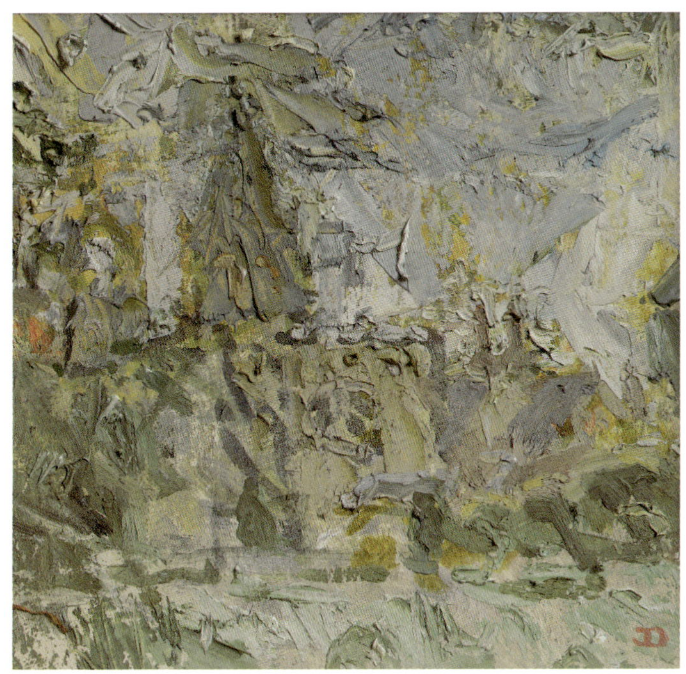

Jane Dowling
Christchurch Cathedral – Oxford
Oil
20 × 20 cm

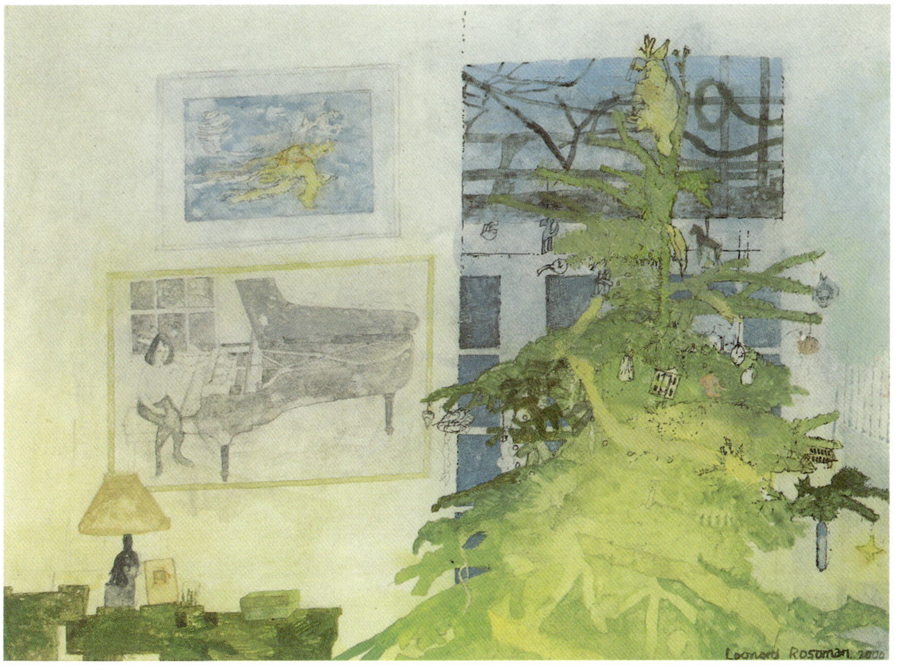

Leonard Rosoman OBE, RA
Christmas
Watercolour
28 × 37 cm

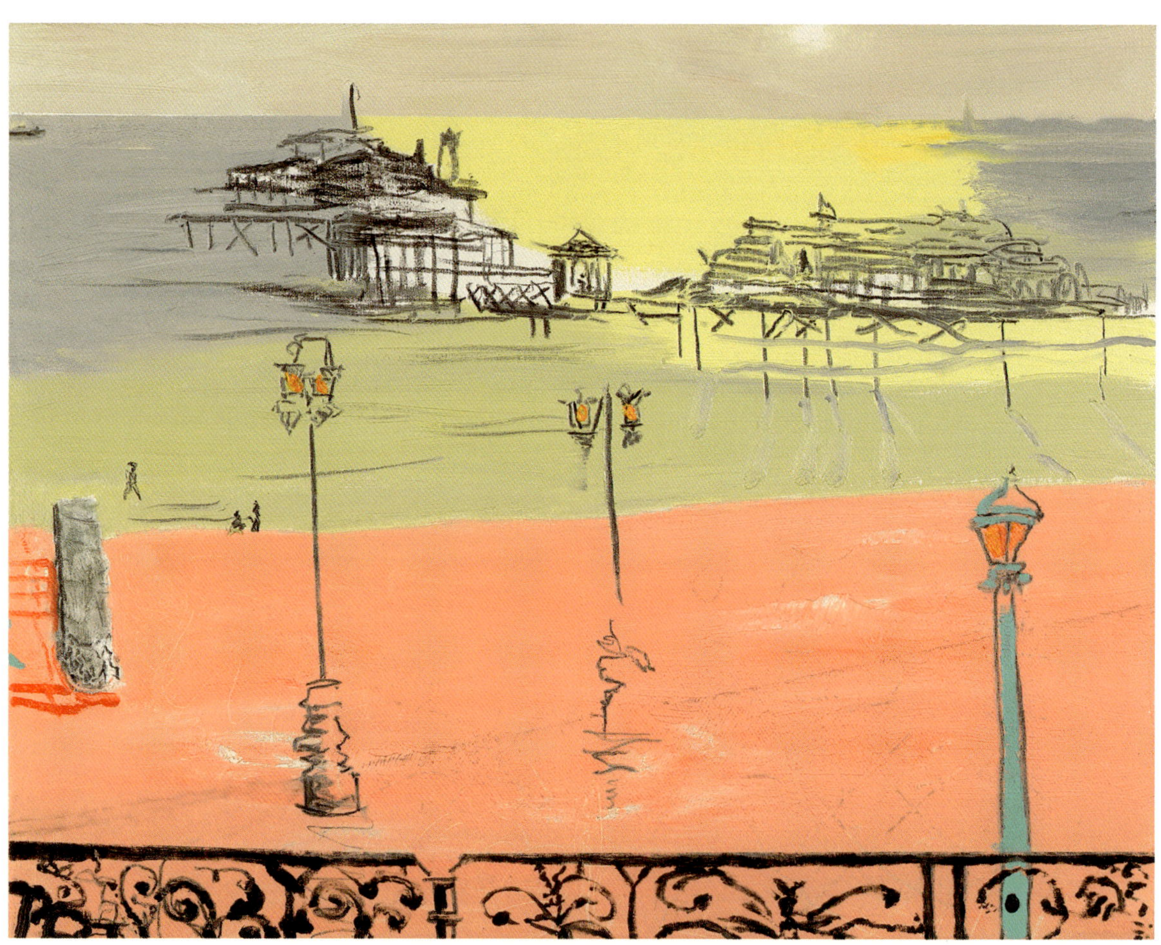

Patrick Procktor RA
Hove
Oil
61 × 76 cm

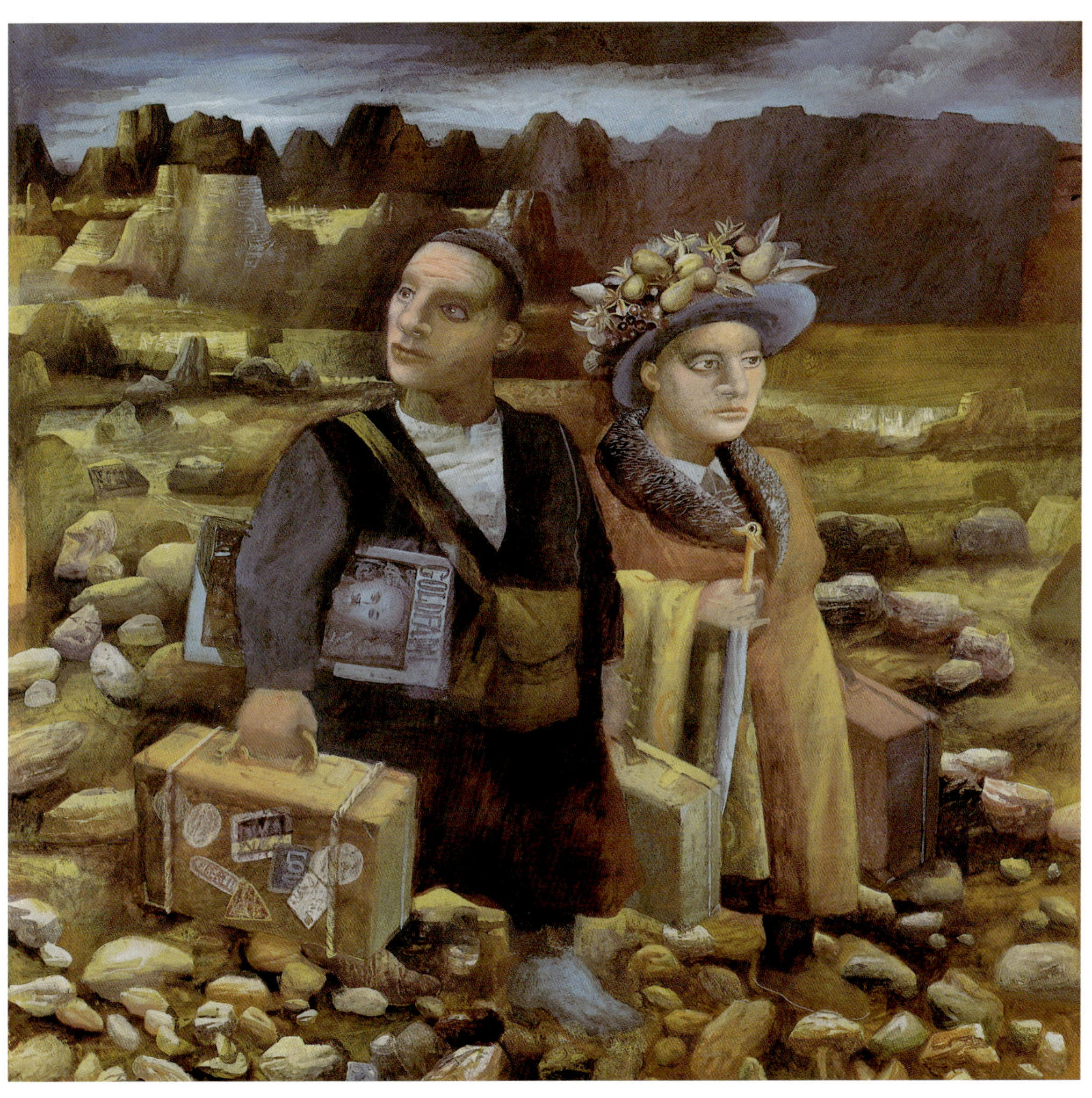

Michael Rooney RA
New World People
Tempera
85 × 85 cm

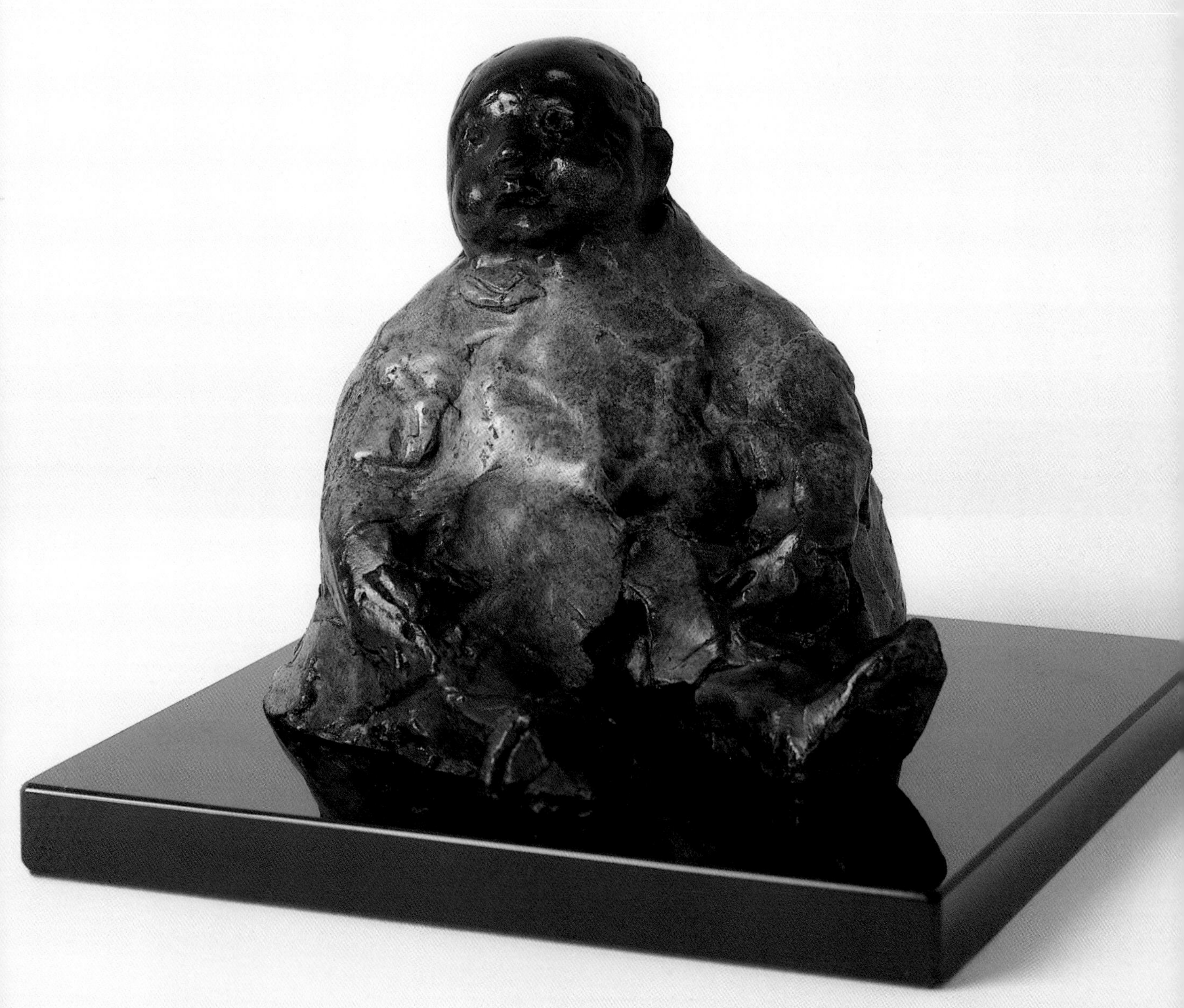

James Butler RA
Babe
Bronze
h 17 cm

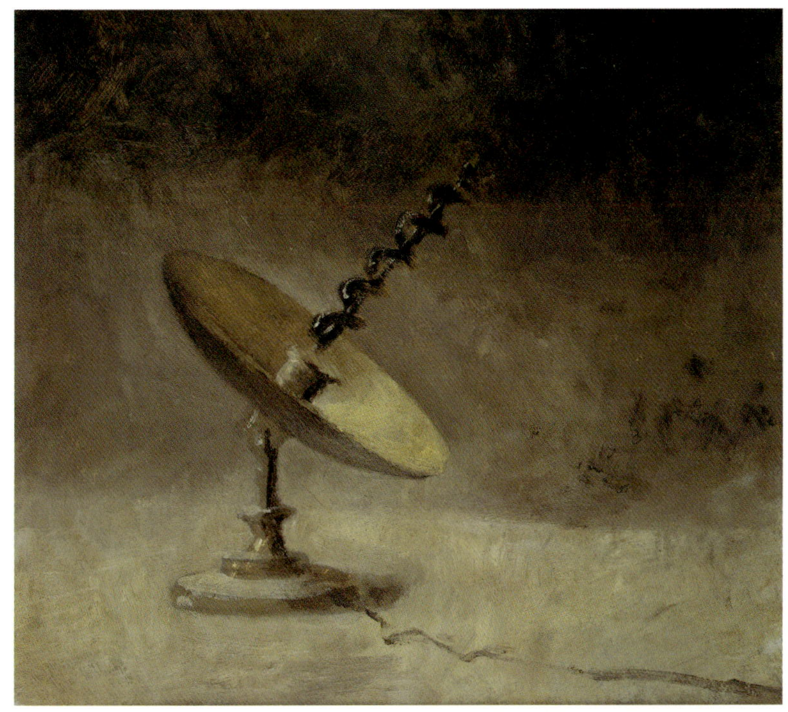

Julian Mitchell
Instrument
Oil
18 × 19 cm

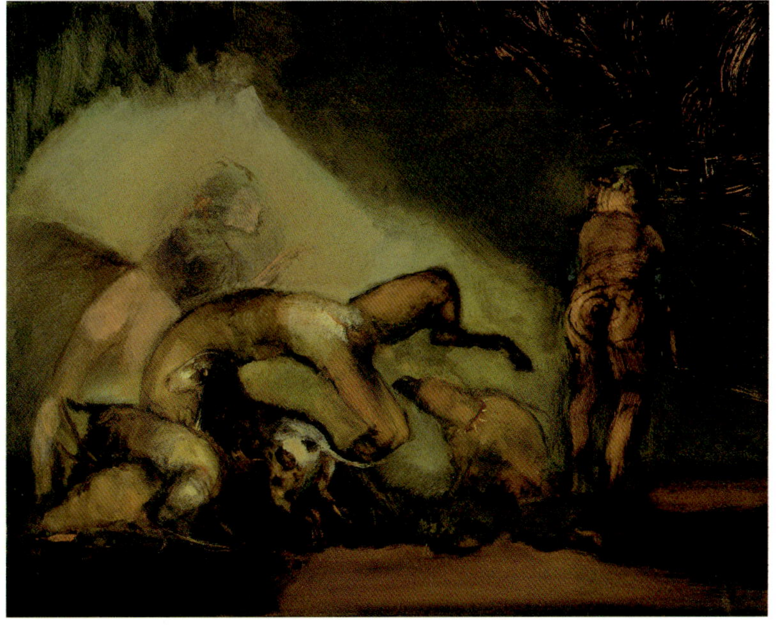

Ansel Krut
The Death of Acteon
Oil on copper
23 × 28 cm

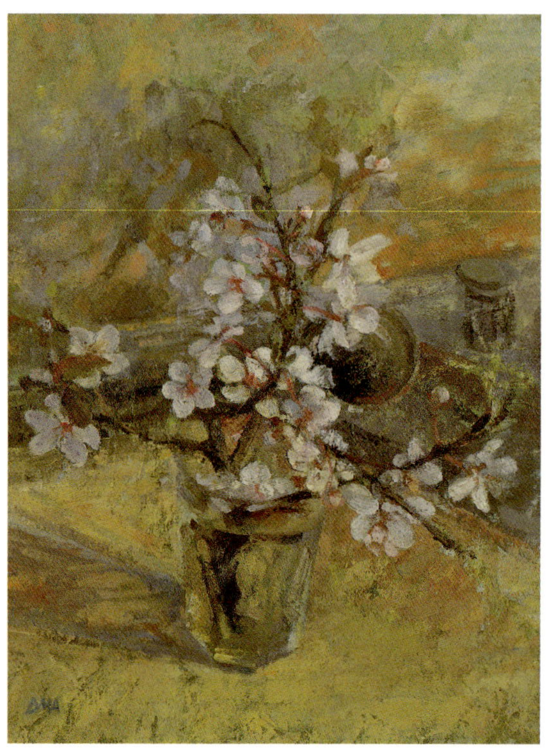

Diana Armfield RA
Early Blossom on the Easel
Oil
28 × 21 cm

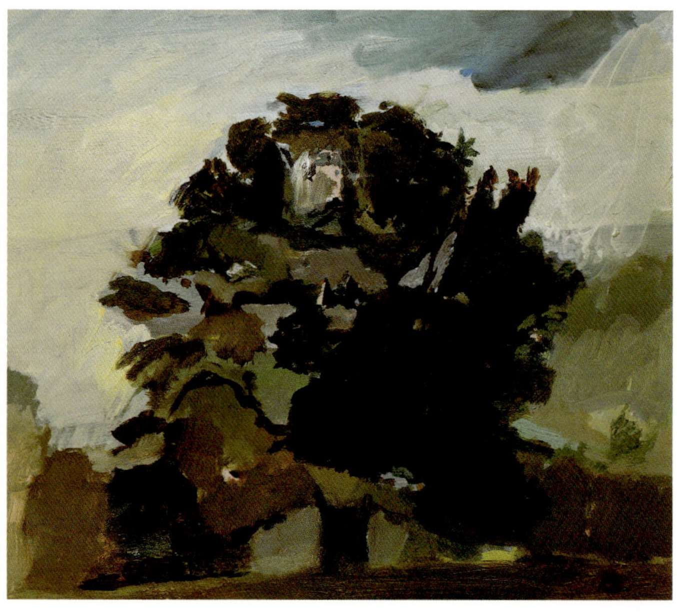

Ben Levene RA
Electric Storm
Oil
25 × 77 cm

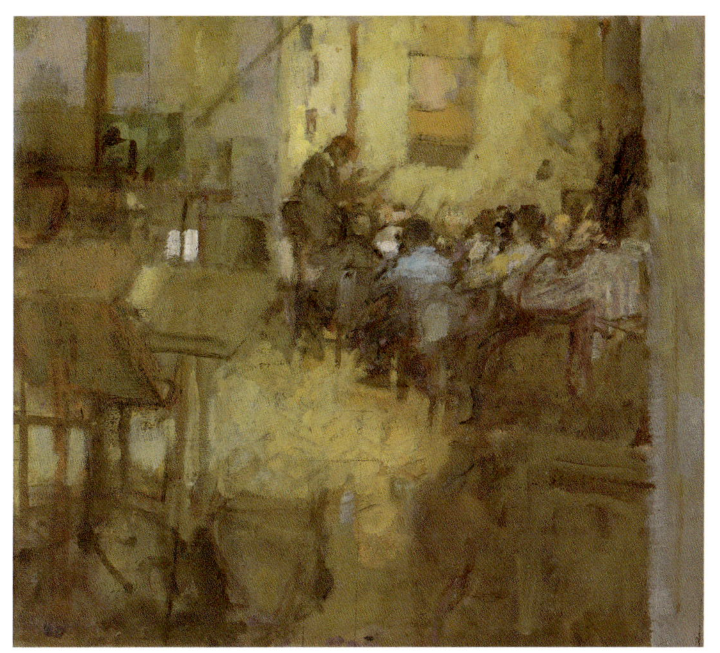

Bernard Dunstan RA
Rehearsal at Maida Vale
Oil
28 × 30 cm

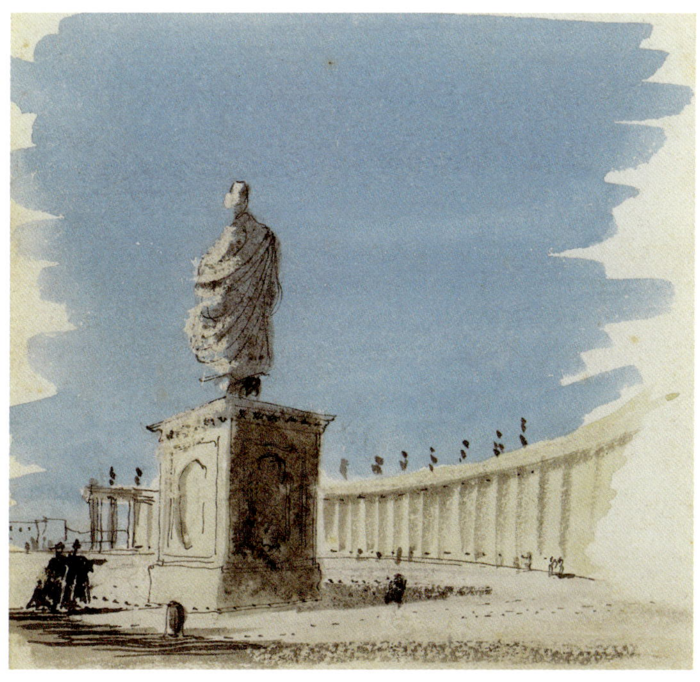

Sir Hugh Casson CH, KCVO, PPRA
Piazza S. Pietro, Rome
Watercolour
11 × 12 cm

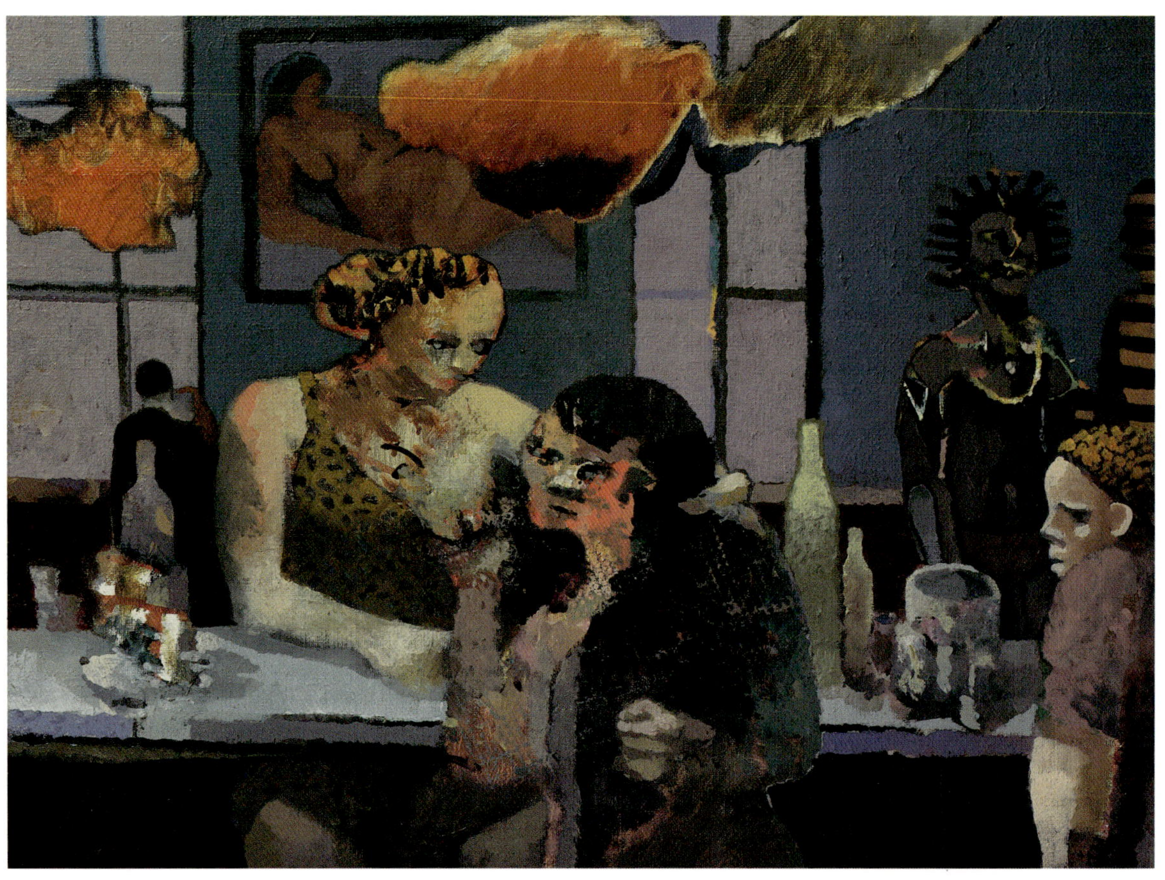

Tom Phillips RA
The Great Bar
Oil
33 × 43 cm

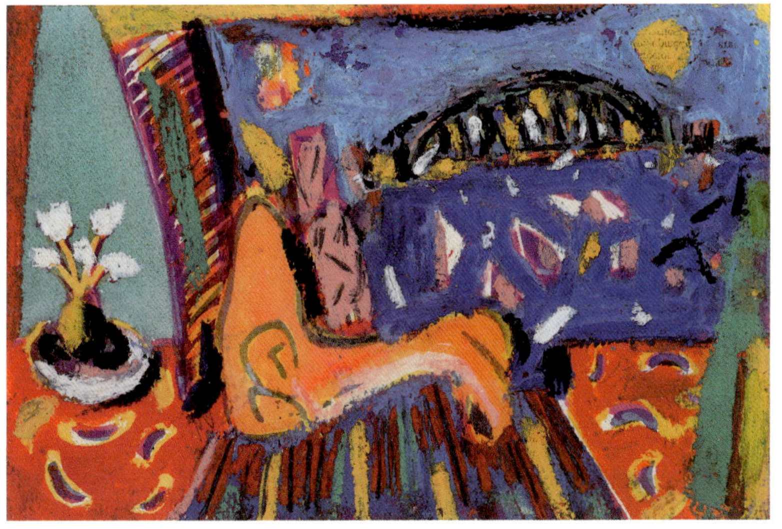

Willie Jasper
Untitled
Pastel
15 × 21 cm

GALLERY III

The largest gallery in the Academy and the centrepiece of the Summer Exhibition has been hung by two Academicians – Paul Huxley and Stephen Farthing the latter being involved with the Summer show for the first time. 'It should really be the room where the *tour de force* paintings are hung,' says Huxley, 'it's got the potential for it.' Given that, it's revealing that Stephen Farthing should thus describe how the process of hanging began: 'We started from the ends. At one end we had Balthus – a wonderful painting of a girl on a bed, which we felt needed to be seen alone' – and at the other Norman Blamey, with six paintings as a posthumous tribute. We worked from those two directions, those two priorities. Because it's predominantly large paintings by Members, when these are in place, what you're effectively doing is finding bridges between them. It would be nice to think there was an exact science by which you found those bridges, but my guess is that it's done through looking at colour and size. It's to do with making a coherent-looking space.'

Farthing continues: 'Very few people have a natural instinct for hanging group shows. It's really an enormous number of compromises. It's not like Nicholas Serota hanging a room in the new Tate. You can't afford yourself the luxury of being pure. It's actually a very interesting exercise because all sorts of chance meetings happen. That's the point of a group show – it's a social thing, the socialisation of artists' work. It's remarkable for me to see how say a painting by John Bellany can sit next to a Balthus, and actually have some interactive qualities. It's a bit like a cocktail party – every now and then people stop hunting out the big names and just chat to the person standing next to them. I would say that is the nature of this room.'

'It has to be said that the arrangements for hanging this show are anarchistic, it's a kind of federal state in which each hanger is given a room and you go for it. What Paul and I have done is pull out works that we like – which is where the elements of taste and favour come into it.' Huxley adds: 'Because of its size, it's the hardest gallery to put any personal stamp on. This is probably the only major group exhibition that is curated by about twelve people, so there is a mixture of anarchy and consensus in the way it's done.'

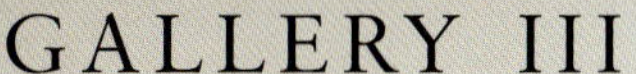
GALLERY III

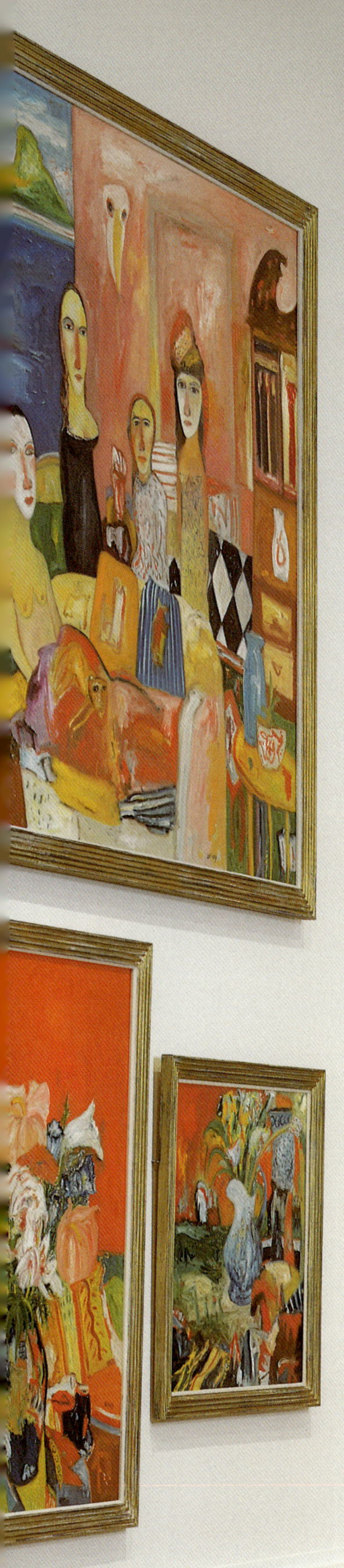

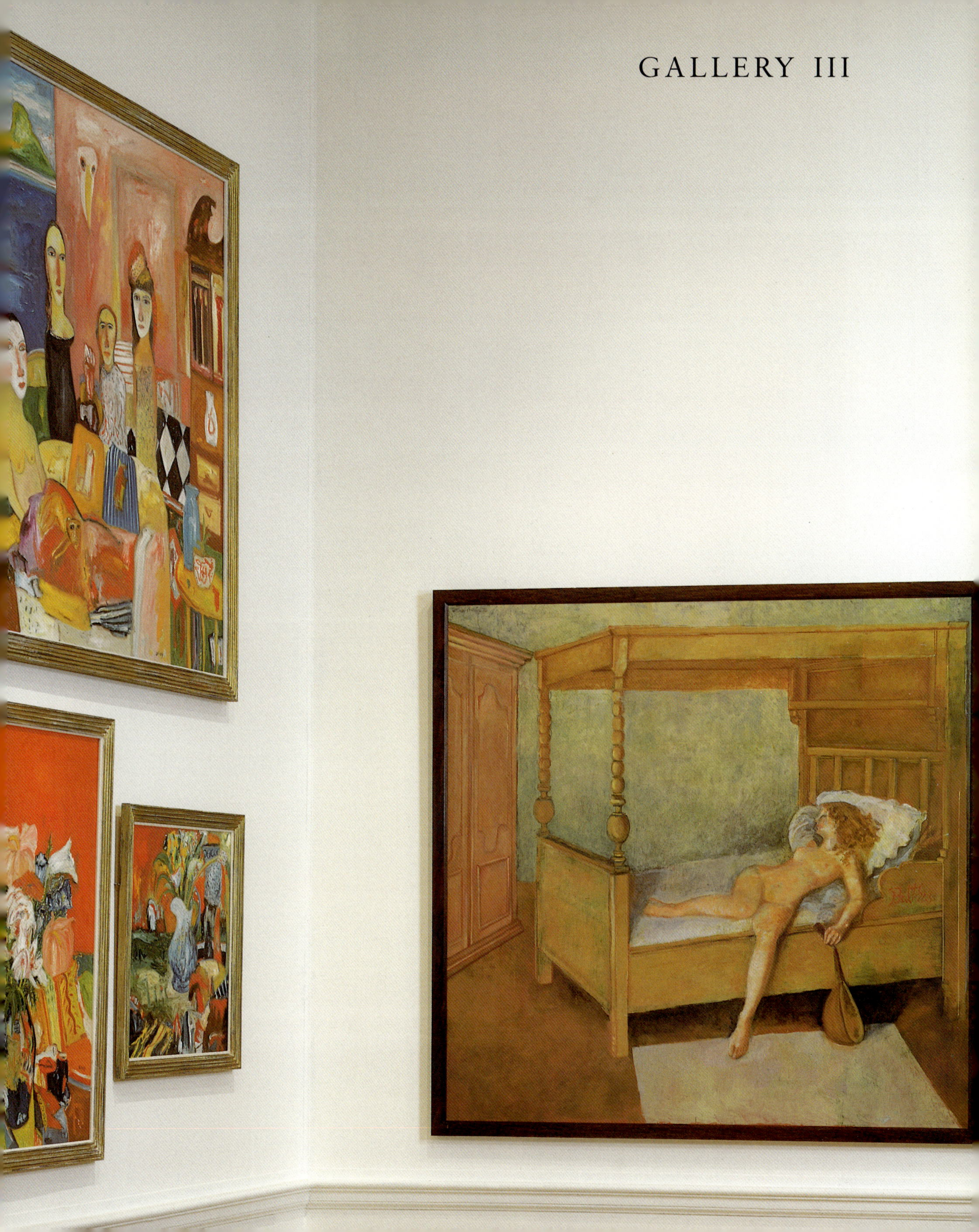

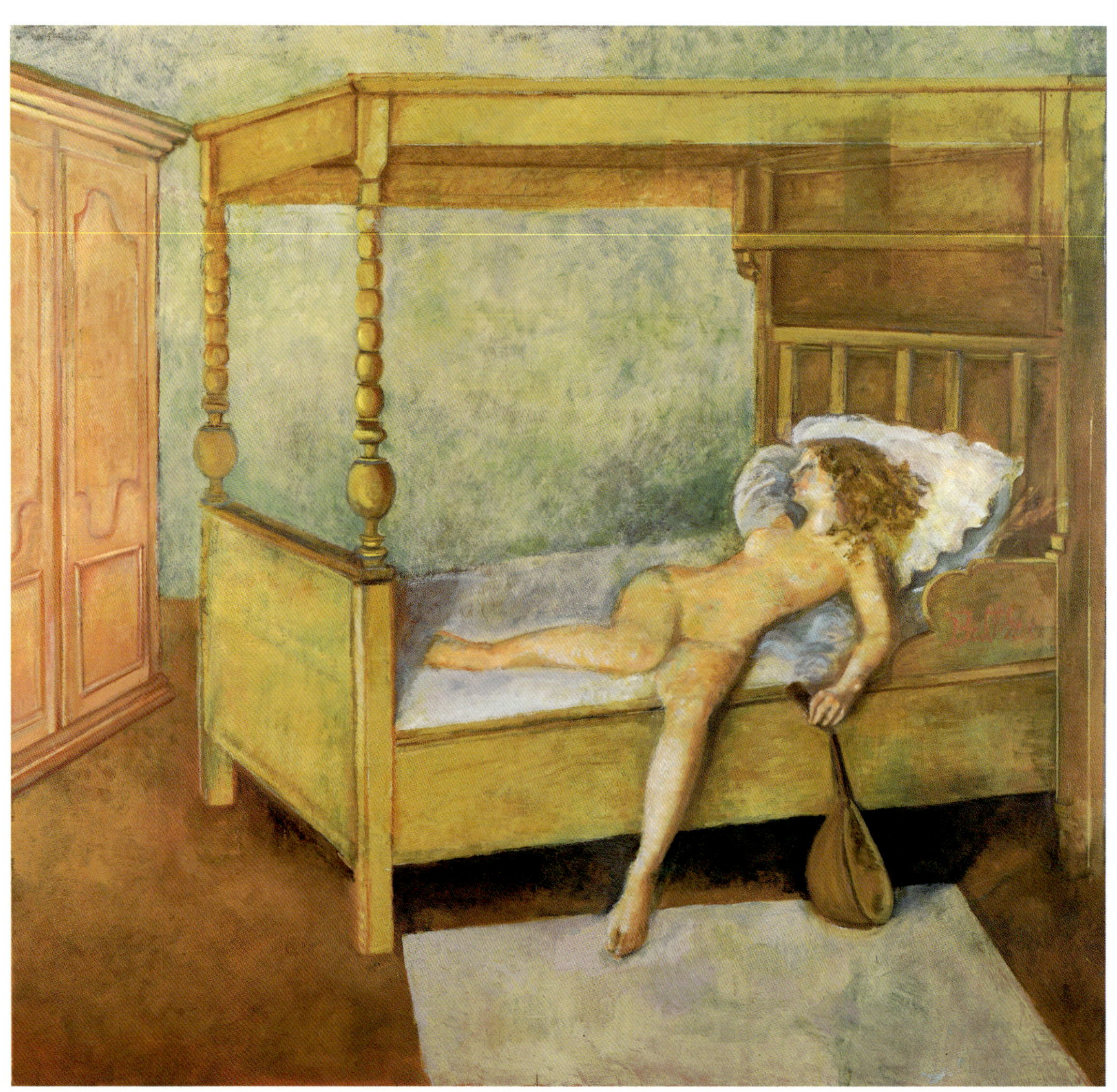

Balthus Hon RA
Odalisque à la Mandoline
Oil
225 × 230 cm

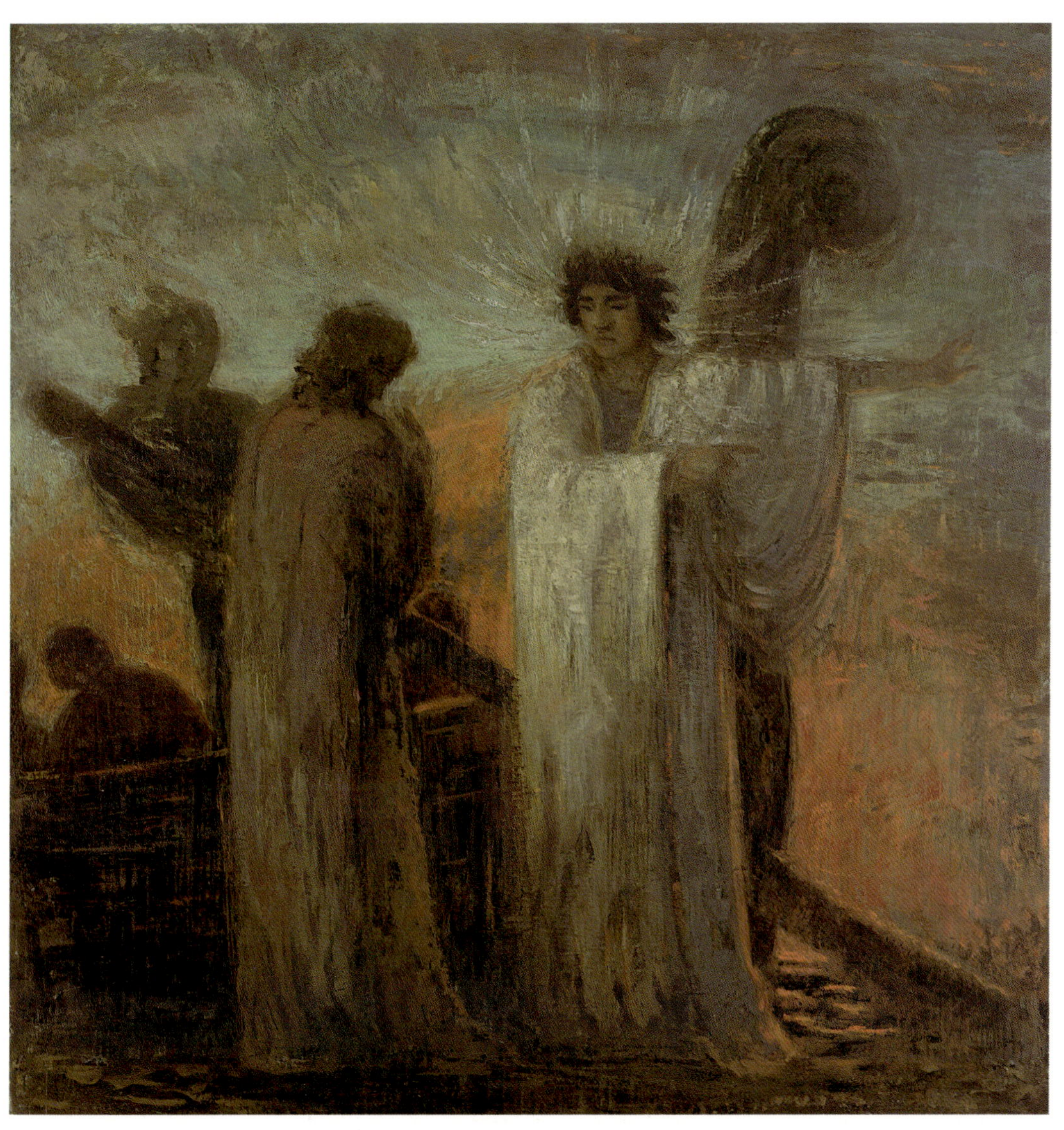

Christopher Le Brun RA
Dante and Virgil: The Embarkation
Oil
191 × 181 cm

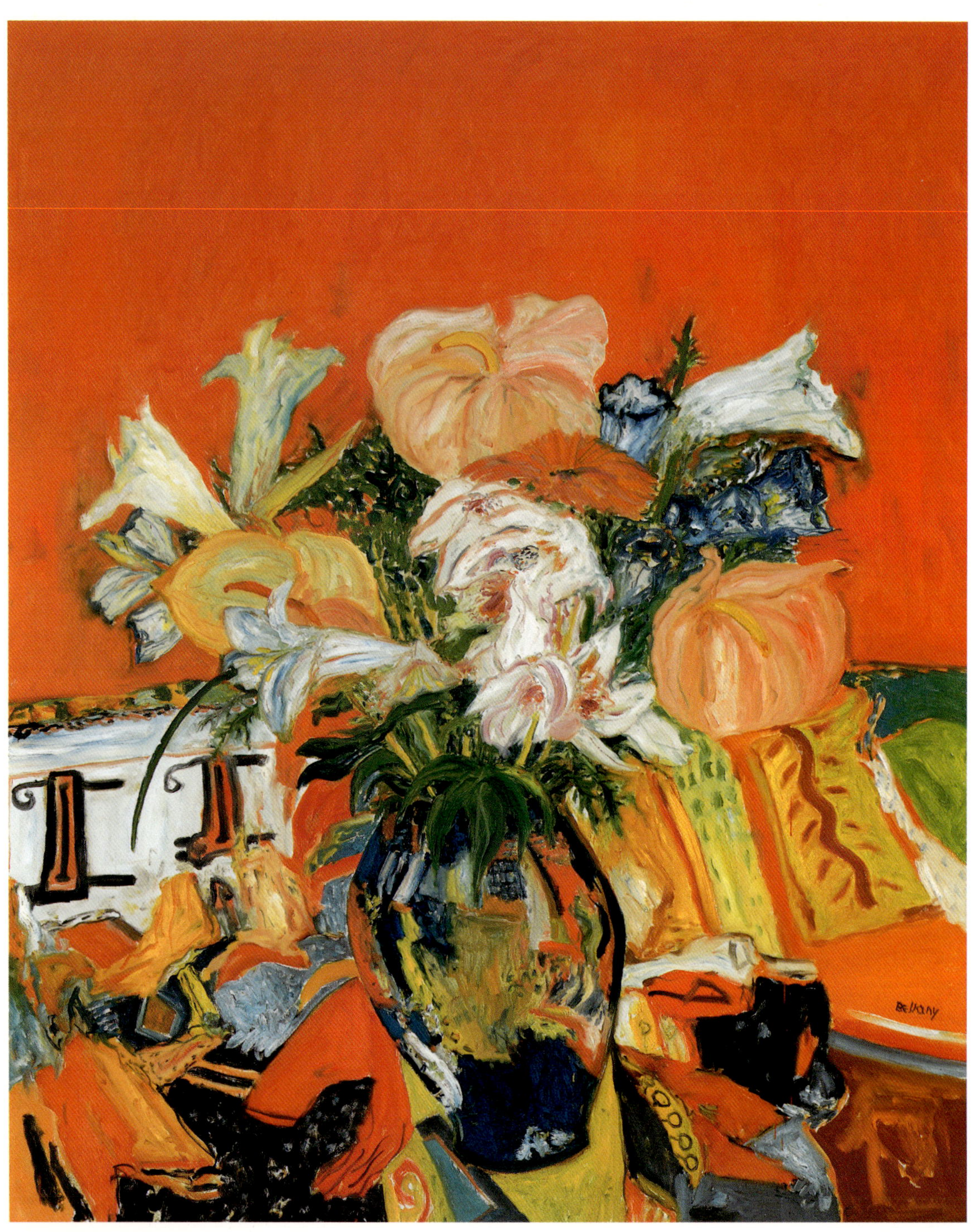

John Bellany CBE, RA
Red Still Life
Oil
152 × 121 cm

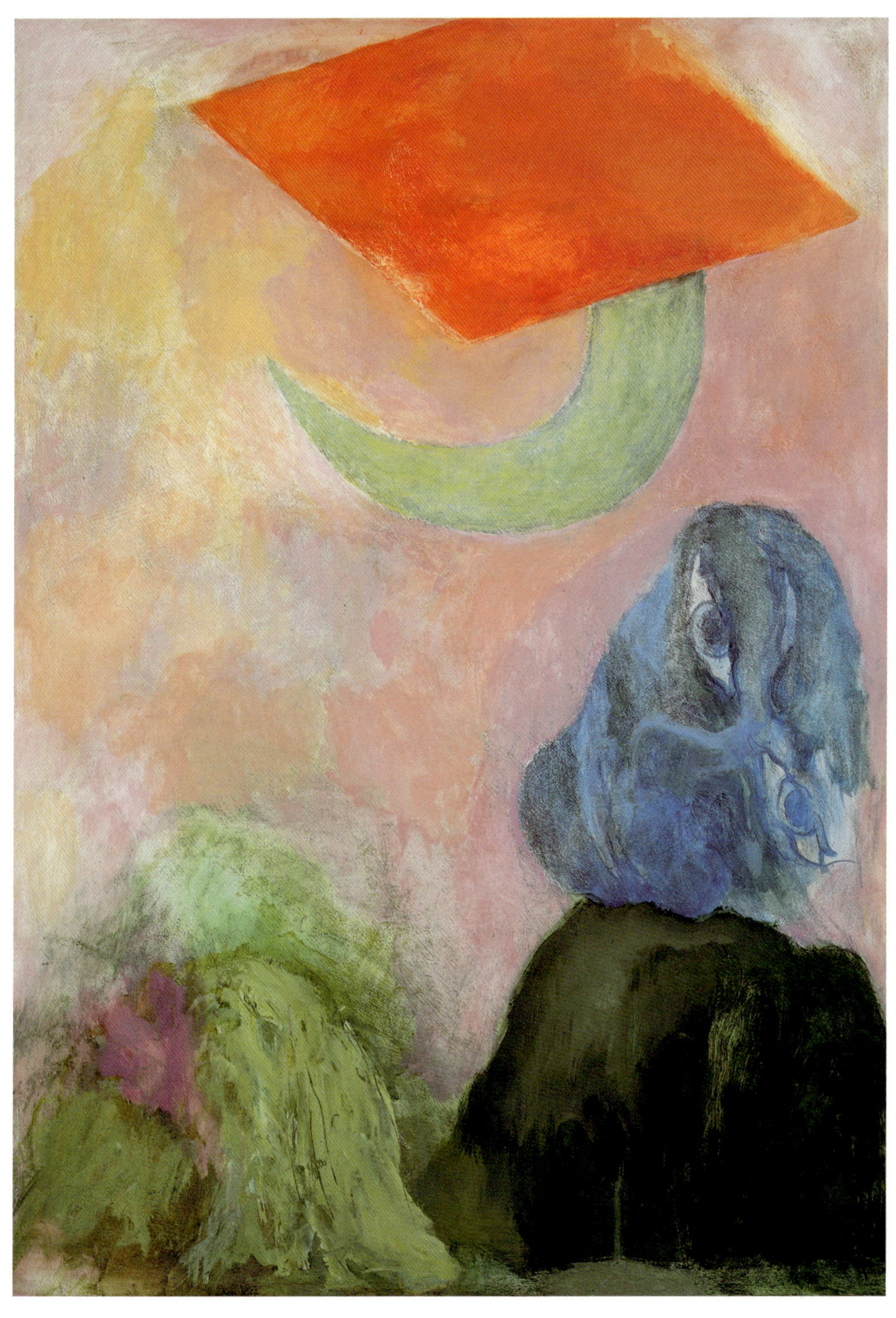

Ken Kiff RA
Resolving the Edges
Acrylic
122 × 82 cm

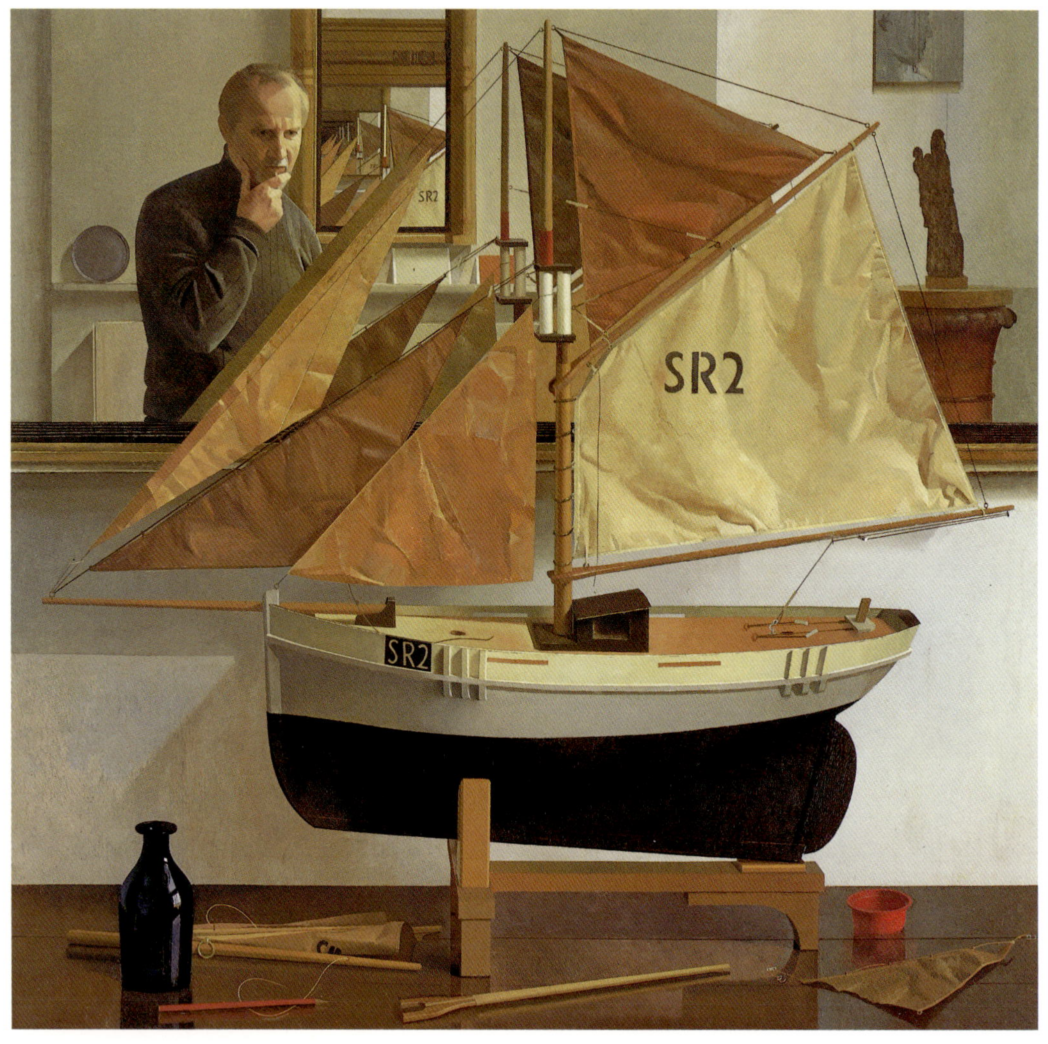

Norman Blamey OBE, RA
The Unresolved Model
Oil
122 × 122 cm

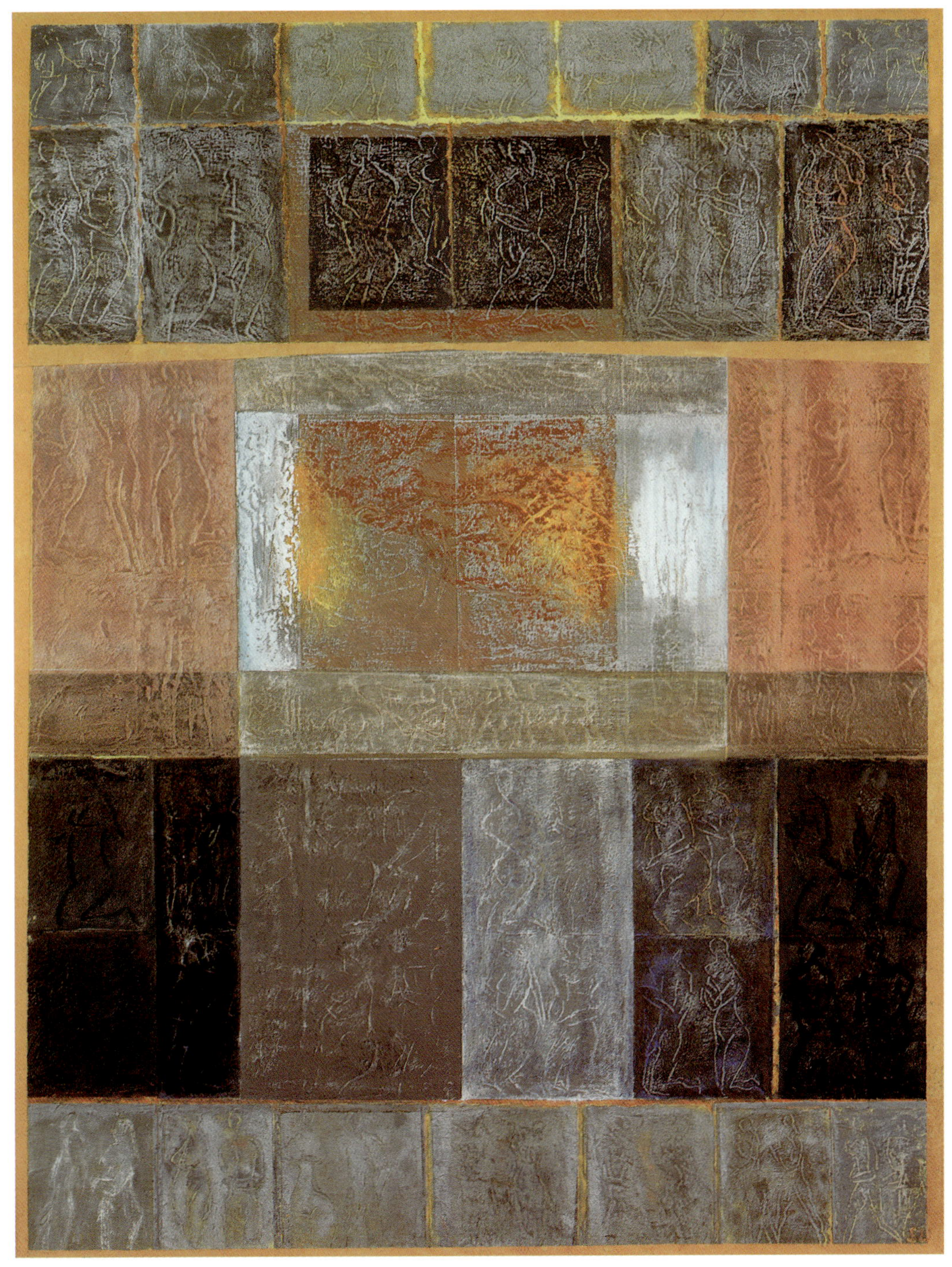

Sonia Lawson RA
Simple Saga
Oil
122 × 91 cm

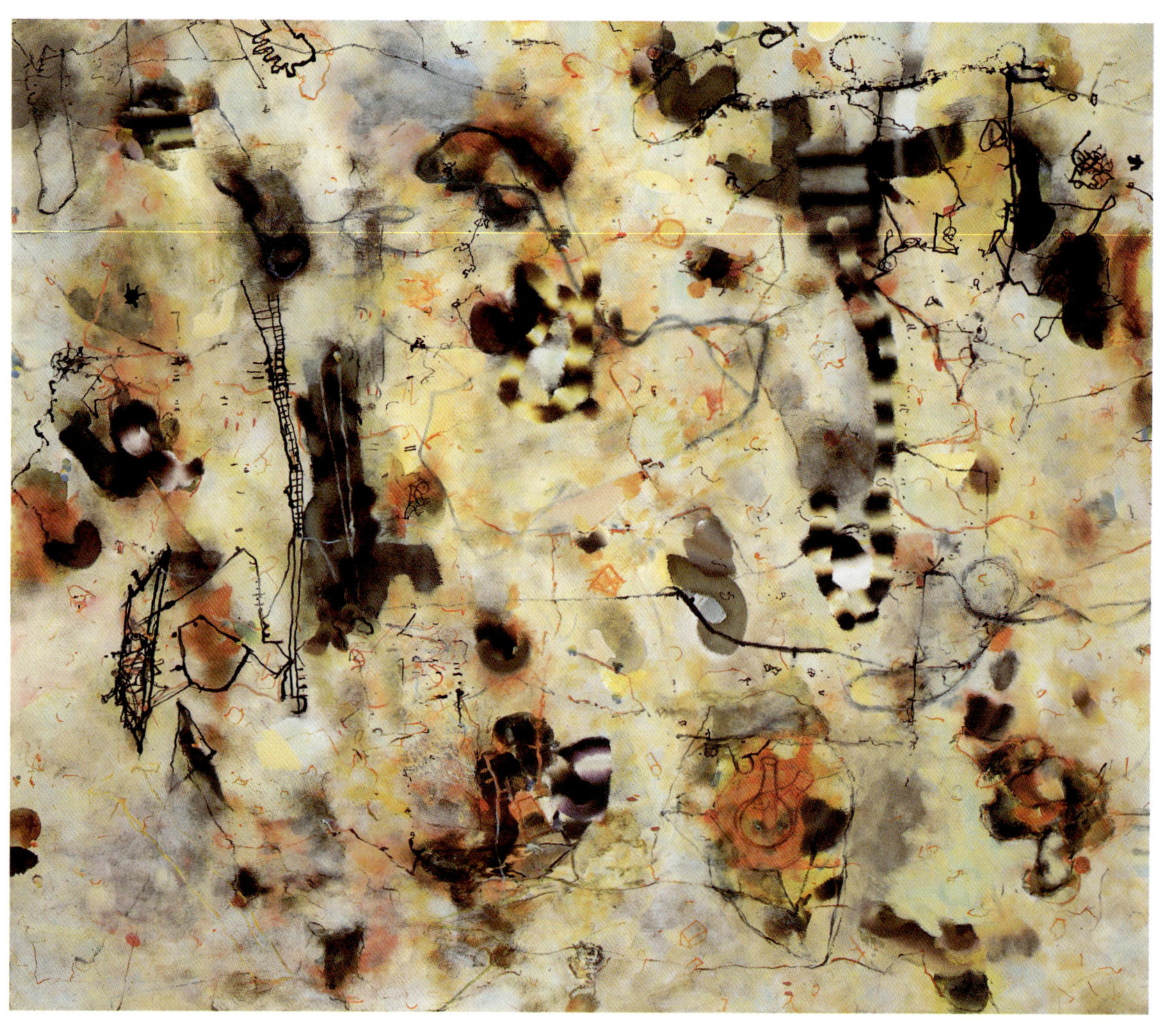

William Henderson
Music for the Storyteller
Acrylic
168 × 191 cm

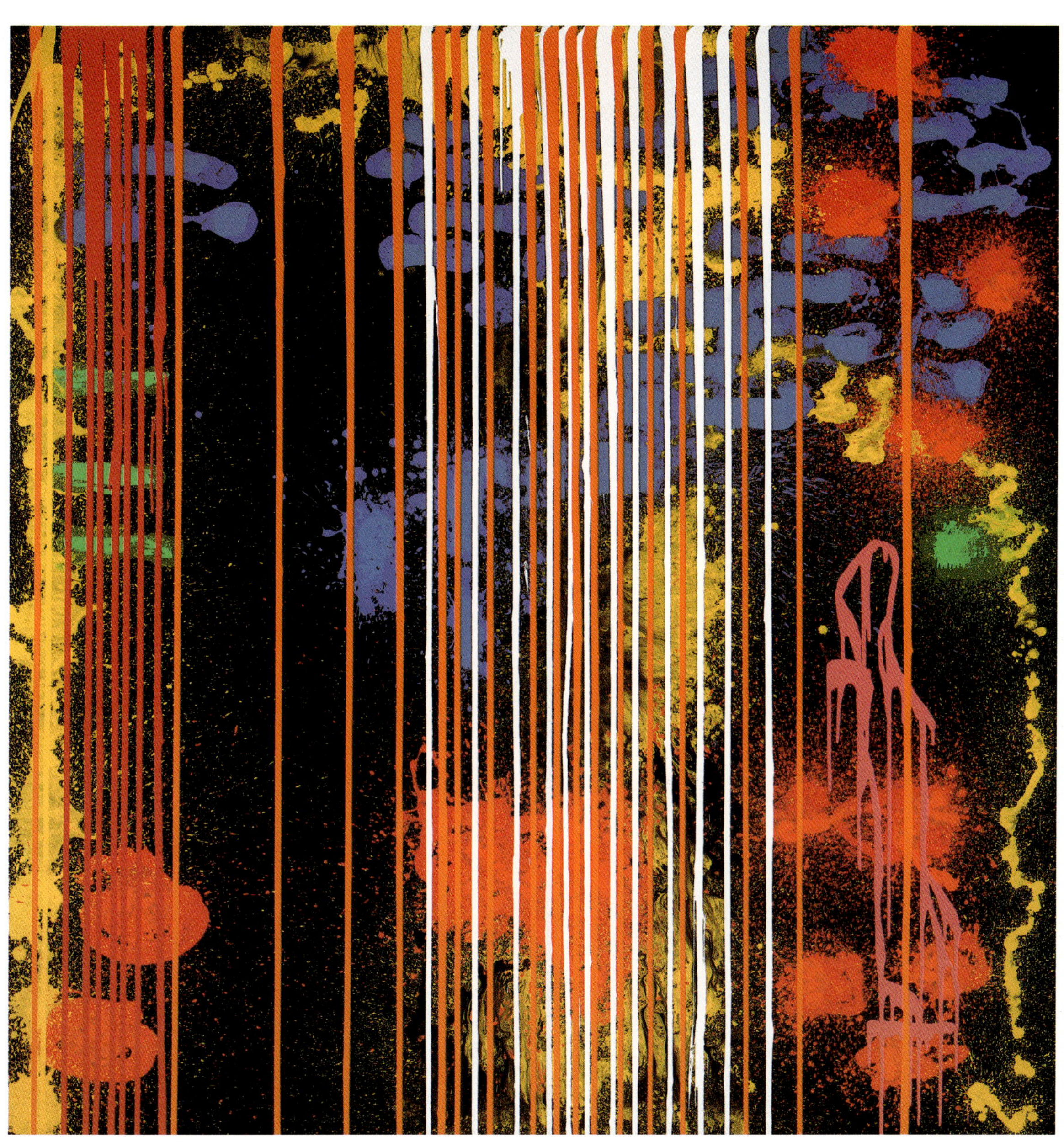

John Hoyland RA
Frontier Song (Viewing the Wilds) 12.4.2000
Acrylic
254 × 236 cm

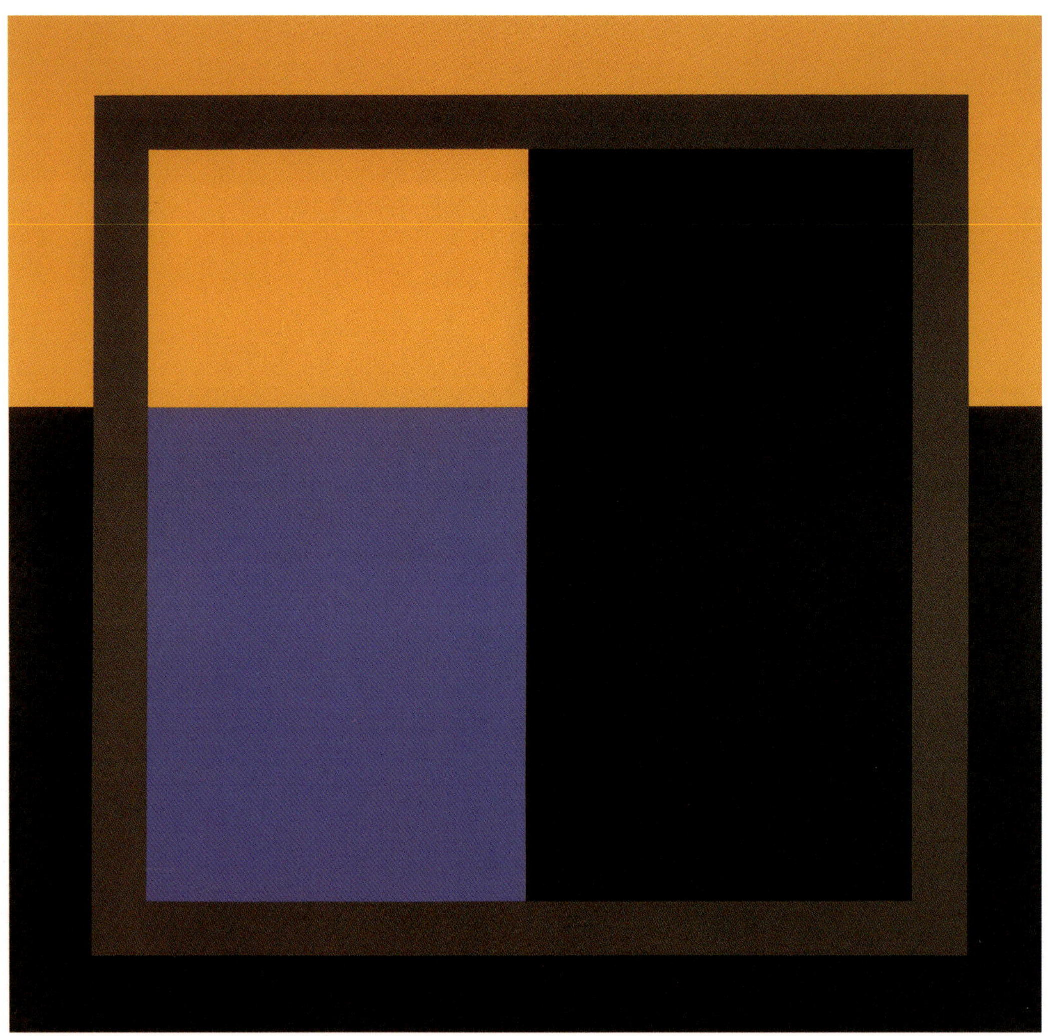

John Holden
The Black Lagoon
Acrylic
183 × 183 cm

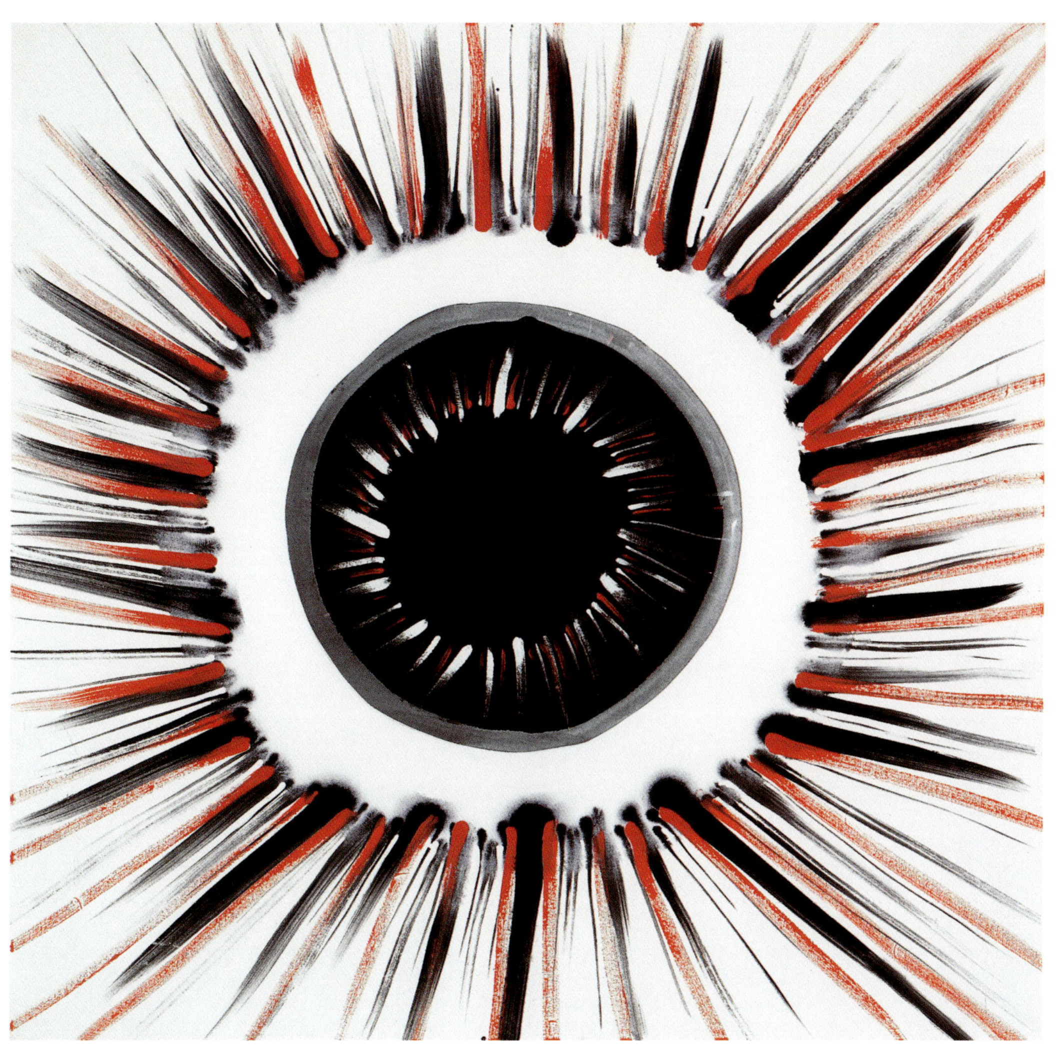

Sir Terry Frost RA
Sunblast, Black and Red
Acrylic/Collage
153 × 153 cm

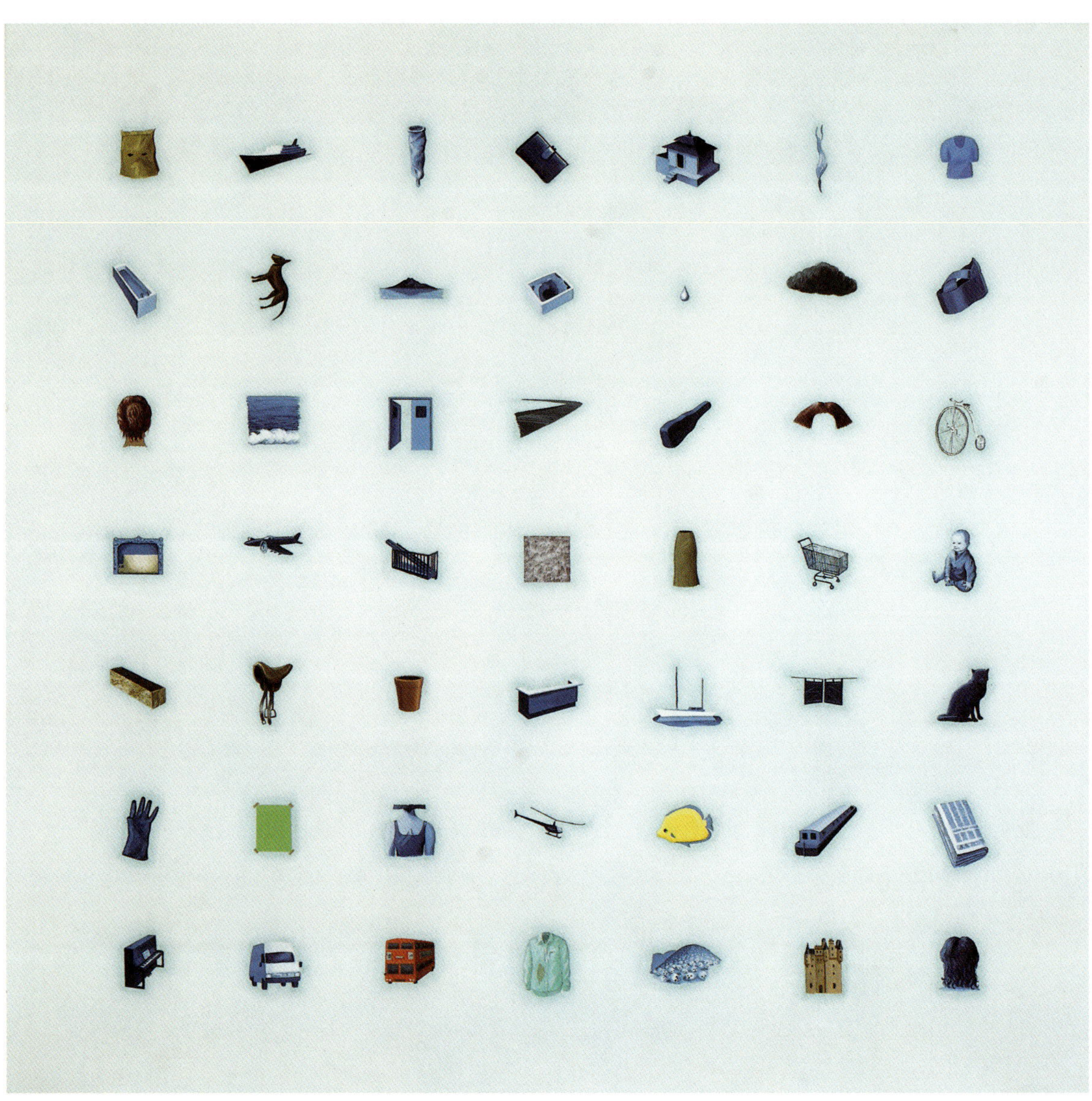

Jane Gifford
Dream Inventory
Acrylic
112 × 112 cm

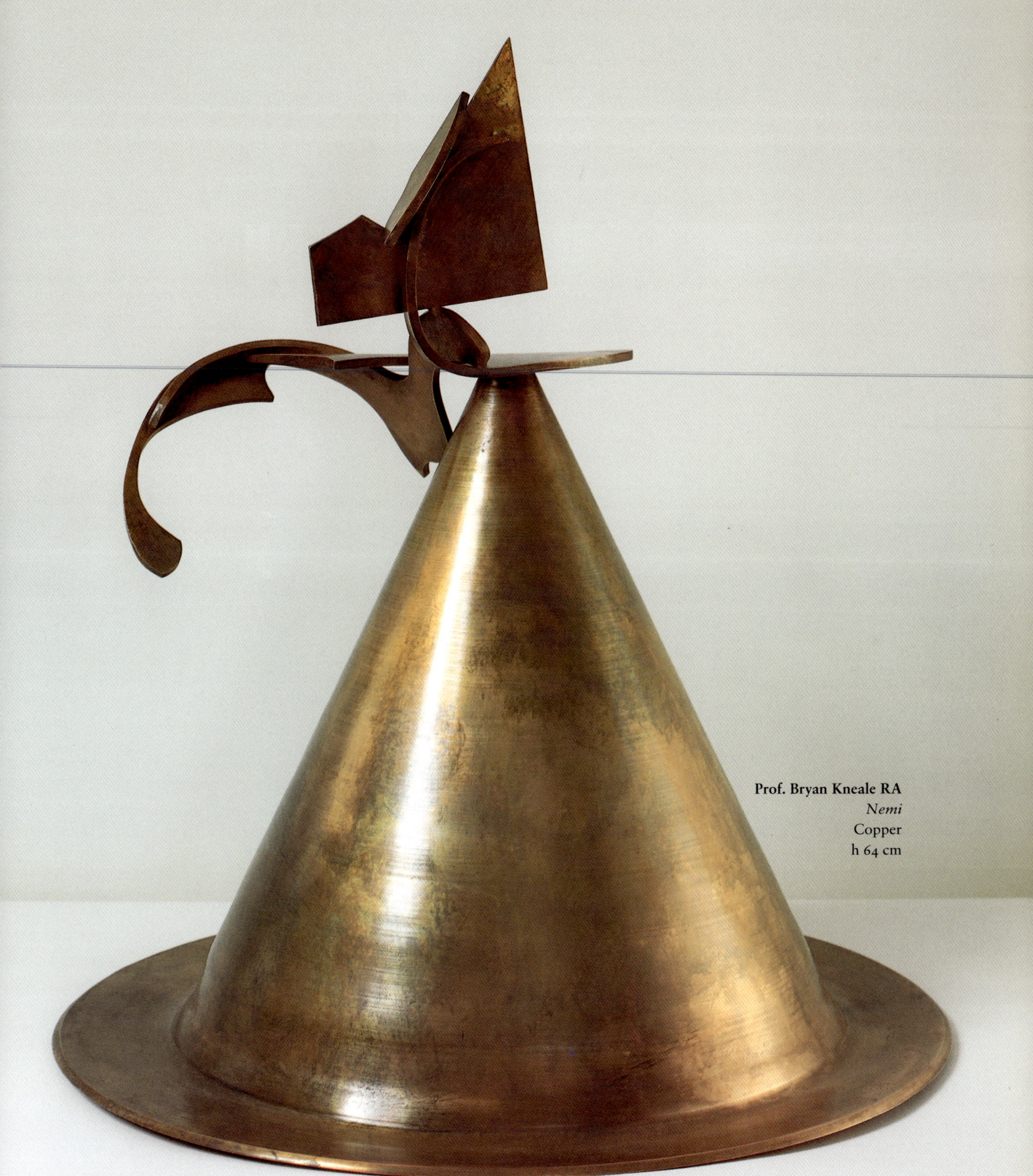

Prof. Bryan Kneale RA
Nemi
Copper
h 64 cm

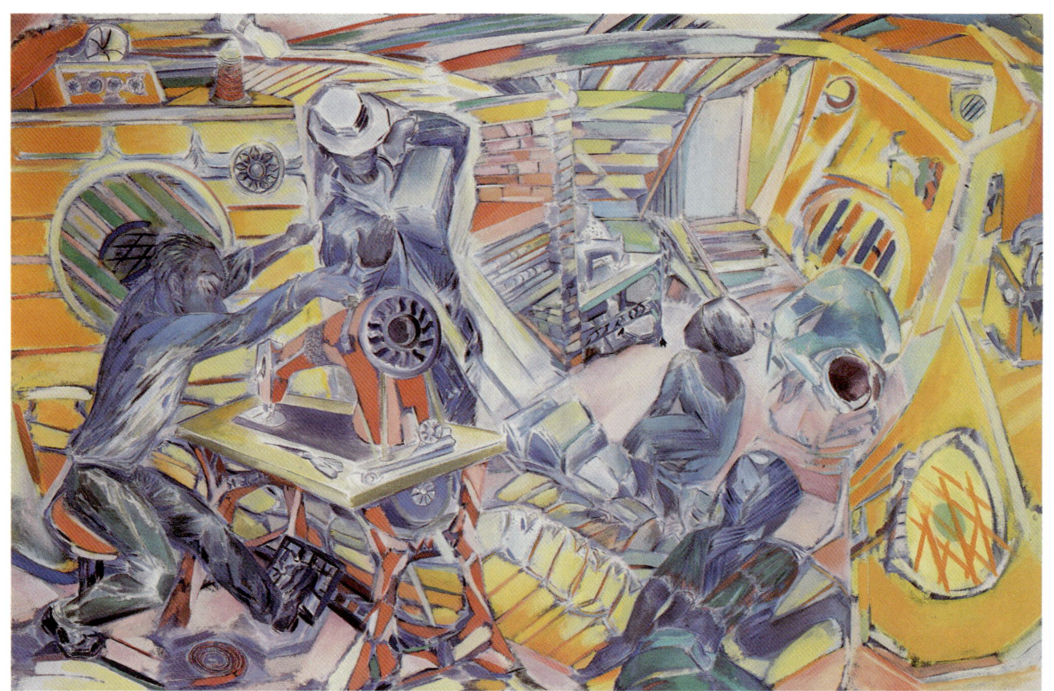

Denzel Forrester
Sewing Machine
Oil
121 × 183 cm

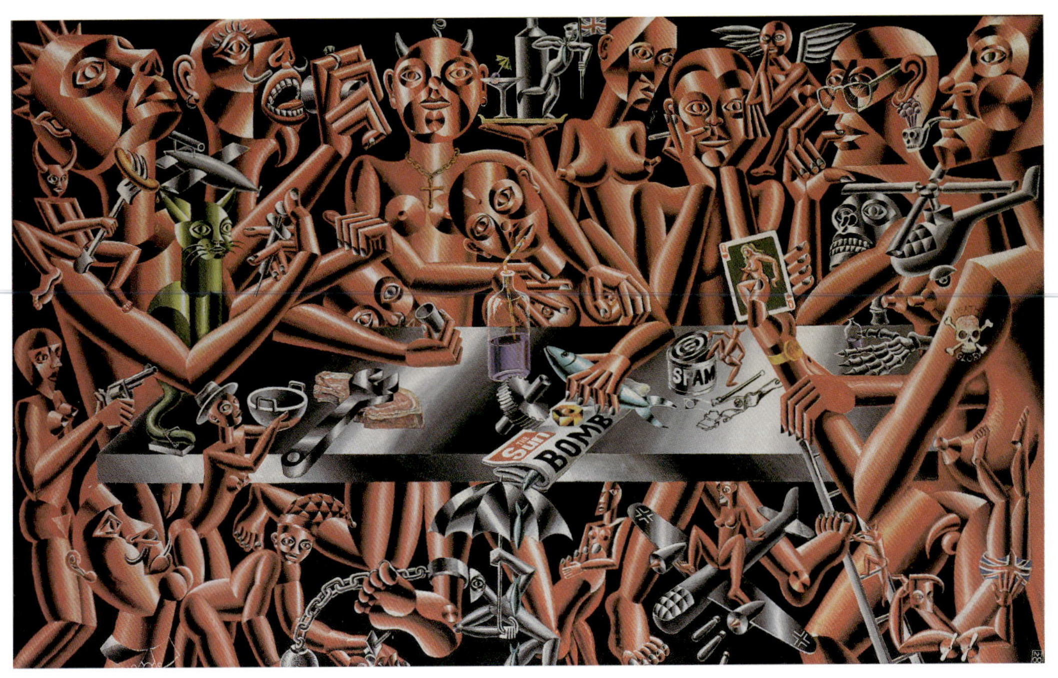

Nichollas Hamper
The Meal
Oil
100 × 156 cm

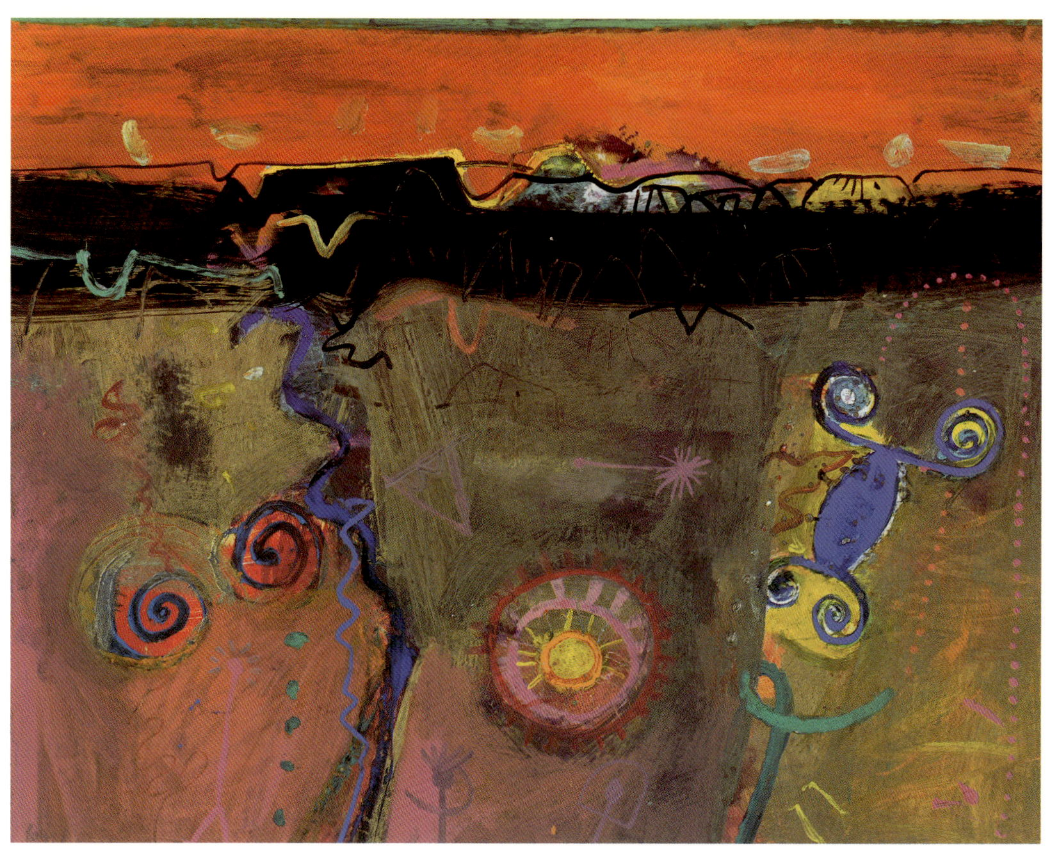

Barbara Rae RA
Hopi Mesa
Mixed media
98 × 122 cm

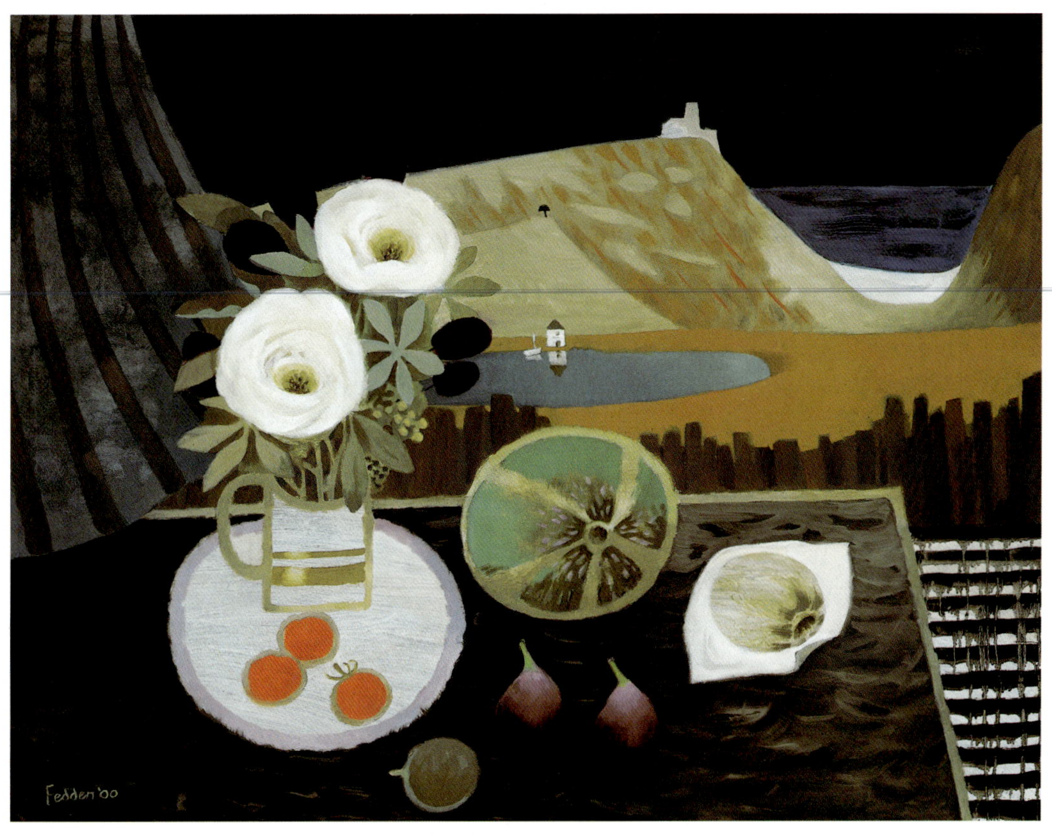

Mary Fedden OBE, RA
Two White Roses
Oil
102 × 127 cm

GALLERY IV

Like a Victorian philanthropist, Anthony Whishaw recommends an early start in the morning to secure the best choice from the huge pool of works that have passed the first round of judging. 'First of all I look for things I immediately like, even though I don't know how I'm going to put them together.' Whishaw gathers more work than he can possibly hang and begins to sort it into groups. 'I don't want to know what the room is going to look like until it's really underway. It's the same with my own pictures, I don't want to know until they really begin to take form; they develop organically. I tend to have an emphasis on work that's quite tactile, but I also like work that uses different languages. By contrasting large scale with very small scale, and bunching paintings with works on paper, I can get in as substantial a hang as possible. The idea is to put together work that might seem incompatible. Strange things start to happen – linear rhythms appear for instance, and make a curious kind of order around the walls.'

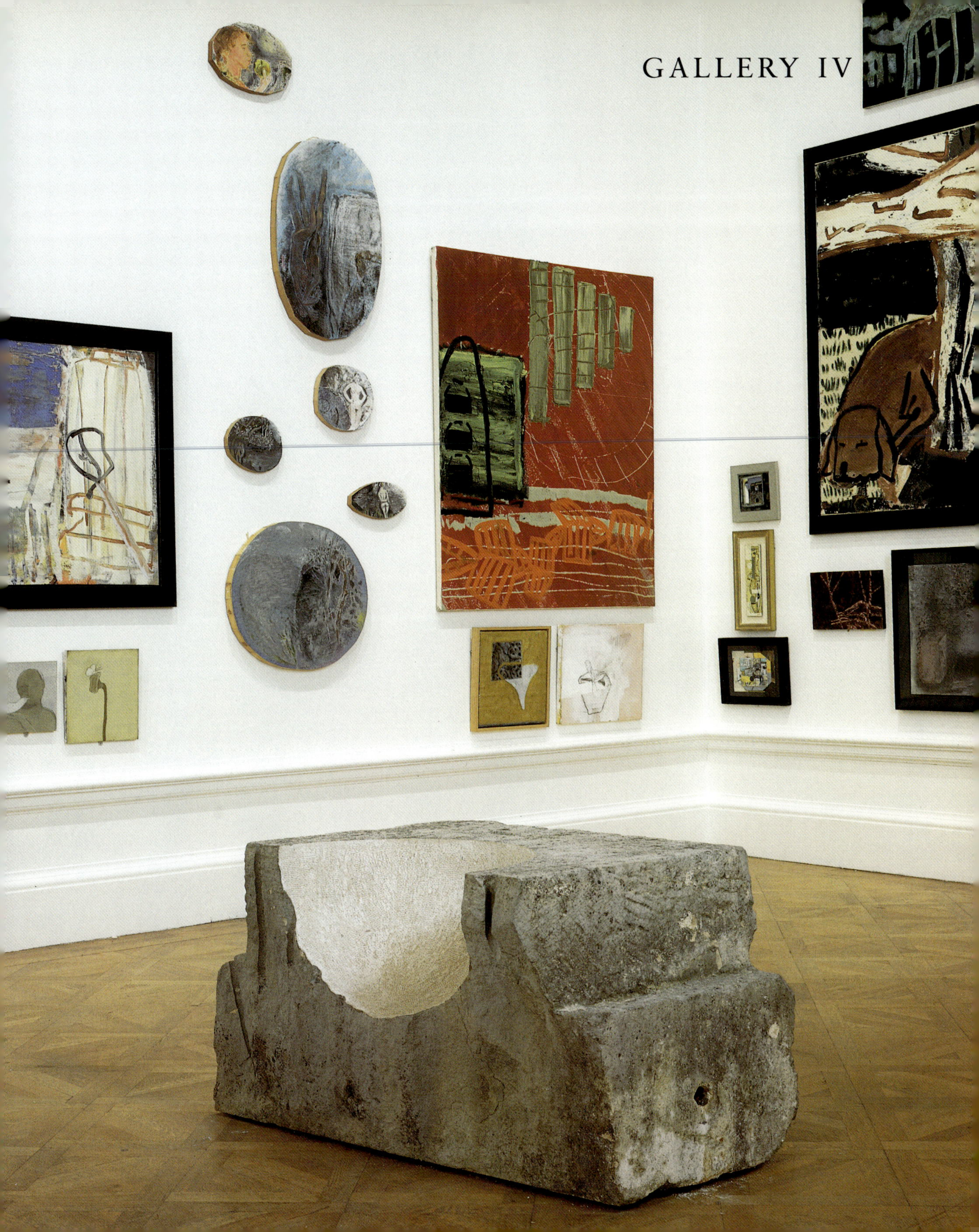

GALLERY IV

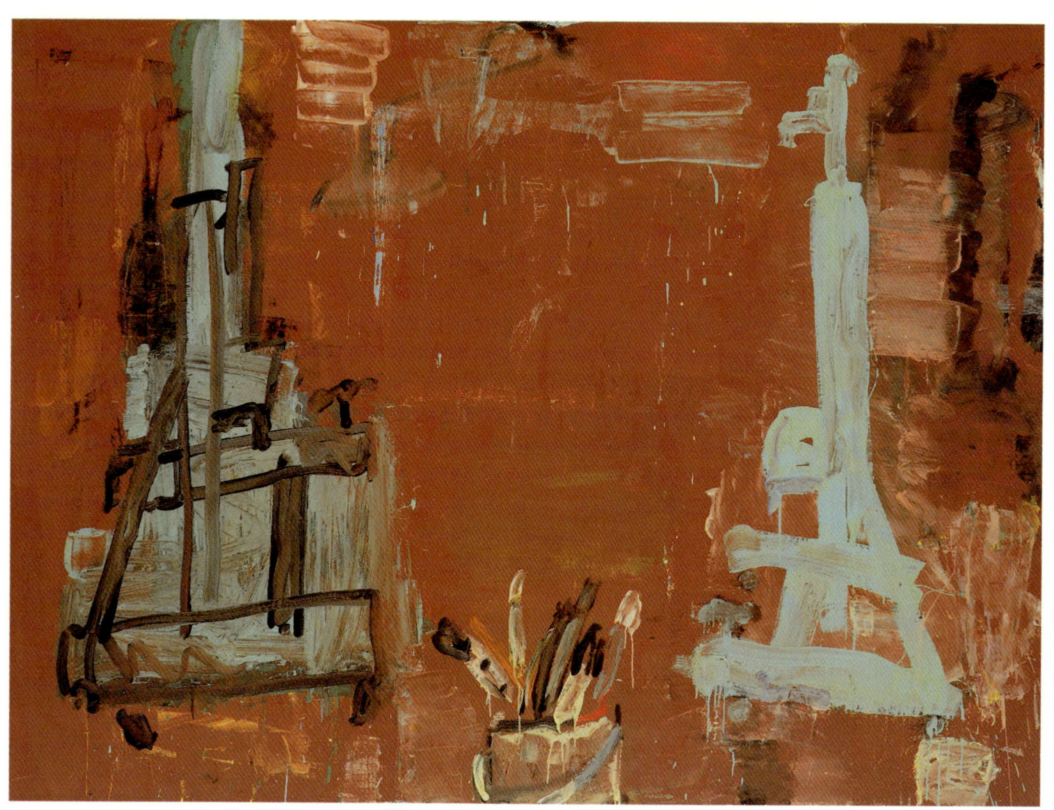

Roy Oxlade
Easels and Brushes
Oil
133 × 173 cm

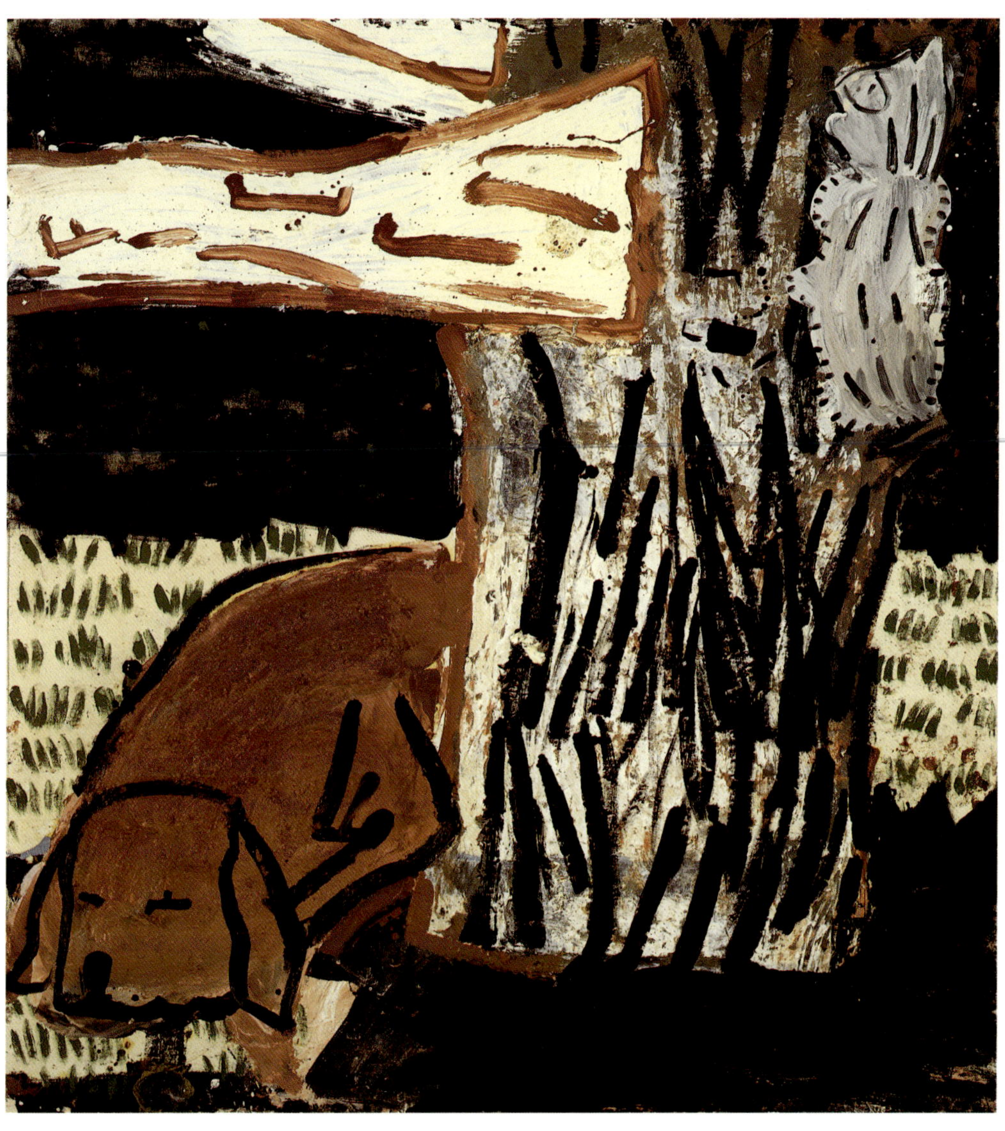

Rose Wylie
Green Grass, White Cat
Oil
184 × 164 cm

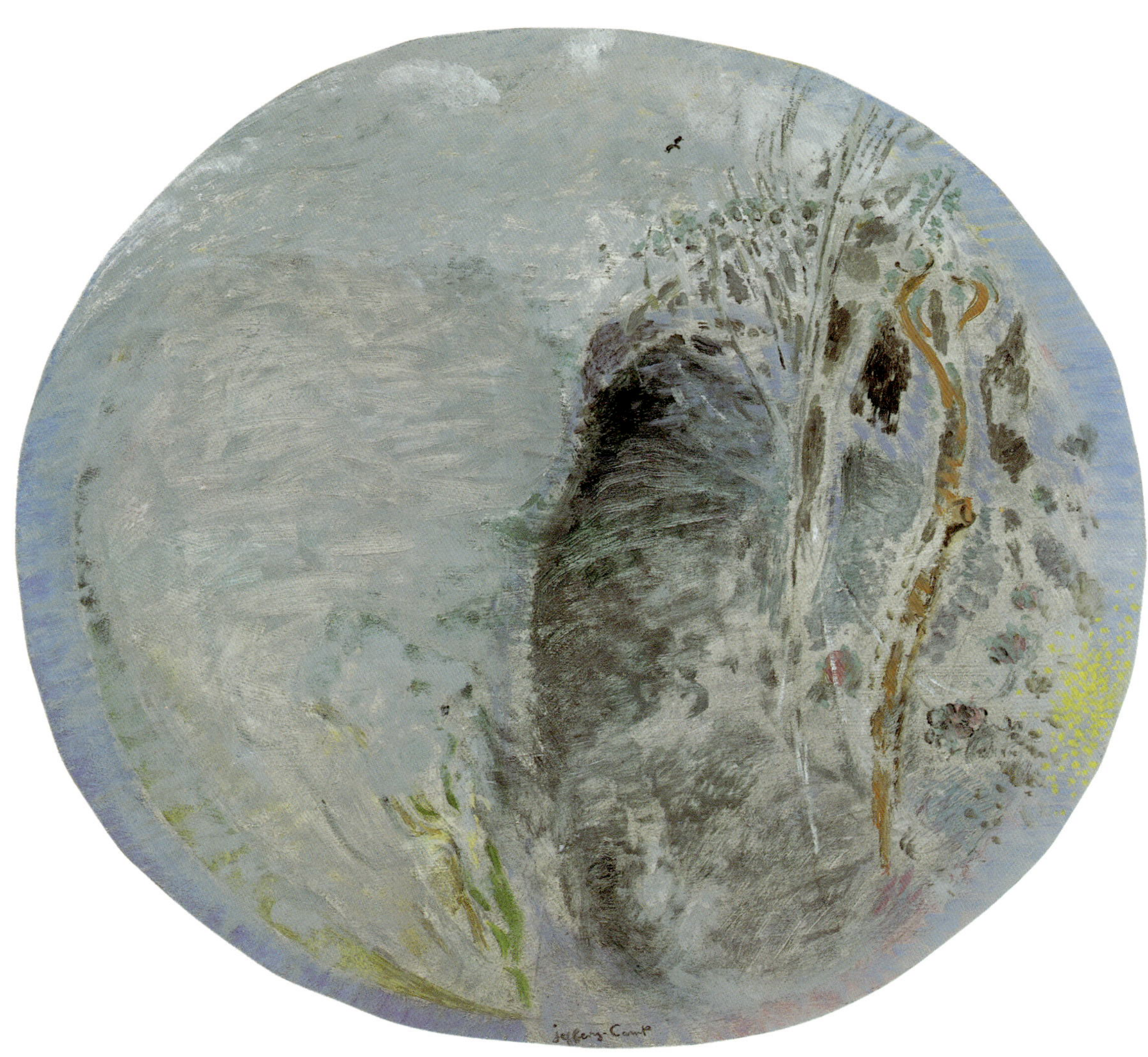

Jeffery Camp RA
Late Springtime
Oil
70 × 76 cm

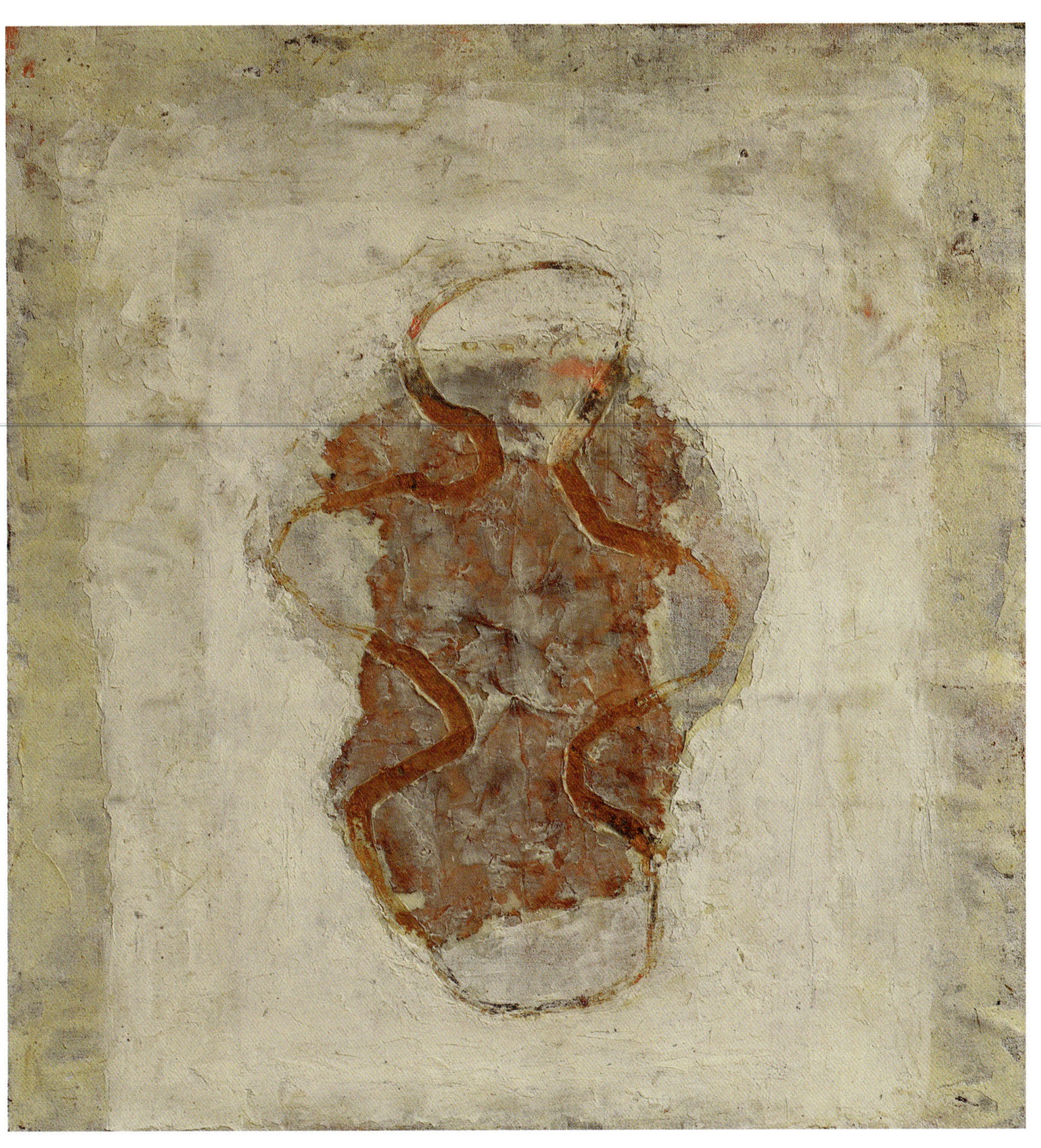

Phillipa Stjernsward
Figurine
Mixed media
54 × 49 cm

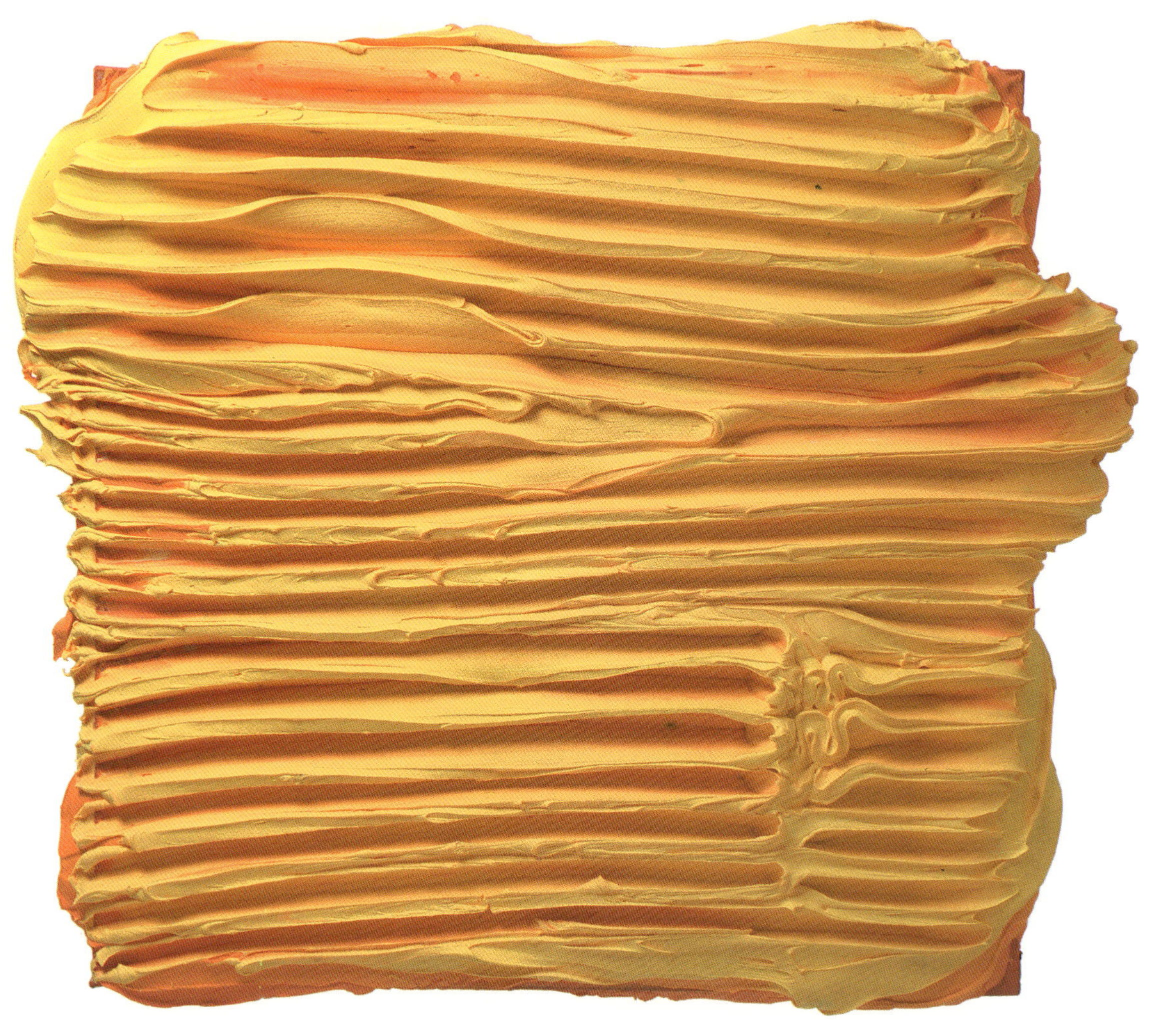

Richard Elliott
Ten
Acrylic
95× 109 cm

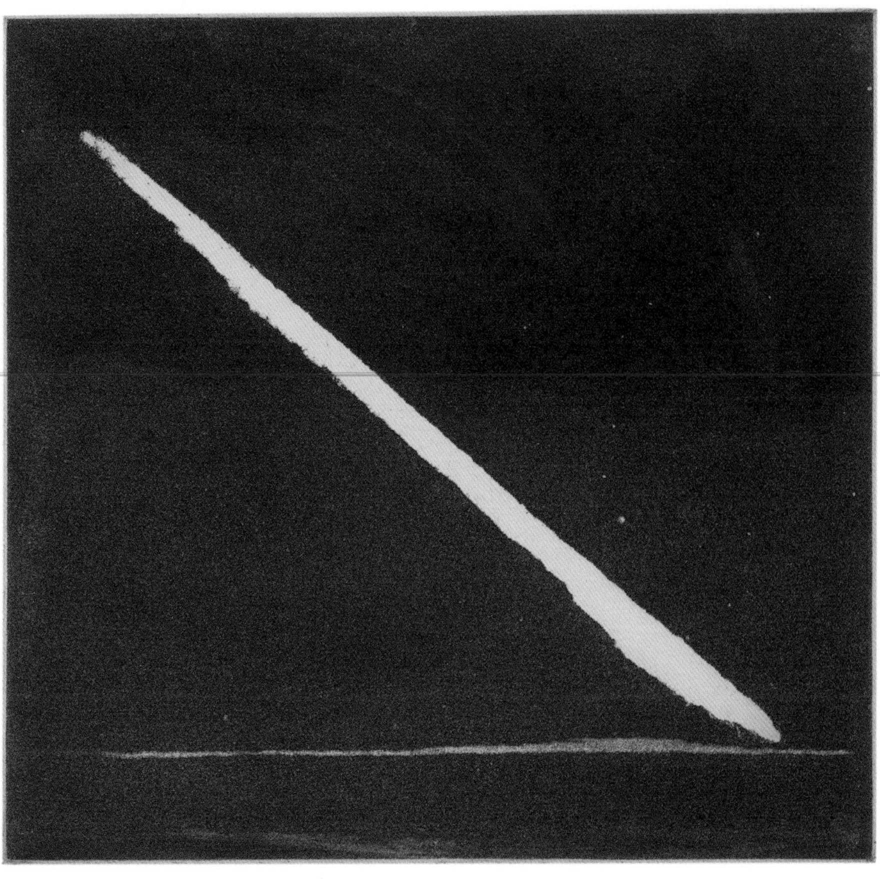

Ian Ritchie CBE, RA
Alba di Milano
Etching
18 × 18 cm

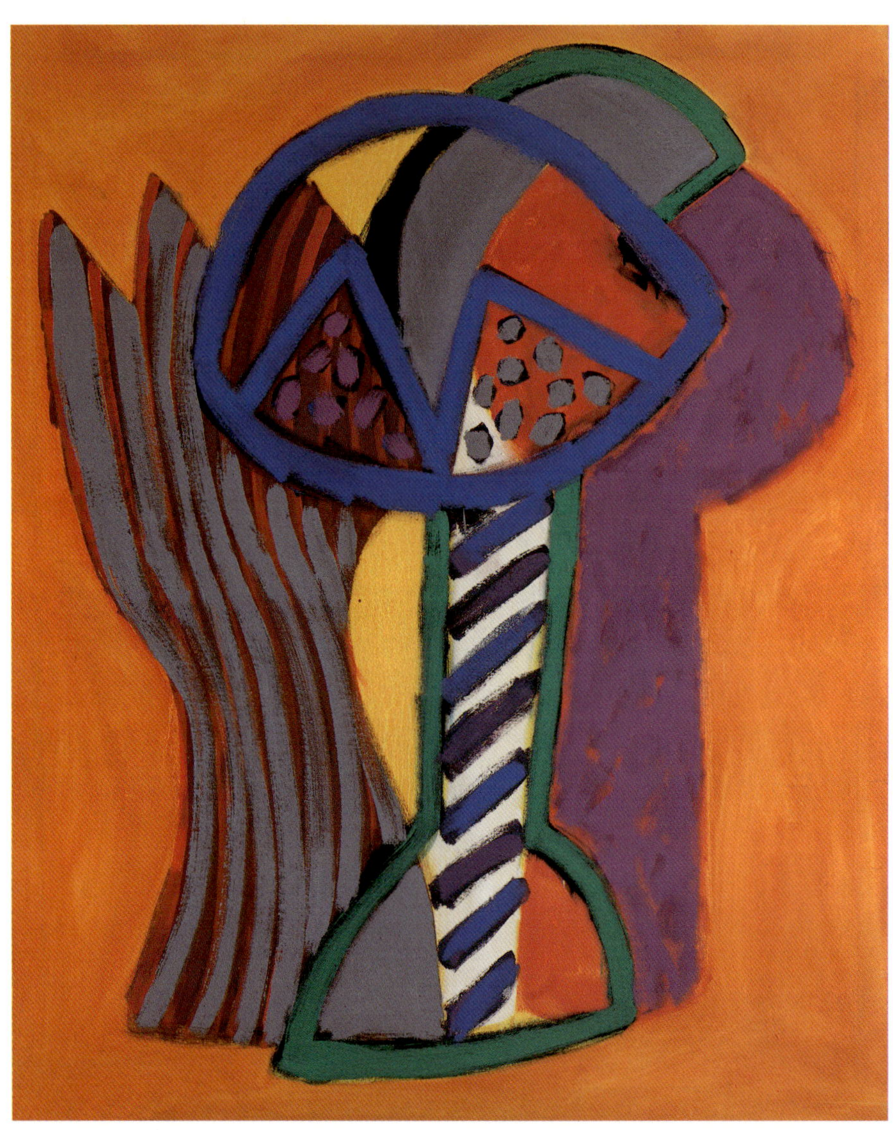

John Edwards
Caussade
Oil
152 × 122 cm

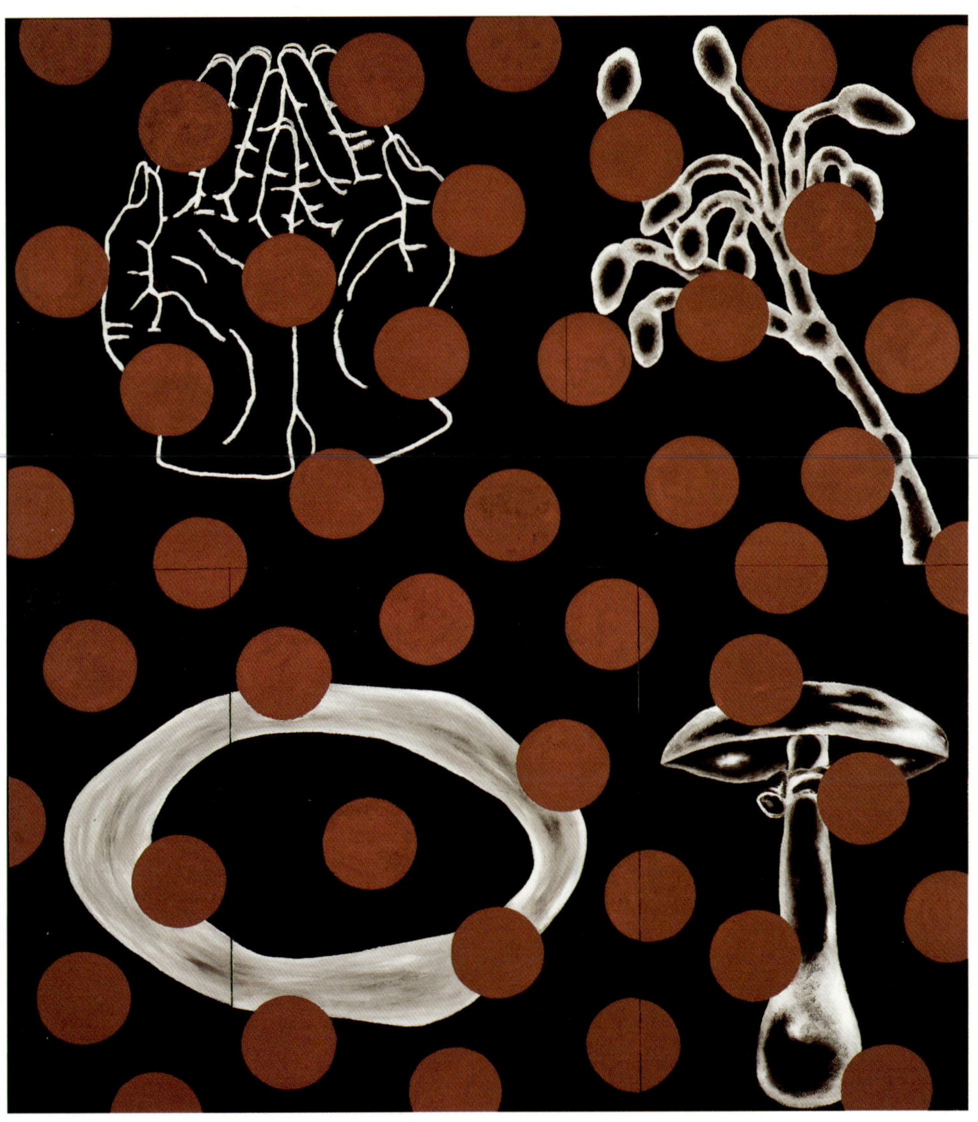

Paulo Rego
Mother Nature
Oil
200 × 174 cm

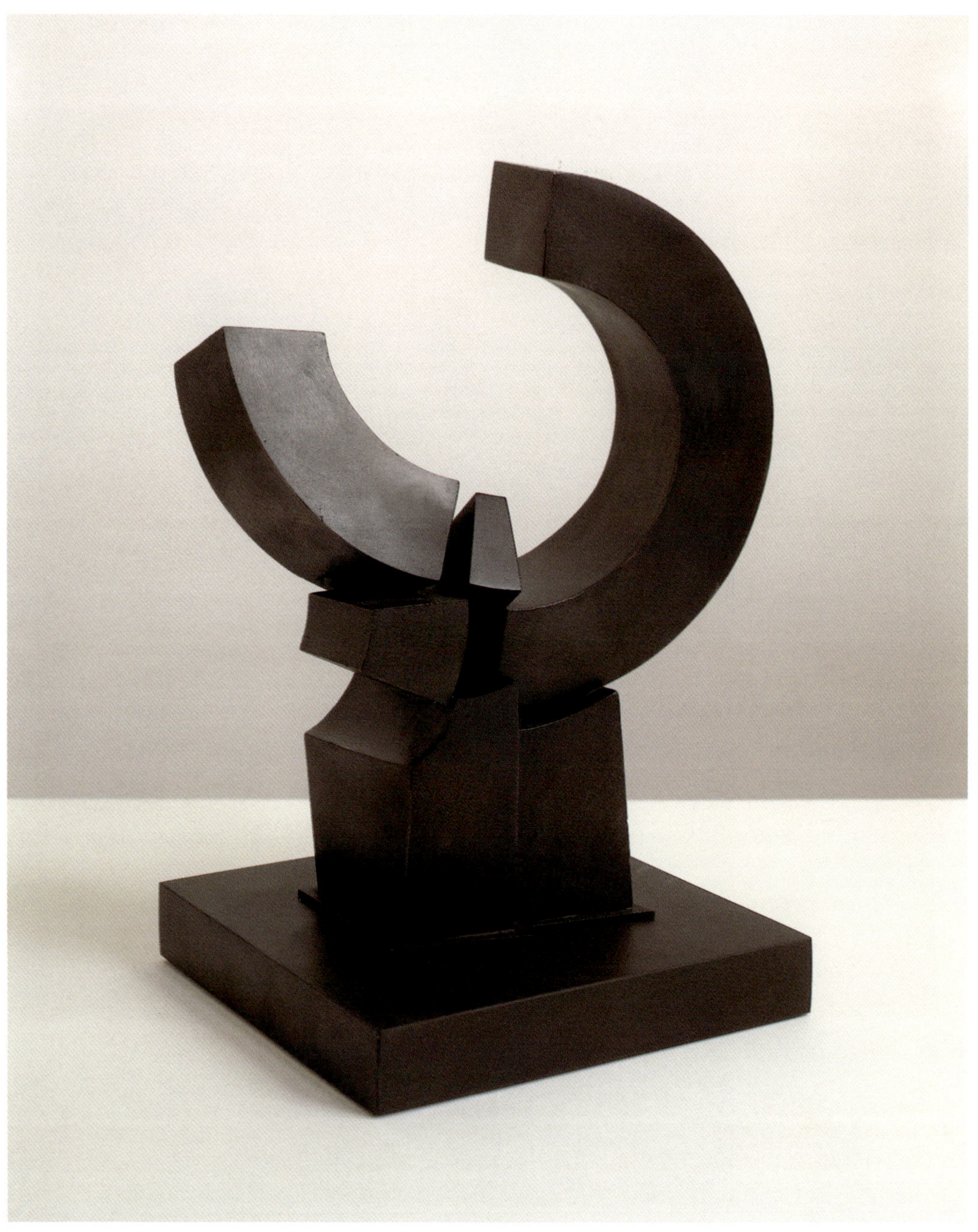

Andrew Stonyer
Broken Circle
Bronze
h 36 cm

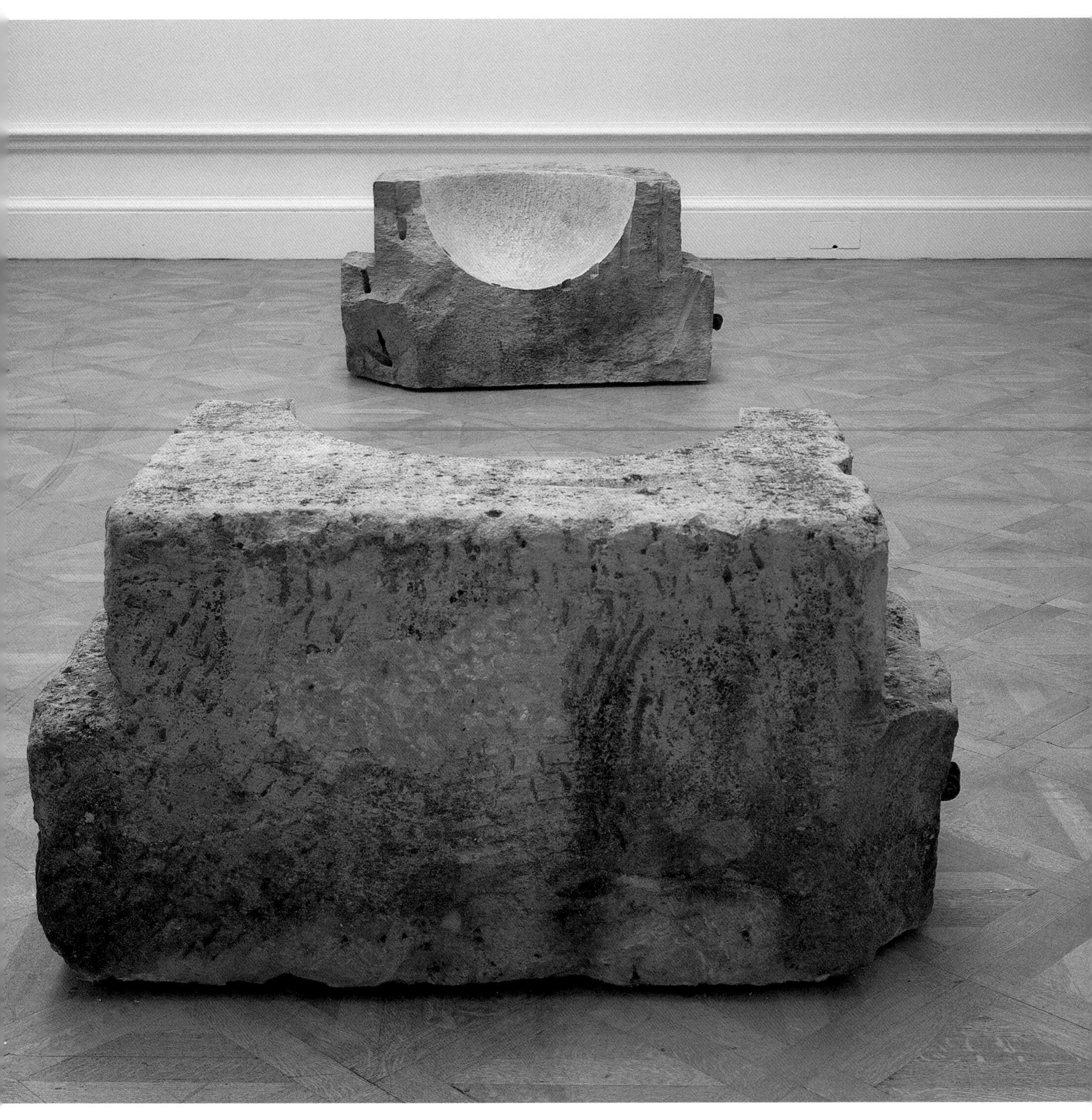

John Maine RA
Hemisphere
Portland Stone
h 80 cm

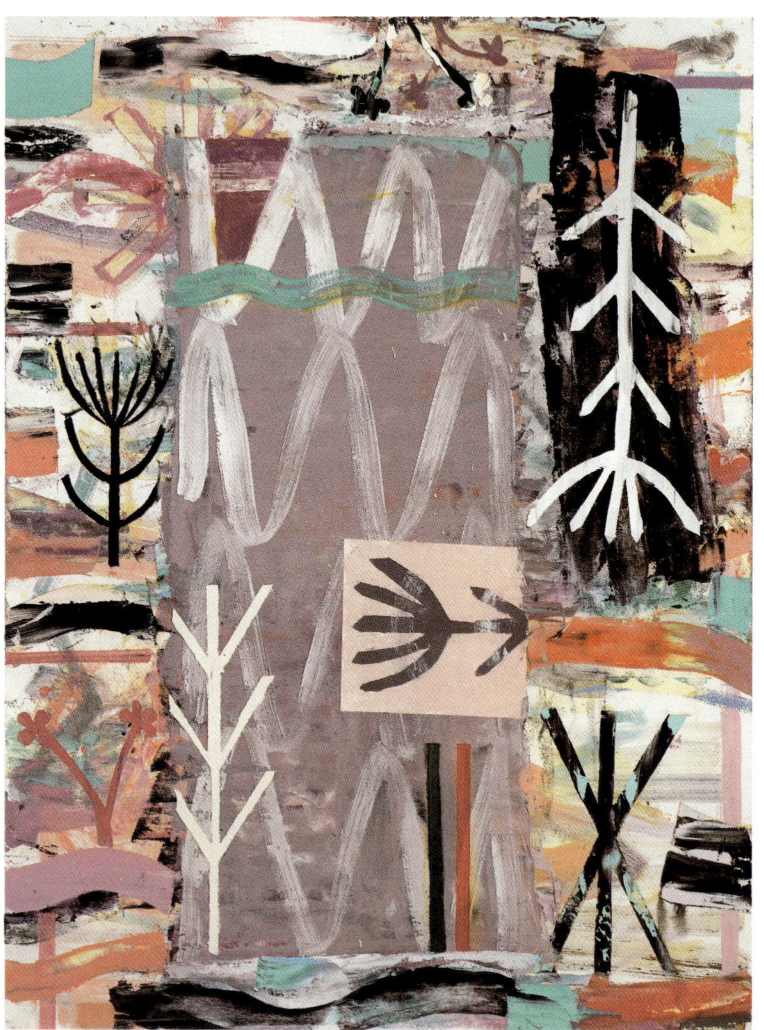

Tricia Gillman
Facing – In
Oil
140 × 102 cm

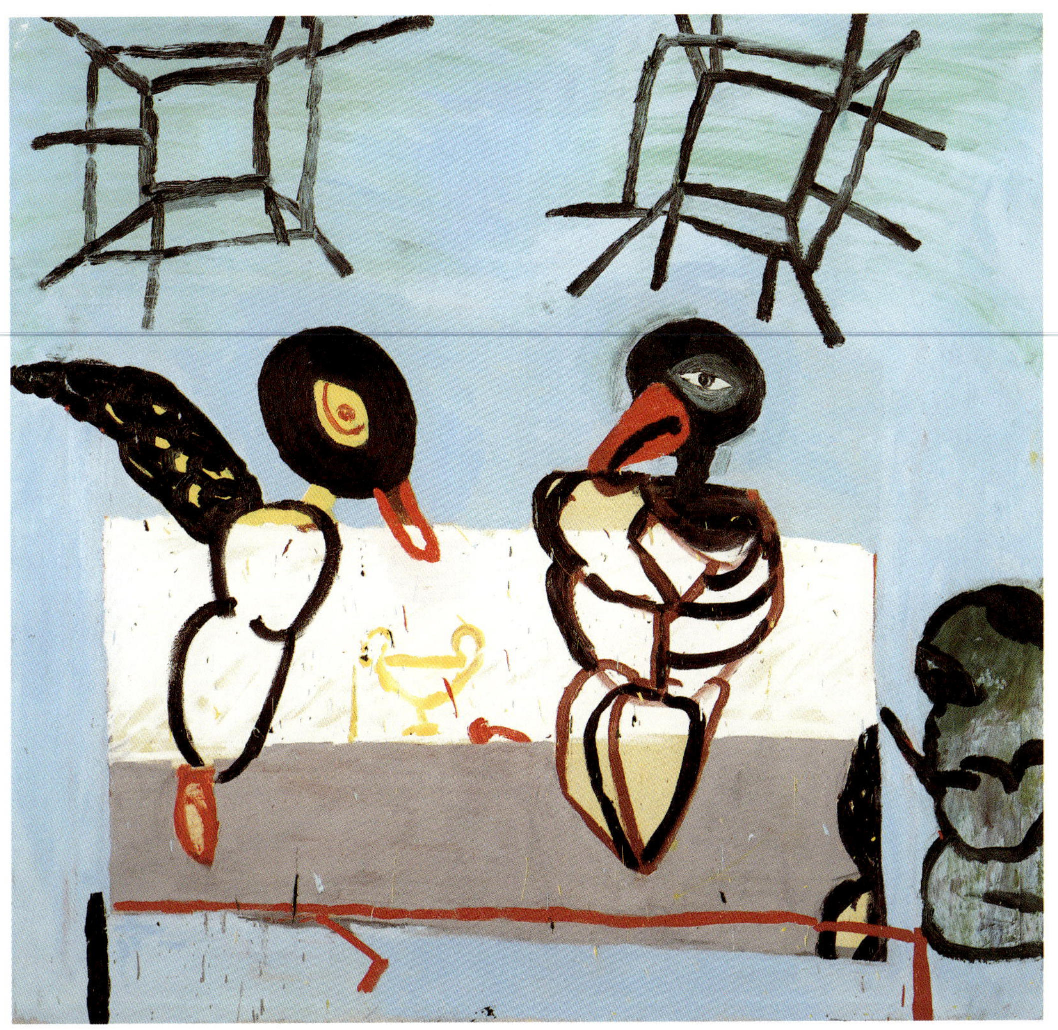

Georgia Hayes
Birds in the British Museum
Oil
181 × 184 cm

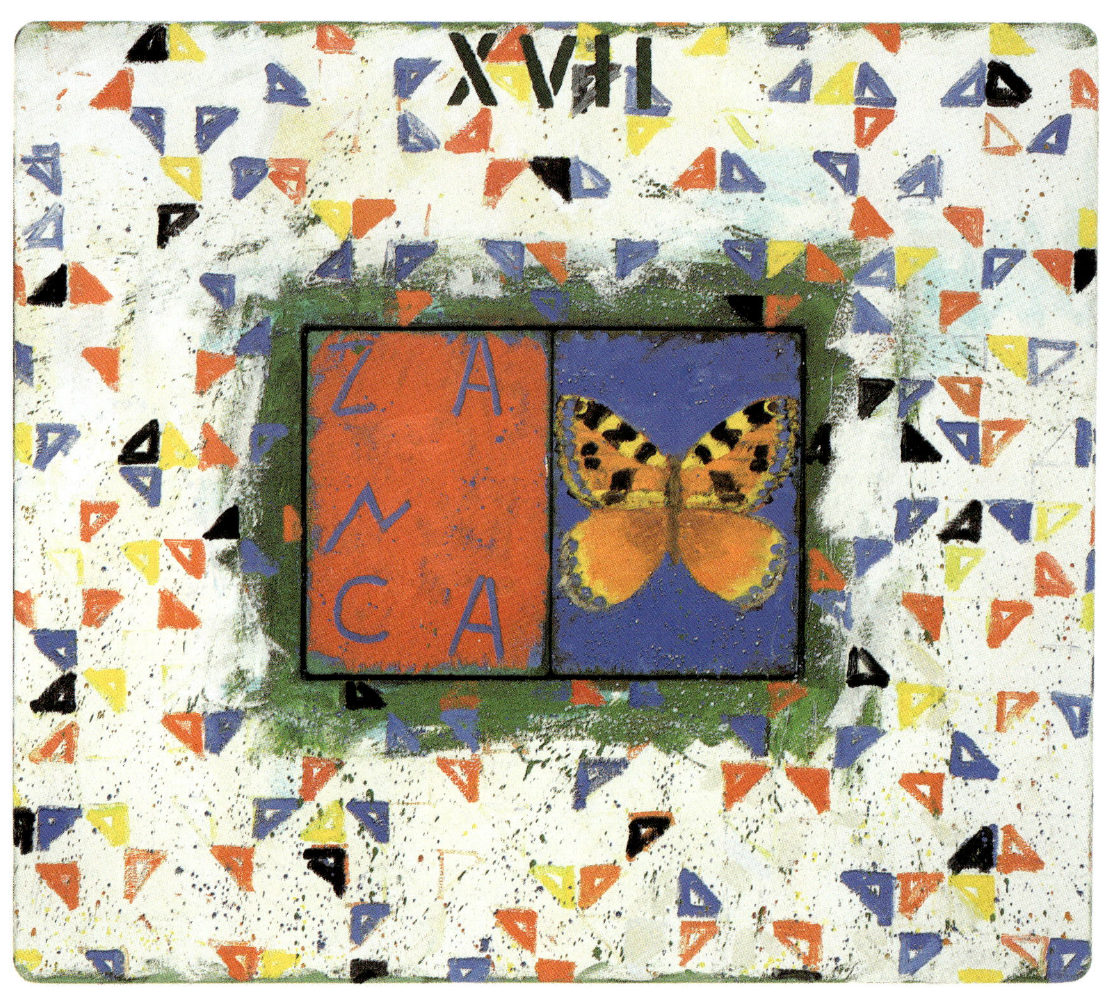

Joe Tilson RA
Conjunction Small Tortoiseshell, Zanca
Oil
137× 152 cm

Ian Stephenson RA
Hardraw
Watercolour
59 × 42 cm

GALLERY V

Bill Bowyer favours an intuitive approach to hanging a gallery. 'I began by hanging all the Academicians first and then built it up gradually and instinctively from there.' Traditionally Gallery V is dedicated to works on paper and this year it is dominated by six very big Norman Adams watercolours. Surveying the work he had selected to hang Bowyer commented: 'it's all got a certain sort of vitality and life about it. The only difference is between one artist and another.' It is his skill, his eye for hanging, which reconciles one painting to another, one drawing to its neighbour. 'Once I've placed them I don't move them around unless I have to. Sometimes it's necessary, but I keep it to a minimum. The process of thinking about placing the pictures goes on all the time. Even when you're not here, you think about it. It's a bit like a jigsaw puzzle to begin with; then when you've got it under your control you can play with it. If I want a light area, for instance, I can bring in a group of drawings.'

GALLERY V

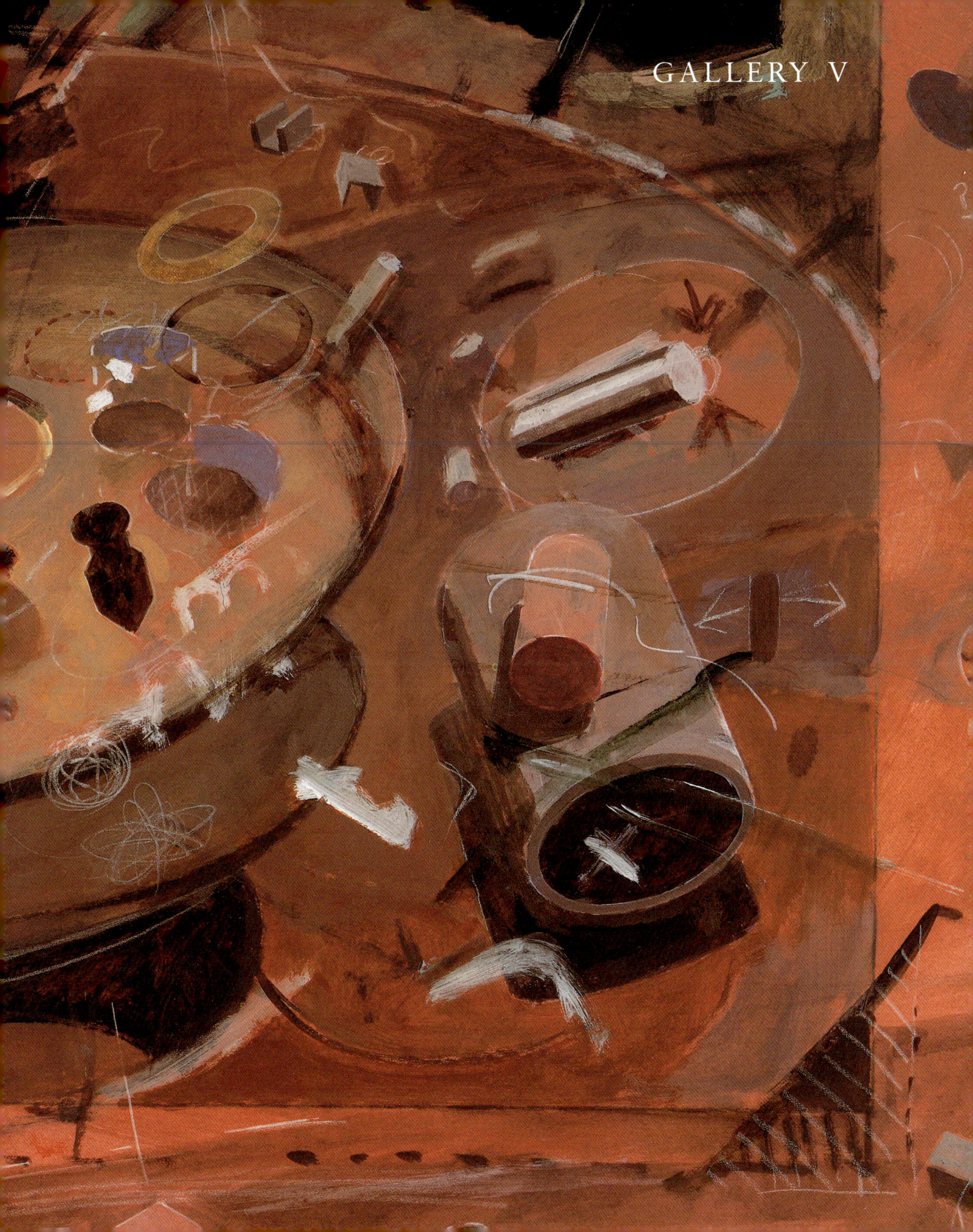

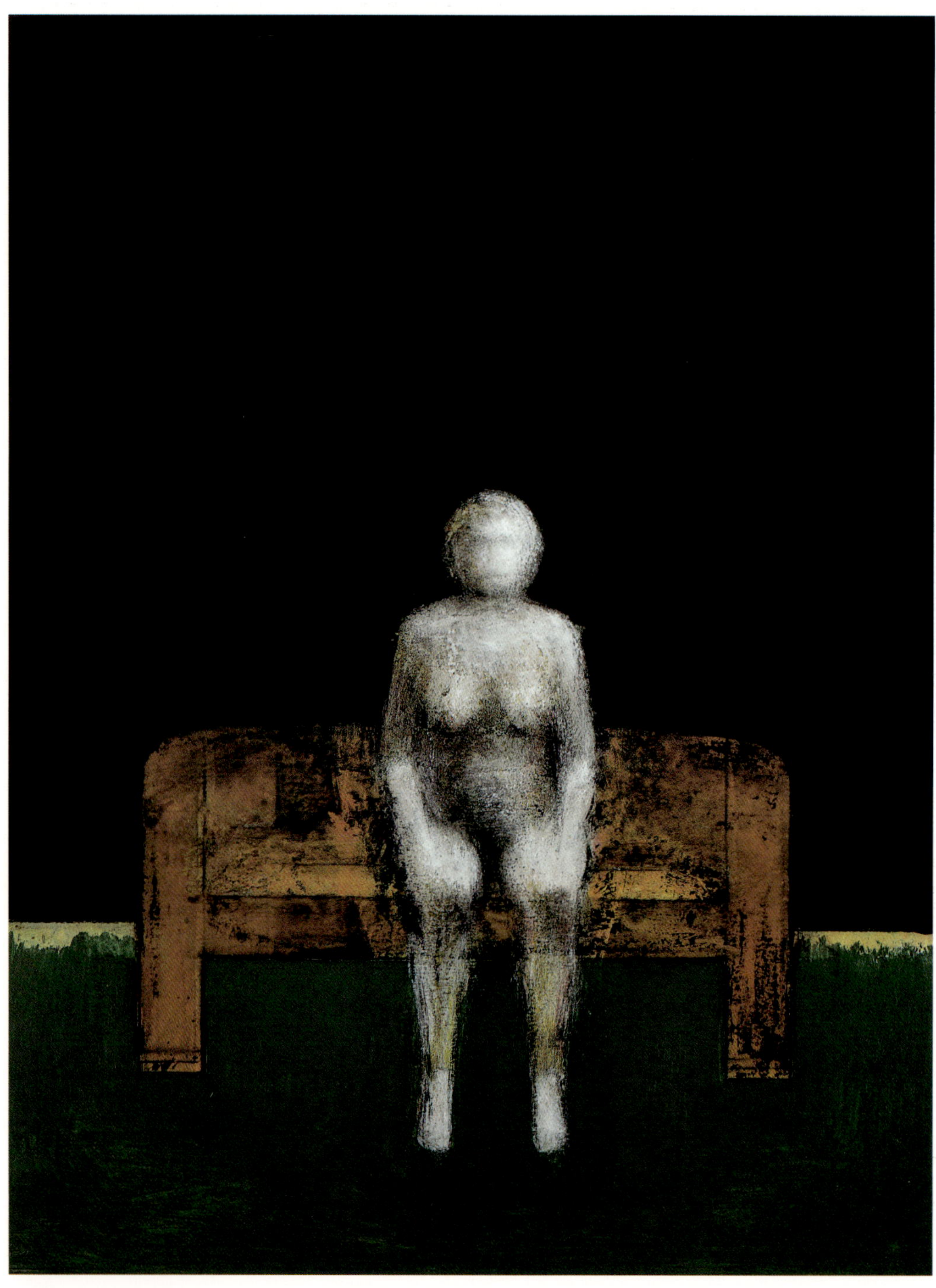

Robert Clatworthy RA
Small Seated Figure
Acrylic
74 × 53 cm

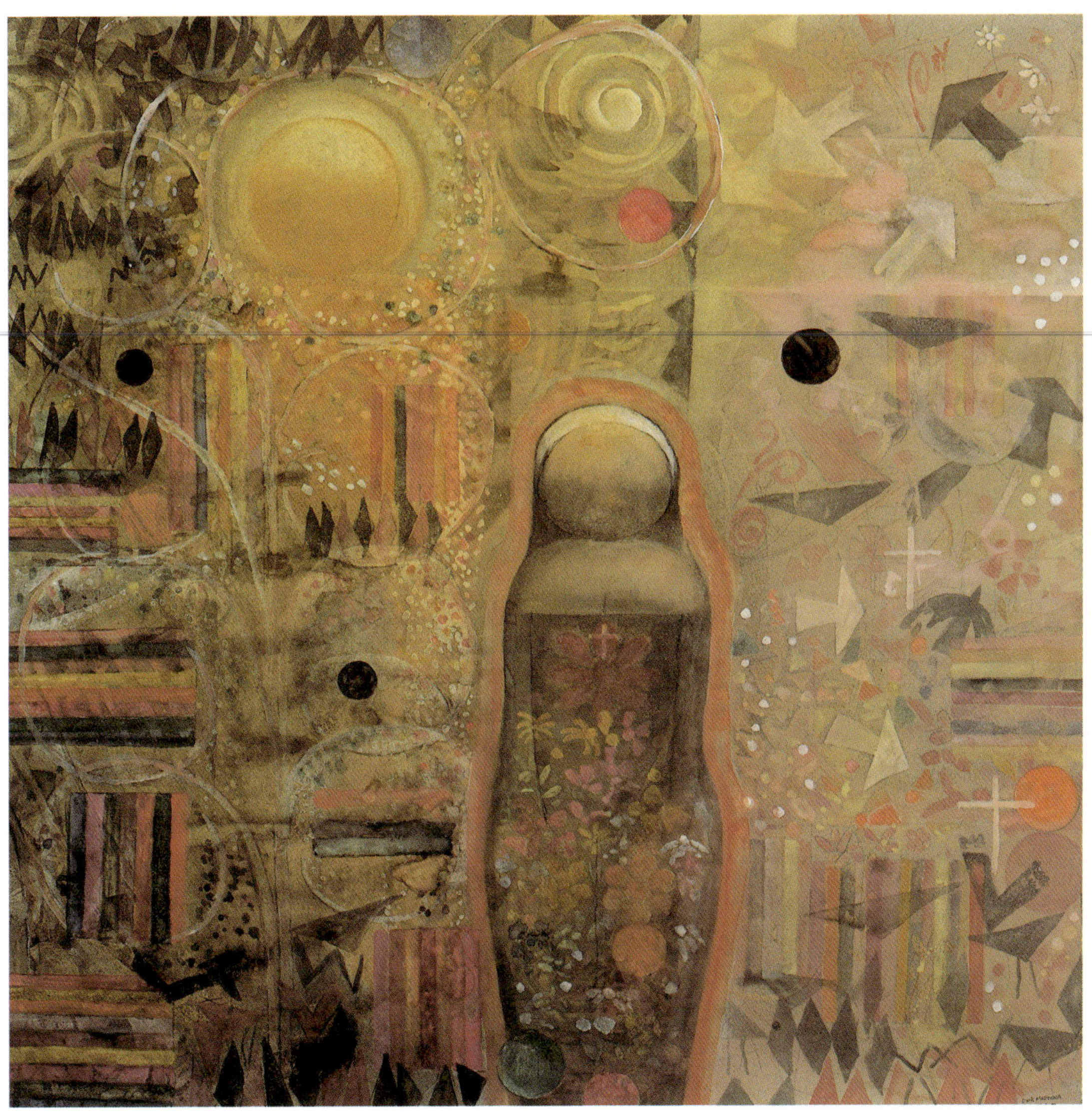

Norman Adams RA
Dark Madonna
Watercolour
125 × 121 cm

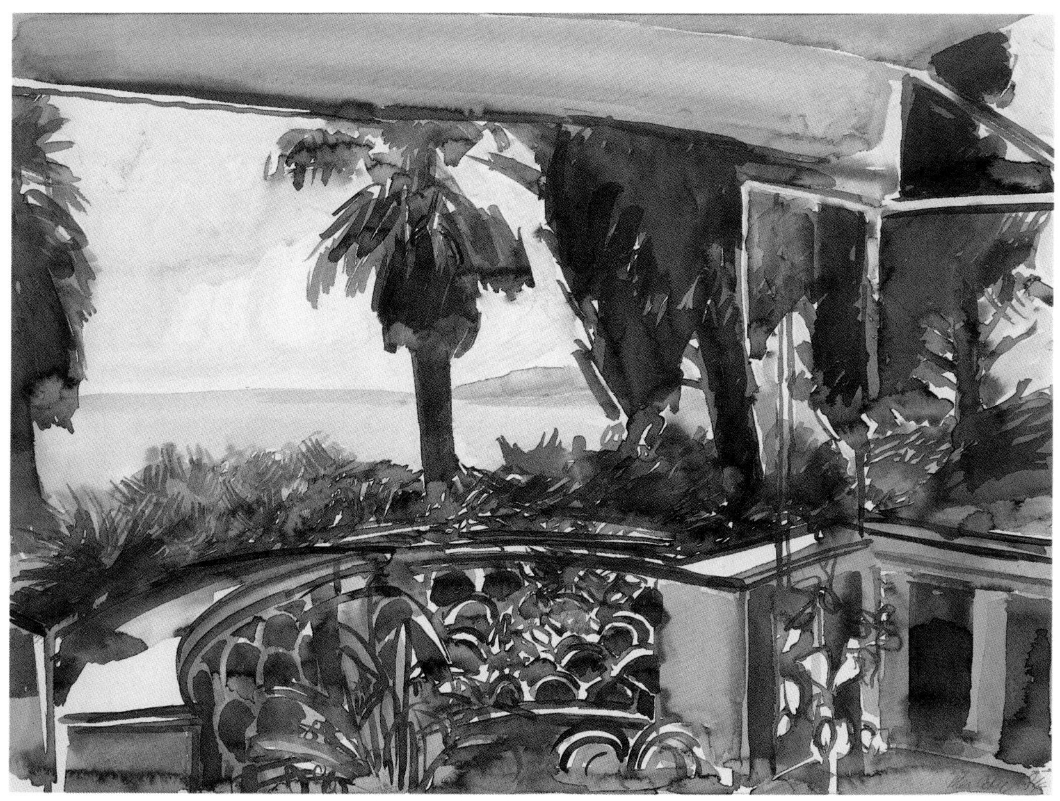

Peter Coker RA
Balcony, Clos du Peyronnet, Garavan
Ink
57 × 76 cm

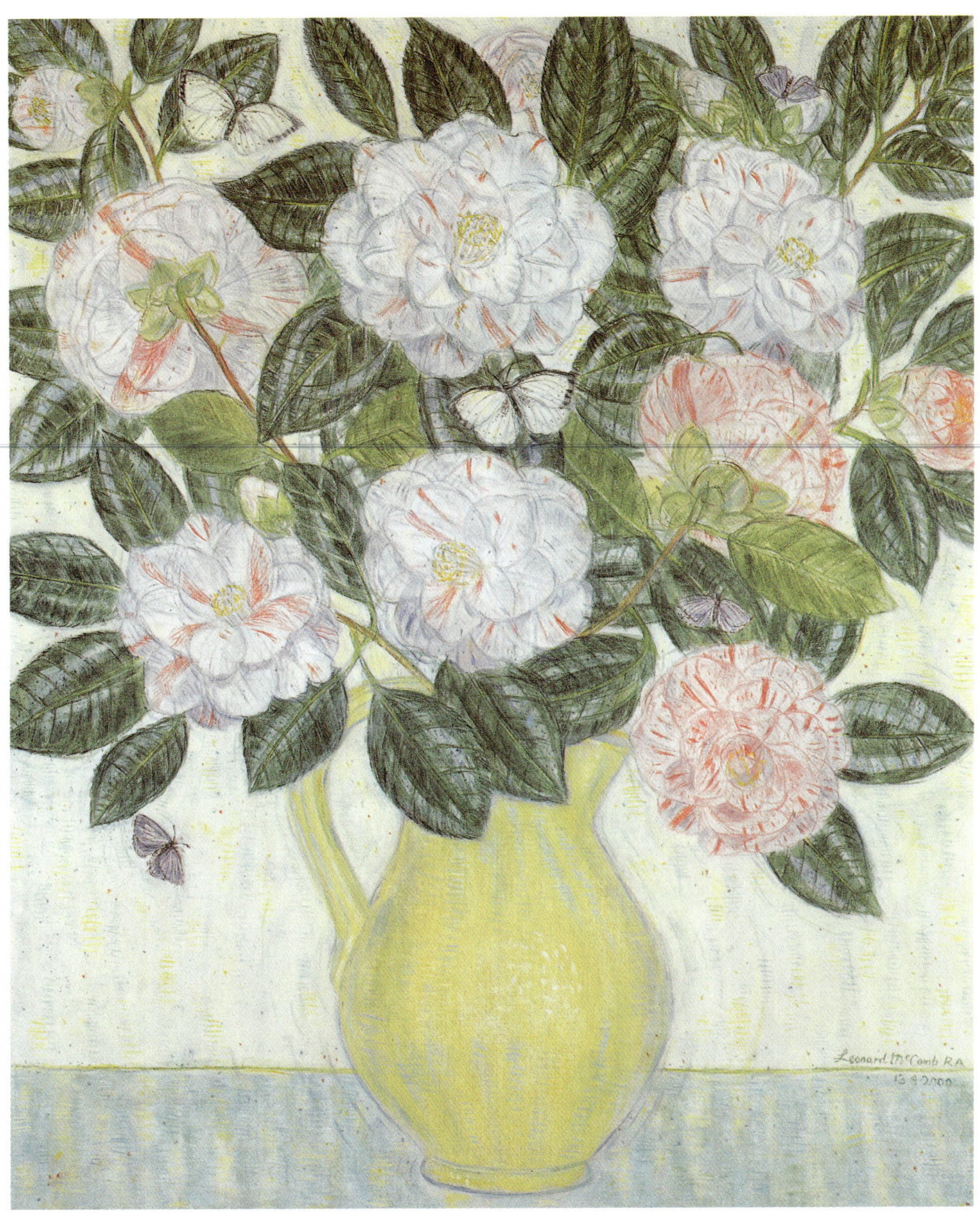

Leonard McComb RA
Camelias
Oil
76 × 61 cm

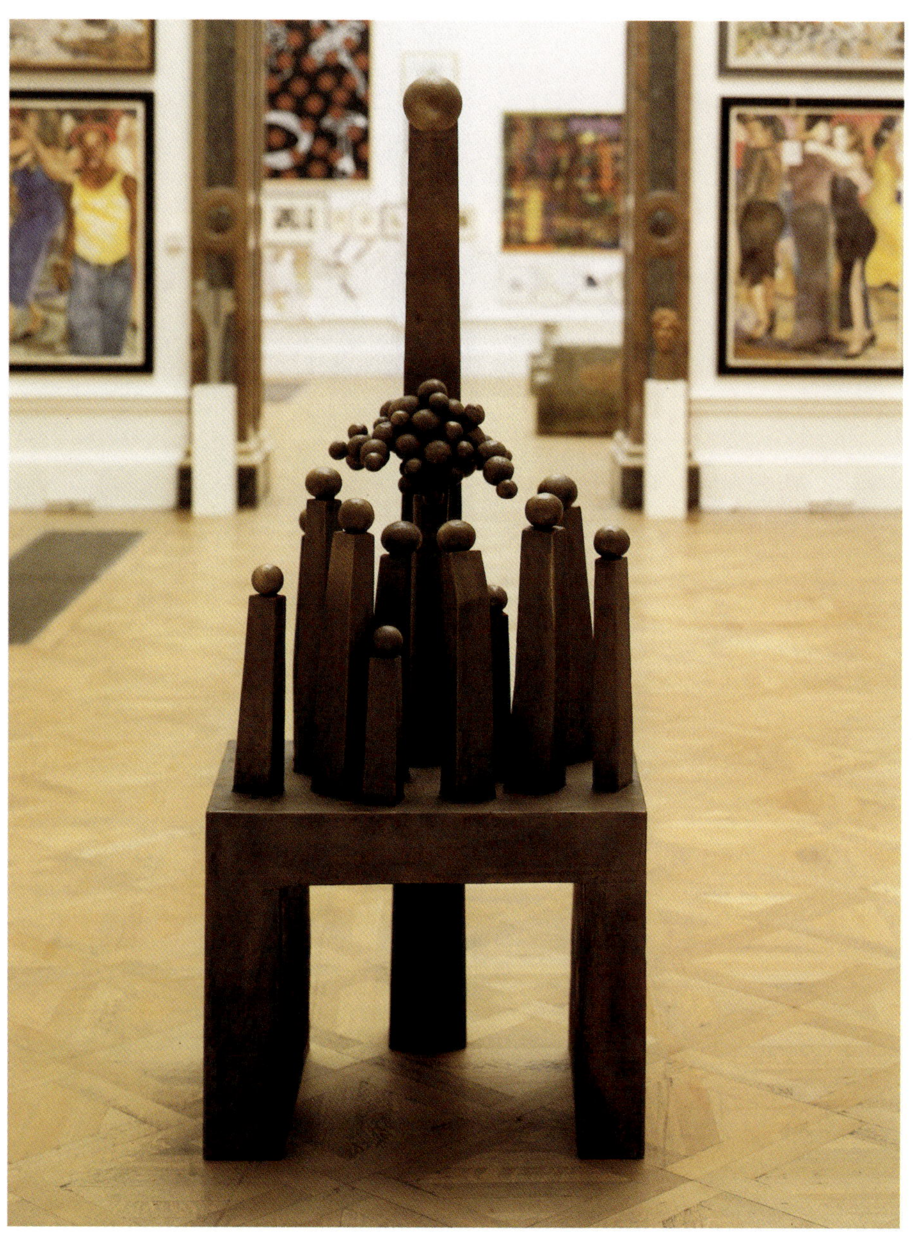

Geoffrey Clarke RA
The Gift (A Symbol) for the Millennium Wood Hartest, Suffolk
Bronze
h 200 cm

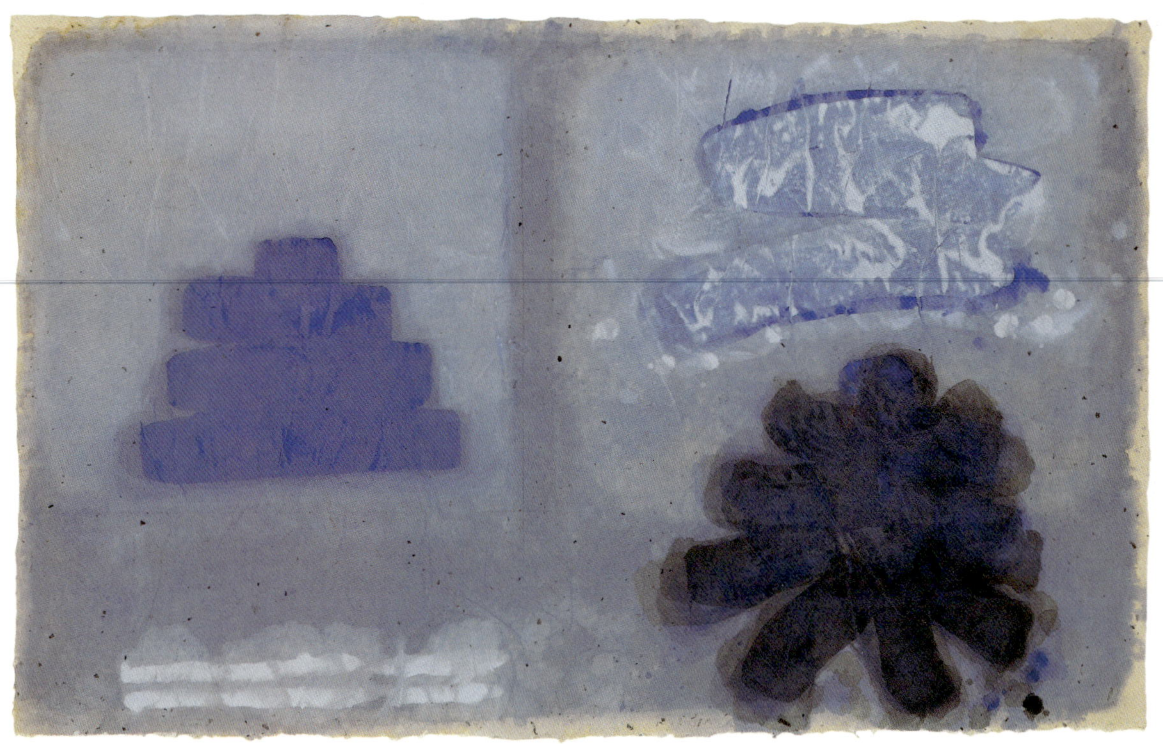

Ian McKenzie-Smith
Hotei's Garden
Watercolour
64 × 102 cm

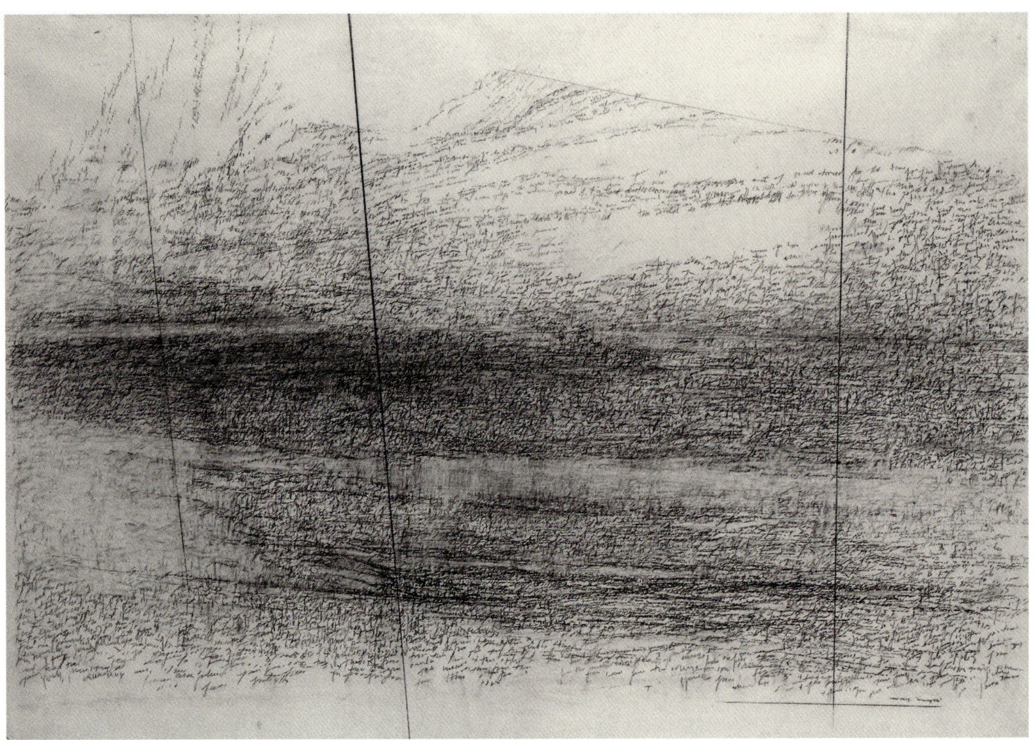

Karn Holly
Incoming tide
Charcoal
120 × 160 cm

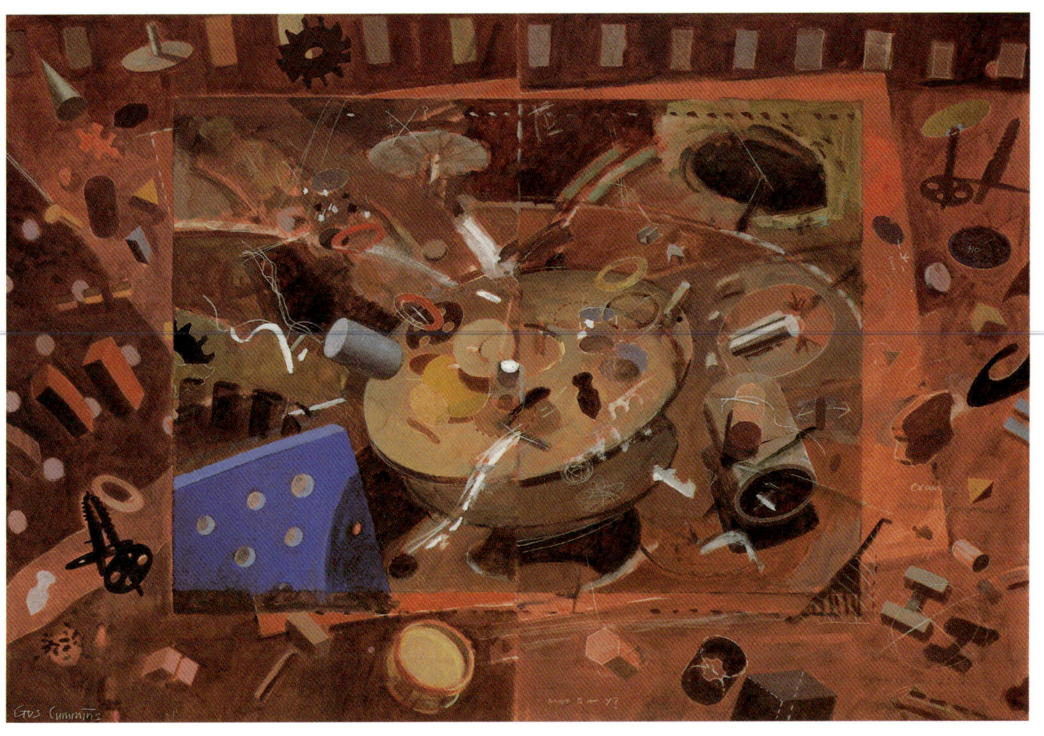

Gus Cummins RA
Circus: (Study)
Acrylic
69 × 98 cm

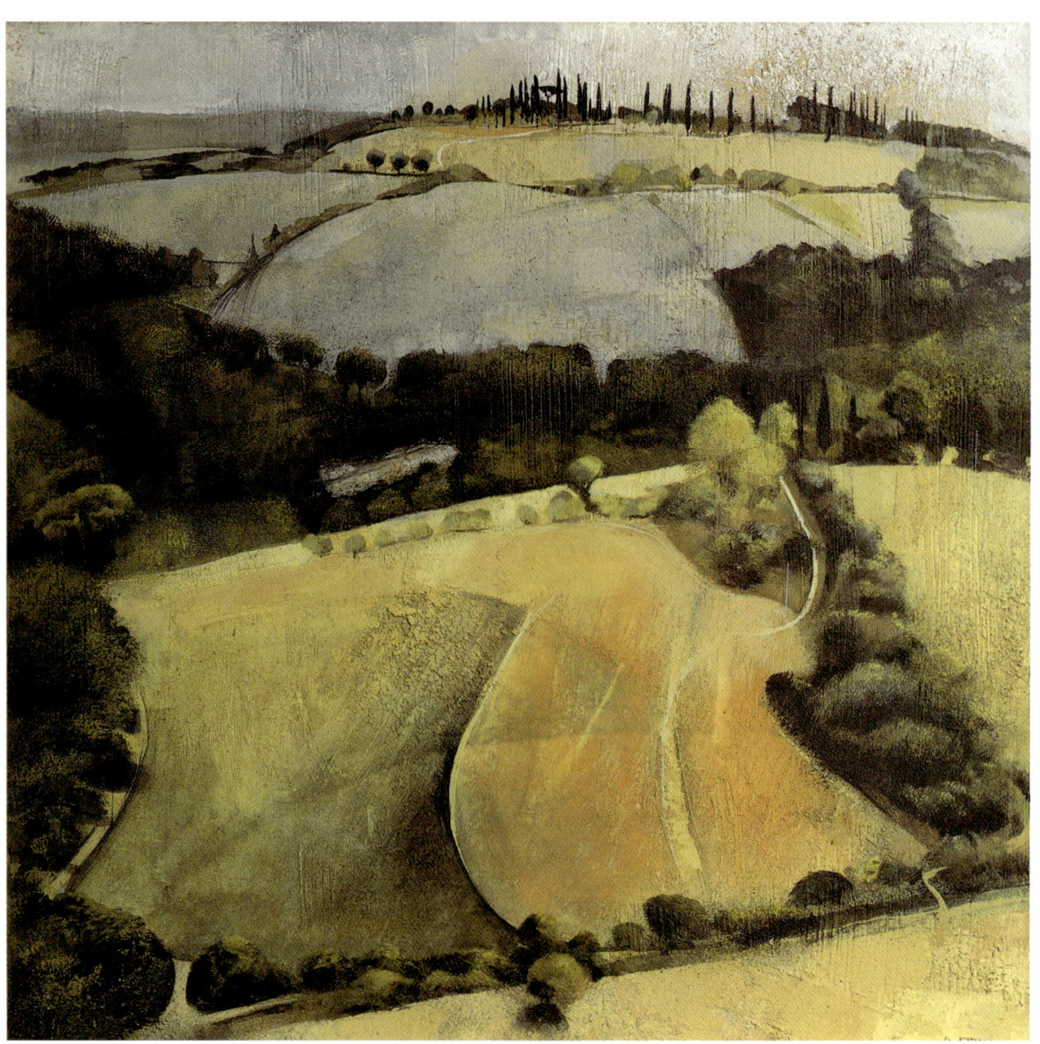

David Firmstone
Celle sur Rigo
Tempera
76 × 76 cm

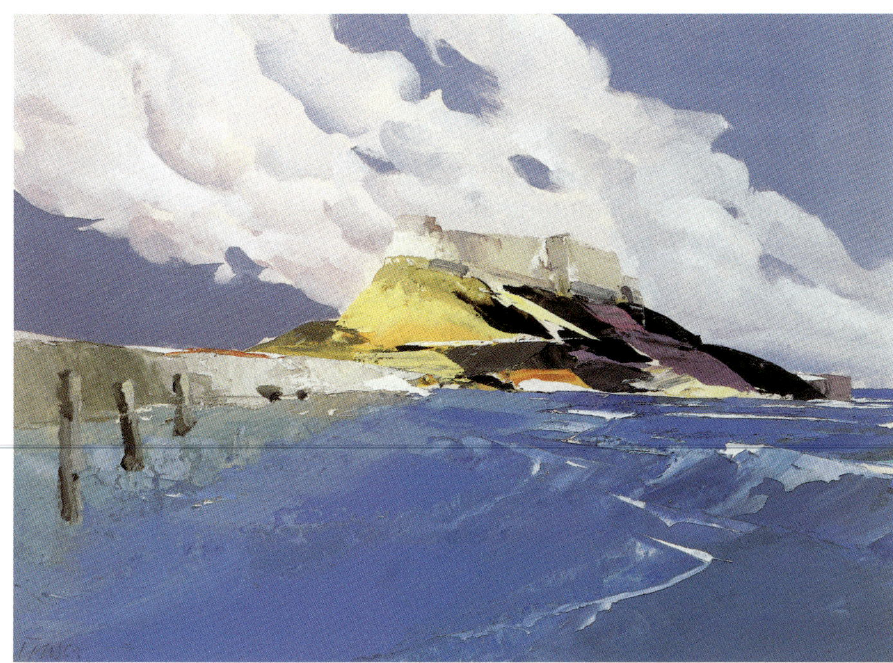

Donald Hamilton Fraser RA
Lindisfarne
Oil
30 × 40 cm

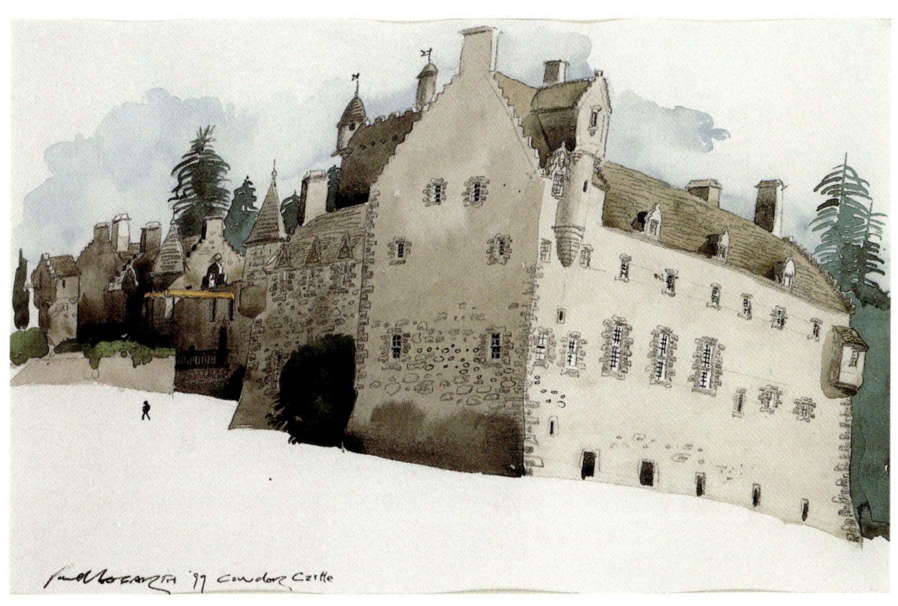

Paul Hogarth OBE, RA
Cawdor Castle
Watercolour
36 × 54 cm

GALLERY VI

The builders are in Gallery VI this year which has reduced the hanging space available and the gallery is only lit by artificial light. As Anthony Green, the hanger directly responsible for this space, effervescently comments: 'This suits us down to the ground because we have a very large sculpture by David Nash purchased by the Chantrey Bequest for the Tate, and their conservators want us to have it in reduced lighting. There will also be two major sculptures by Neil Jeffries as well as works by Ken Draper and as the cherry lobbed in like a Molotov Cocktail, a Jean Cooke.'

GALLERY VI

David Nash RA
Pyramid, Sphere, Cube
Wood and Charcoal

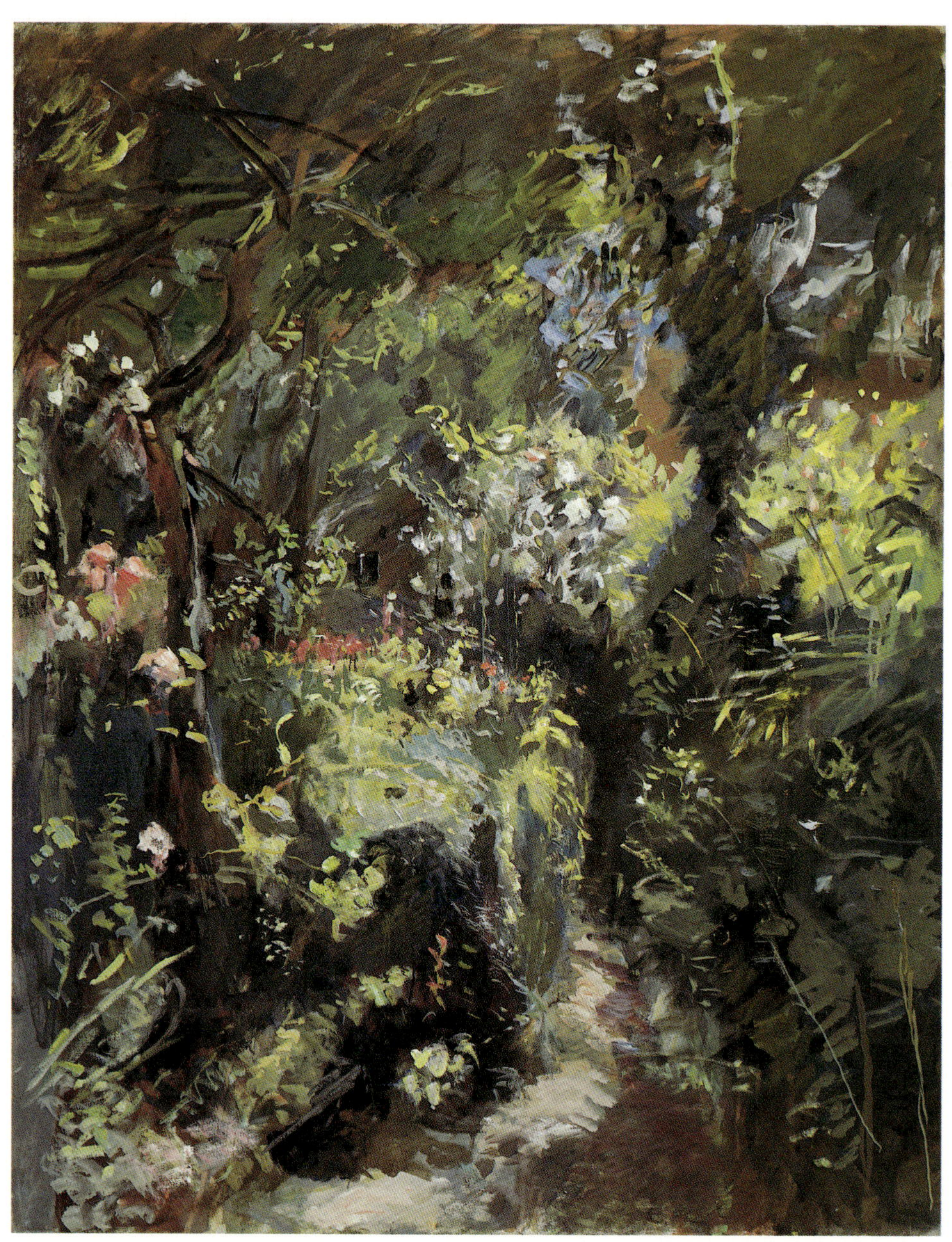

Anthony Eyton RA
Brixton Garden
Oil
152 × 117 cm

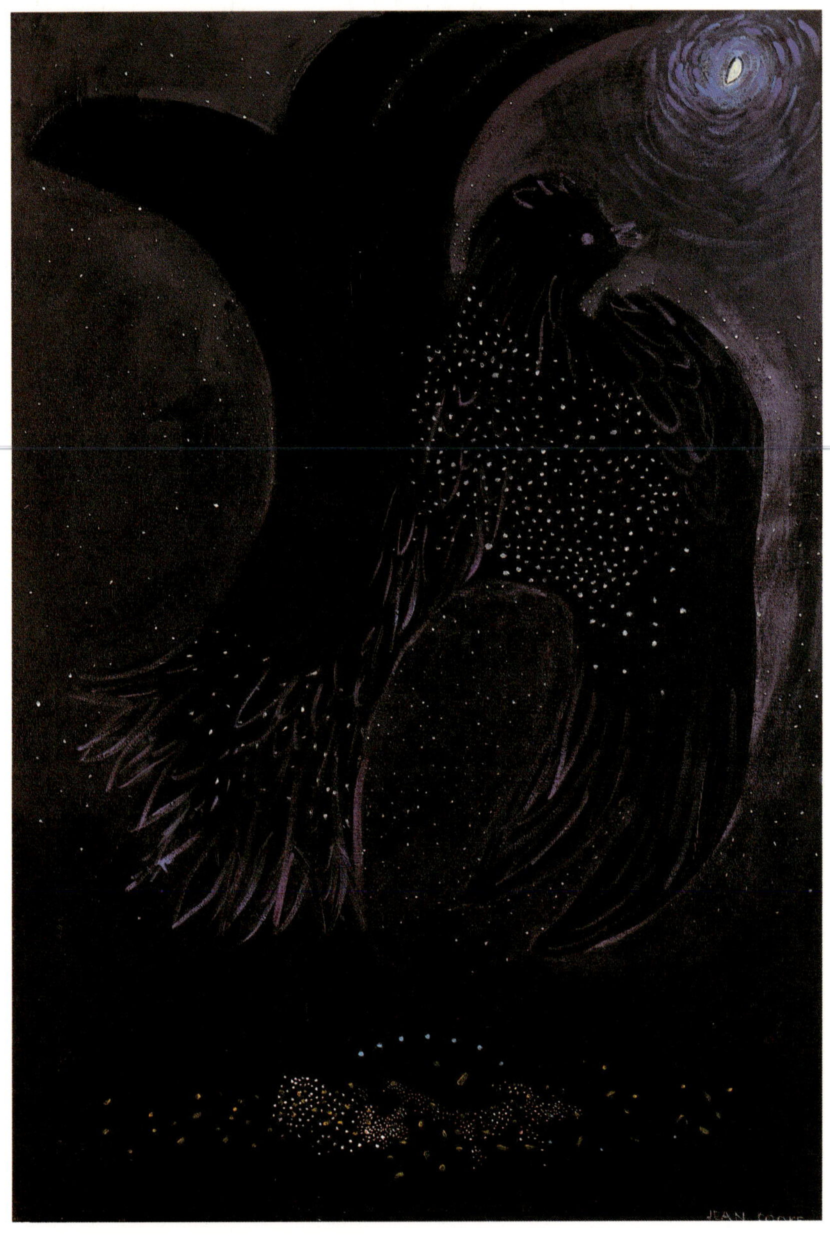

Jean Cooke RA
Rumour…shrieking through darkness
Acrylic
183 × 122 cm

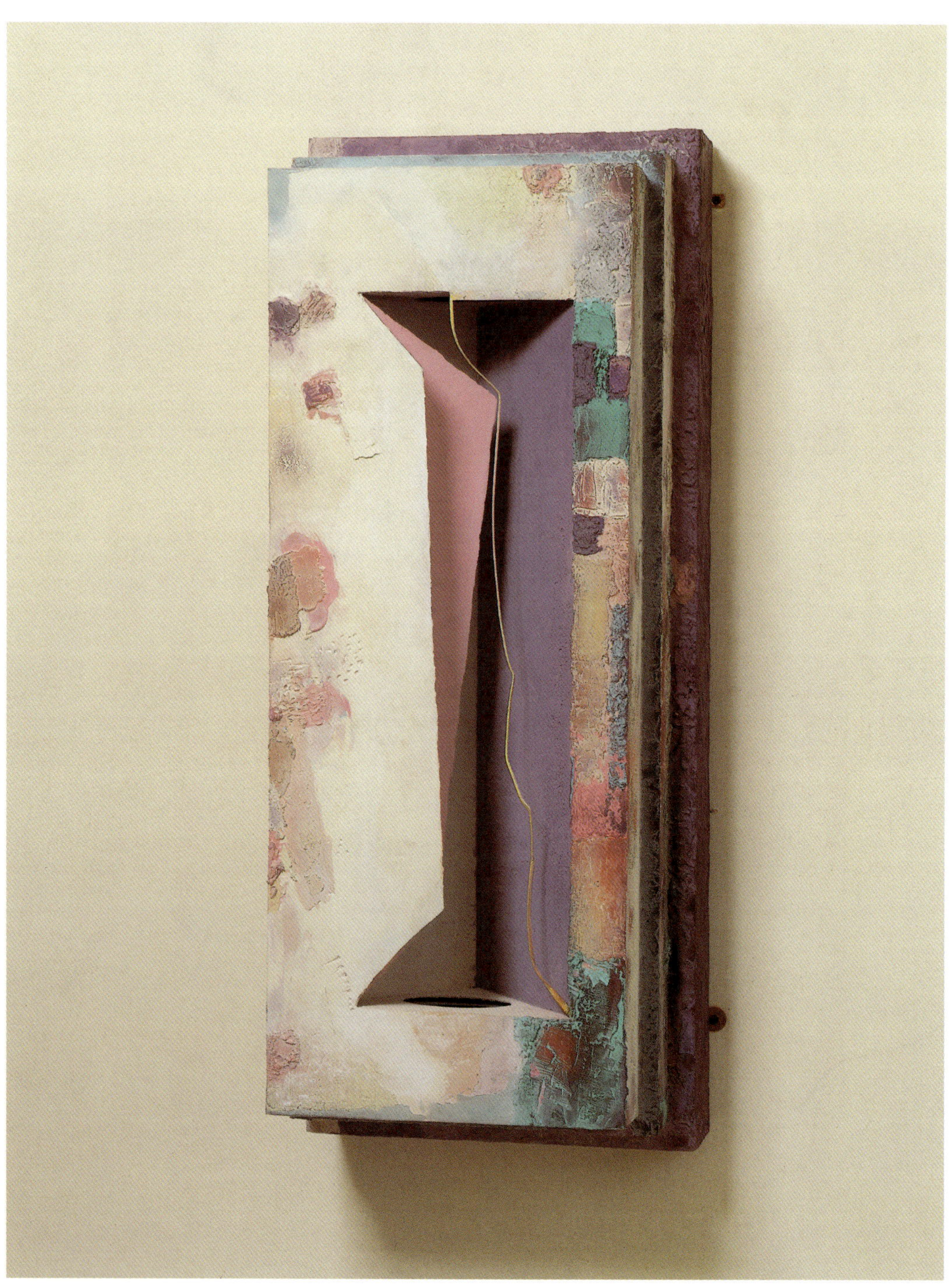

Ken Draper RA
Through the Yellow Fall
Mixed media
h 92 cm

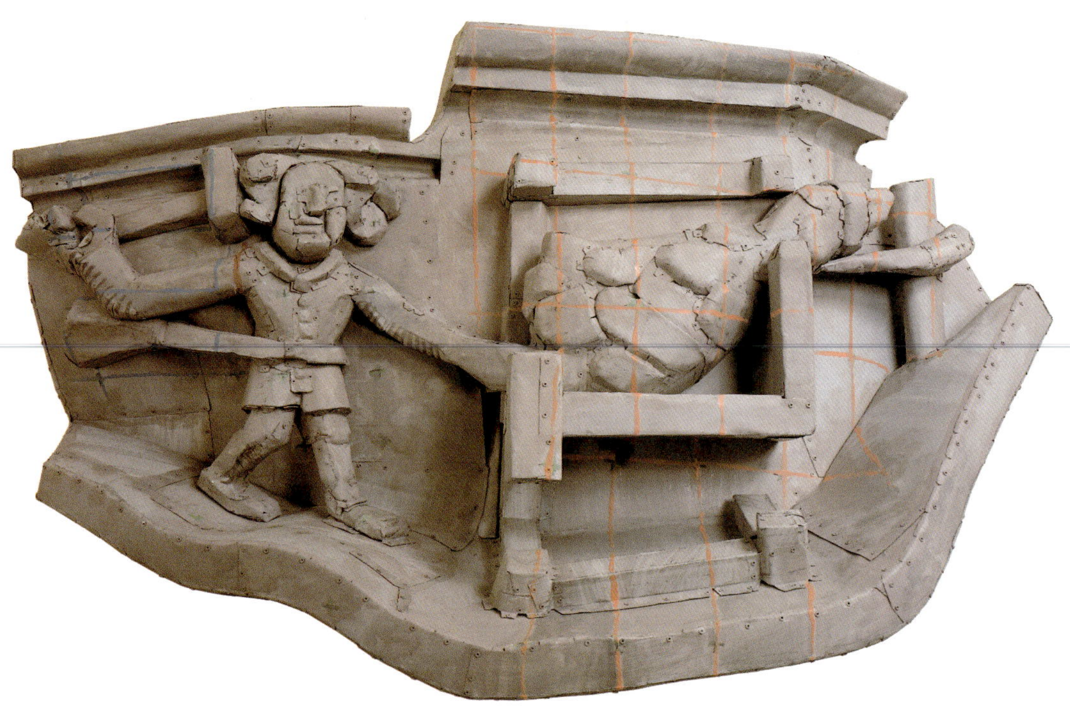

Neil Jeffries
A Man Shoeing a Goose
Oil on metal
h 95 cm

GALLERY VII

Peter Blake explains the inimitable look of his gallery: 'I'm continuing the idea that I've done twice before. I did it originally with Craigie [Aitchison] about fifteen years ago when we looked for all the kittens and the Queen Mothers, all the Sunday painters and popular art, and we hung a whole room of that kind of picture. Then seven or eight years ago I hung a room with lots of small pictures going right up to the picture rail. I thought I couldn't honestly repeat that this year over the whole room so I'm only continuing the concept on one side – lots of small pictures, some Sunday paintings, some primitives, some very serious little paintings.'

Blake moves over to look at the work laid out on the floor opposite. 'On this other wall, one area will be given over to a series of black and white drawings, a combination of very serious figurative drawings and quite amusing things. Another area will be the memorial to Josef Herman with a distinguished and serious group of pictures. Around it will be larger paintings, quite densely hung. I think what's always interesting about the Summer Show is that although we are a team, we're all disparate people, we do things differently. To walk from a room which is quite lightly and elegantly hung to a room which is, in a way, overhung, can be a nice contrast. This gallery is not far from Anthony Whishaw's room, which is always a serious, beautifully hung room. You come into this room and you giggle a bit – you read it in a different way. It's not quite a kitsch thing, it's very much a concept. It's to keep something going which has always been a part of the Academy – the amateur painter, the Sunday painter – which sometimes can be overlooked. I'm all for what everybody else is doing too – it would be awful if every room was like this – but to come into one room and to understand that it is a concept, is important.'

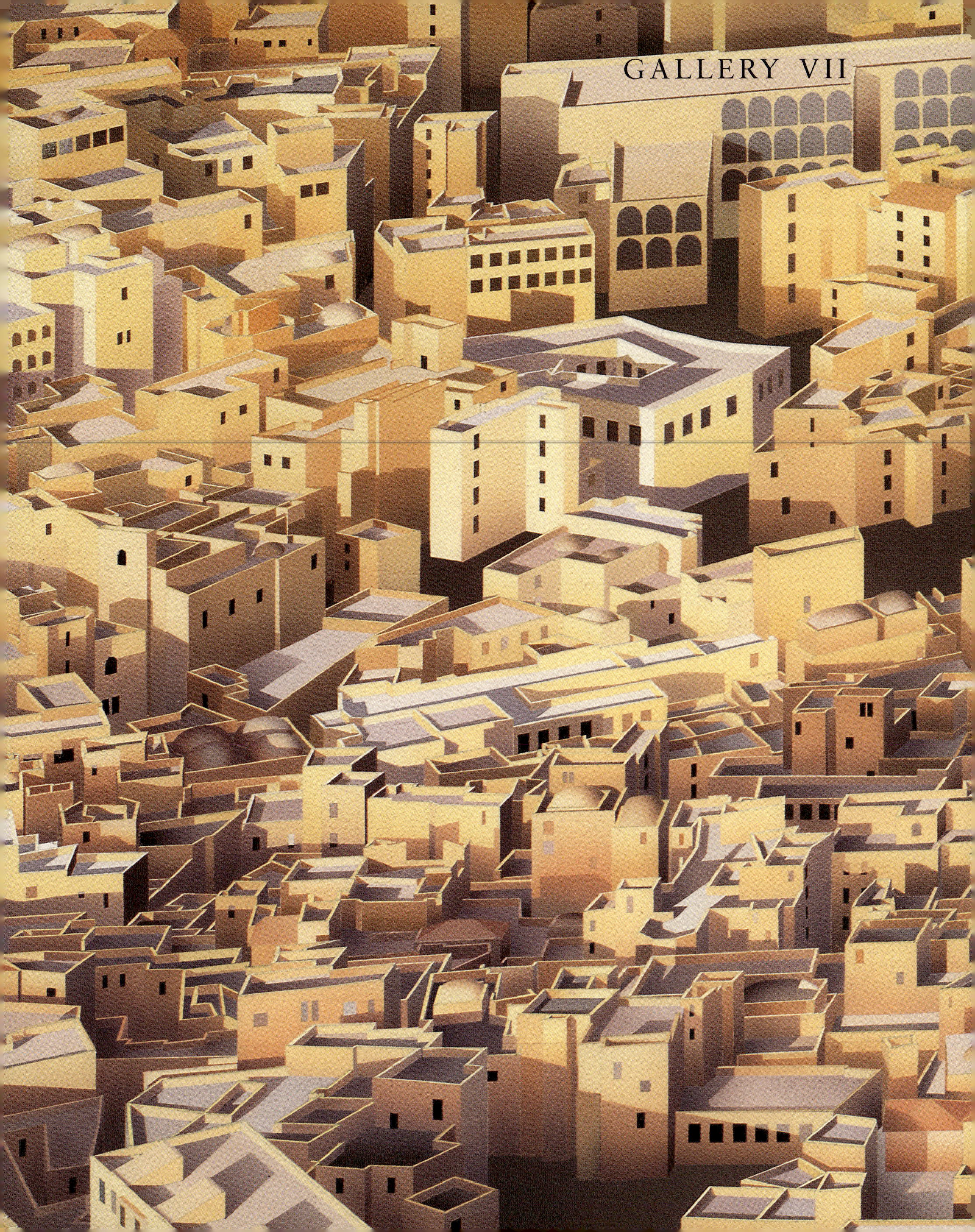
GALLERY VII

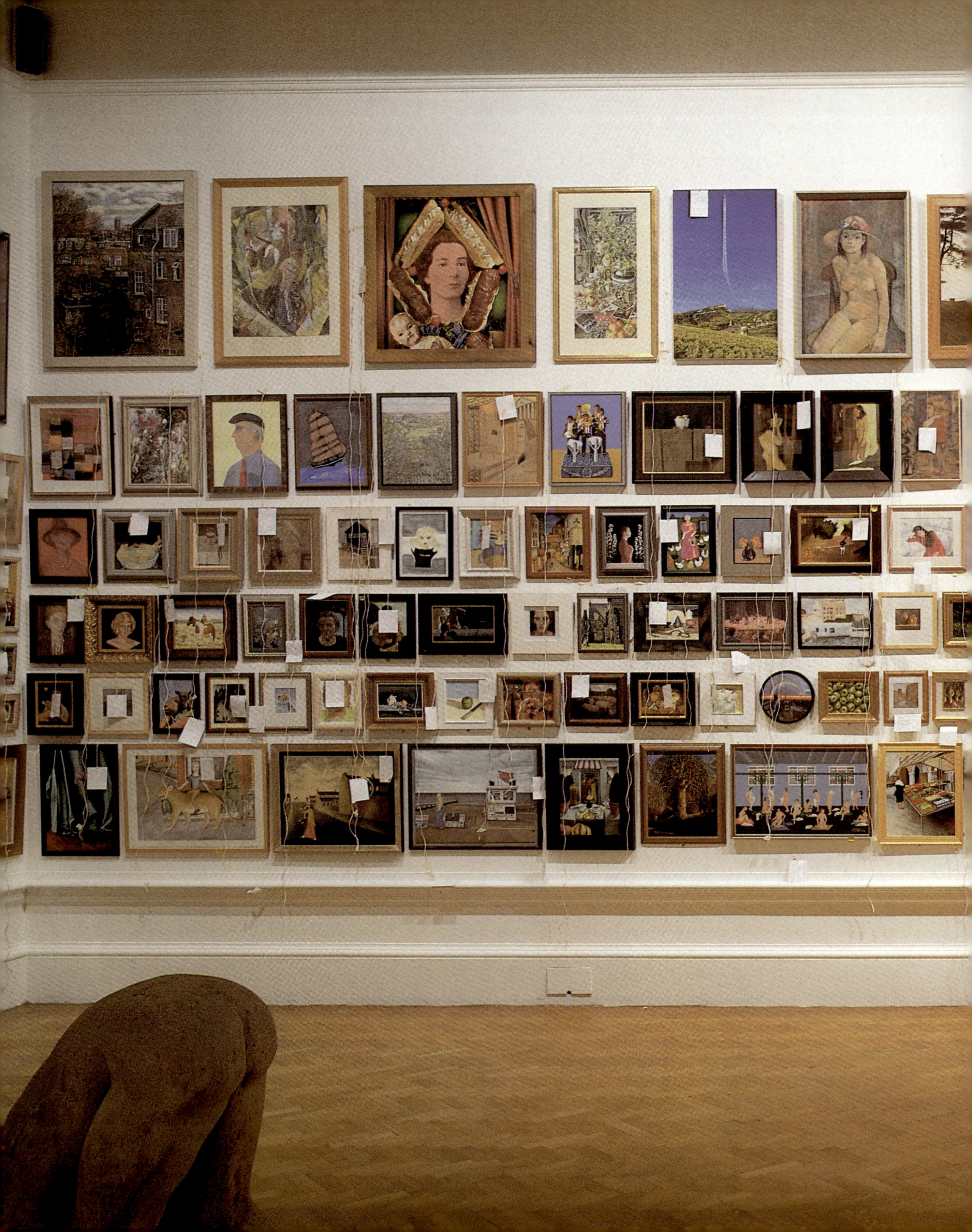

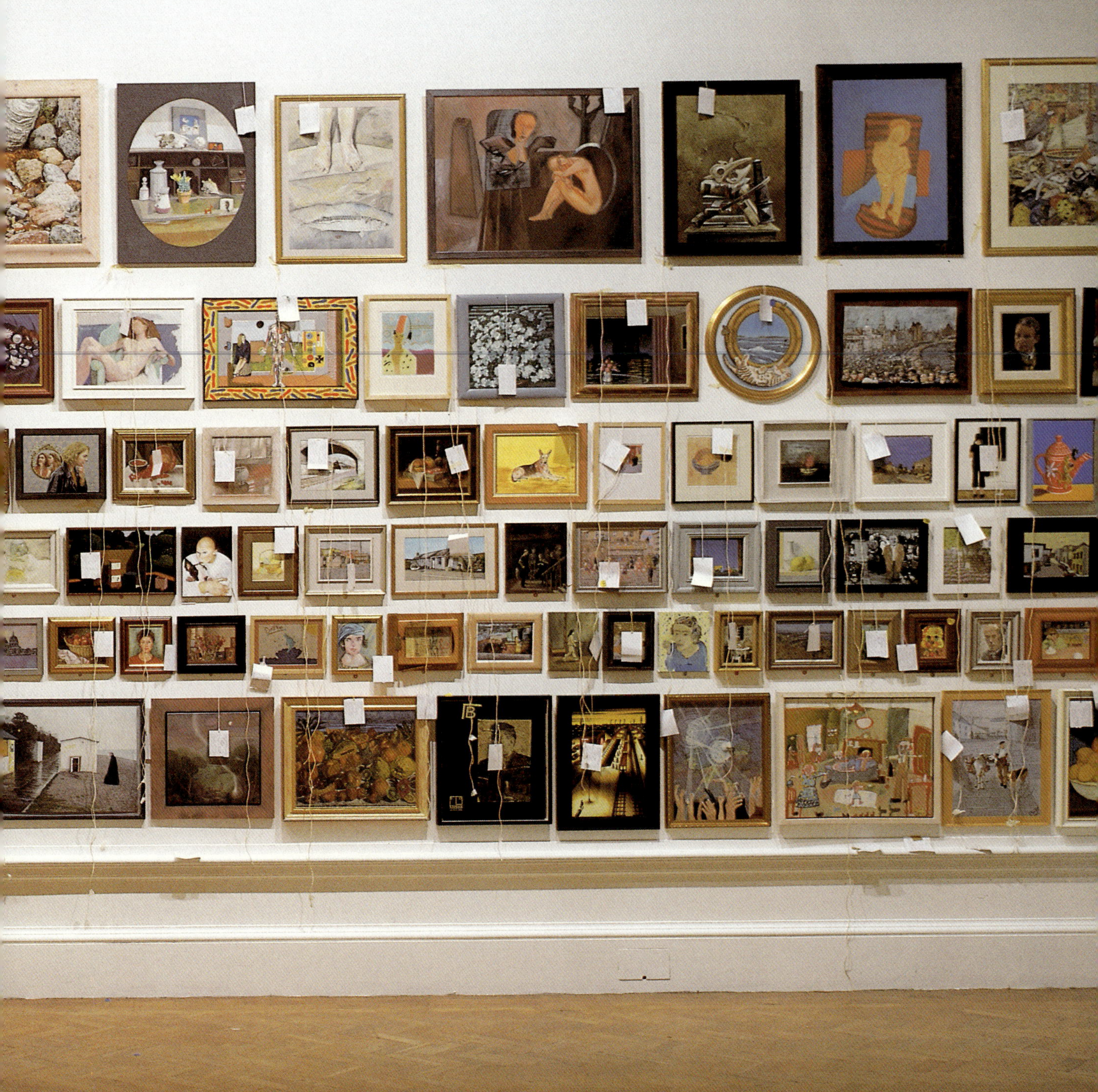

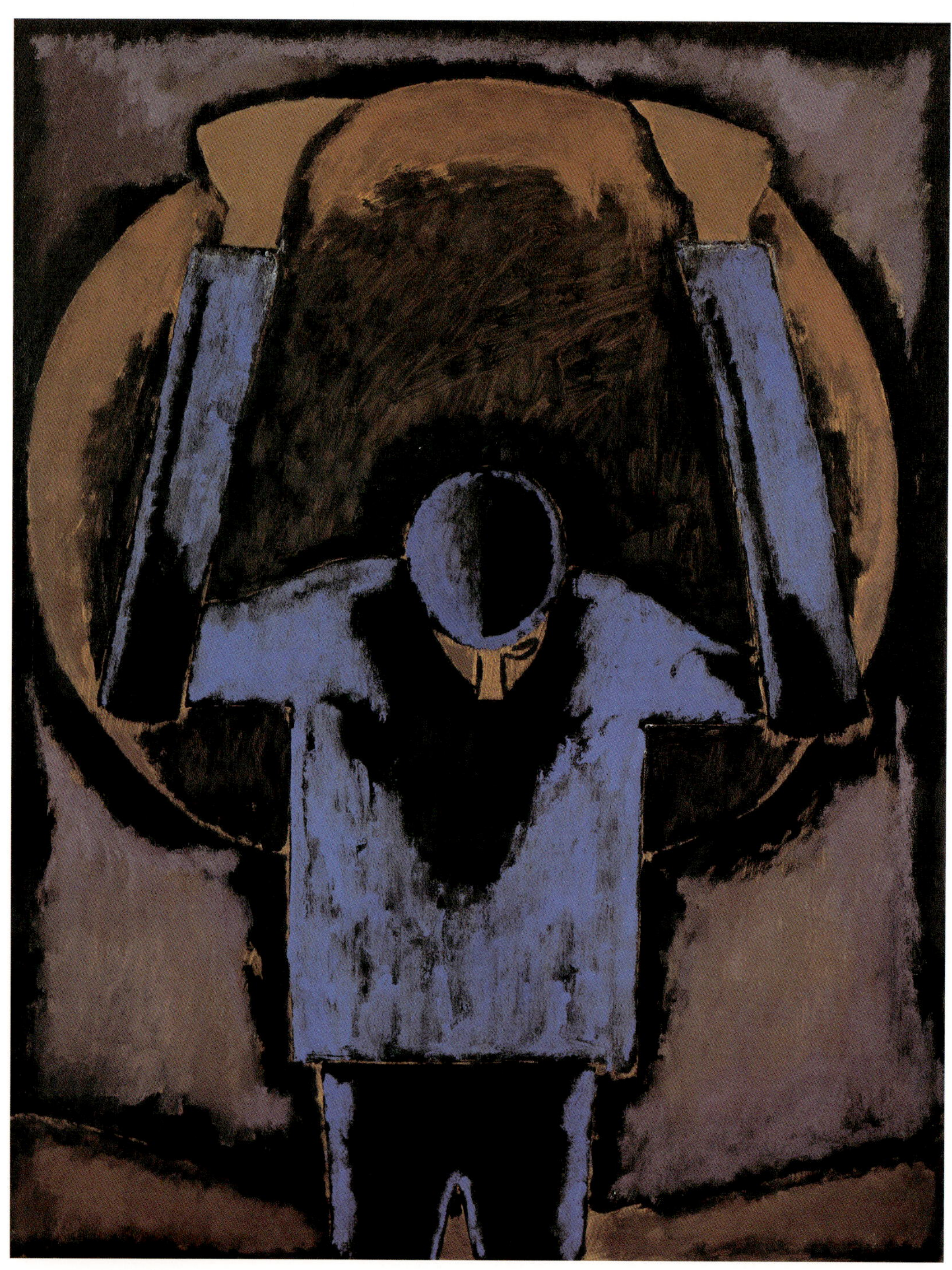

Josef Herman OBE, RA
Fisherman with Nets
Oil on canvas
121 × 91 cm

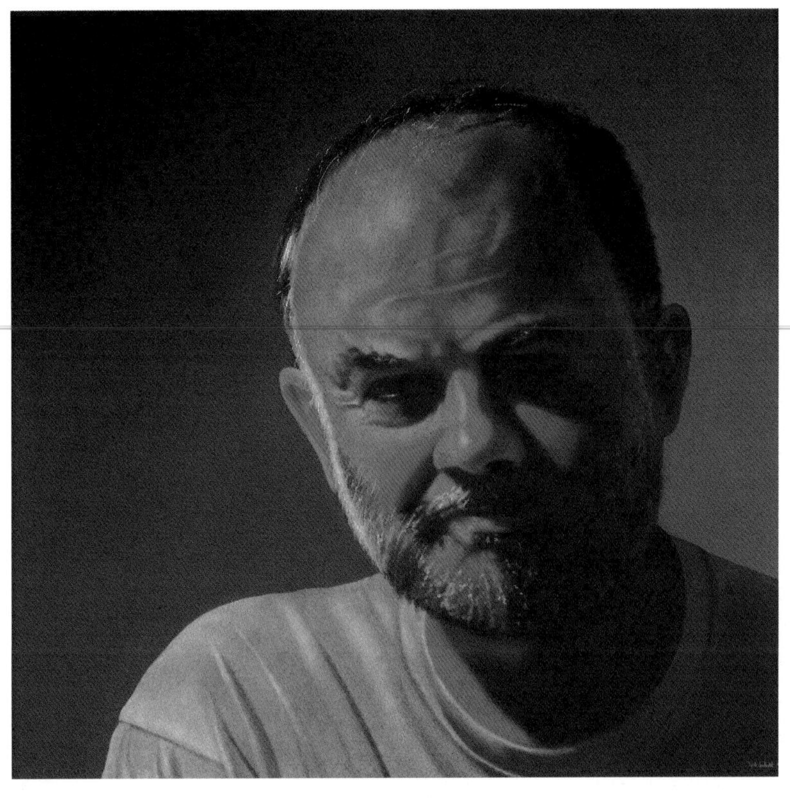

Nick Cudworth
John Peel O.B.E.
Pastel
54× 54 cm

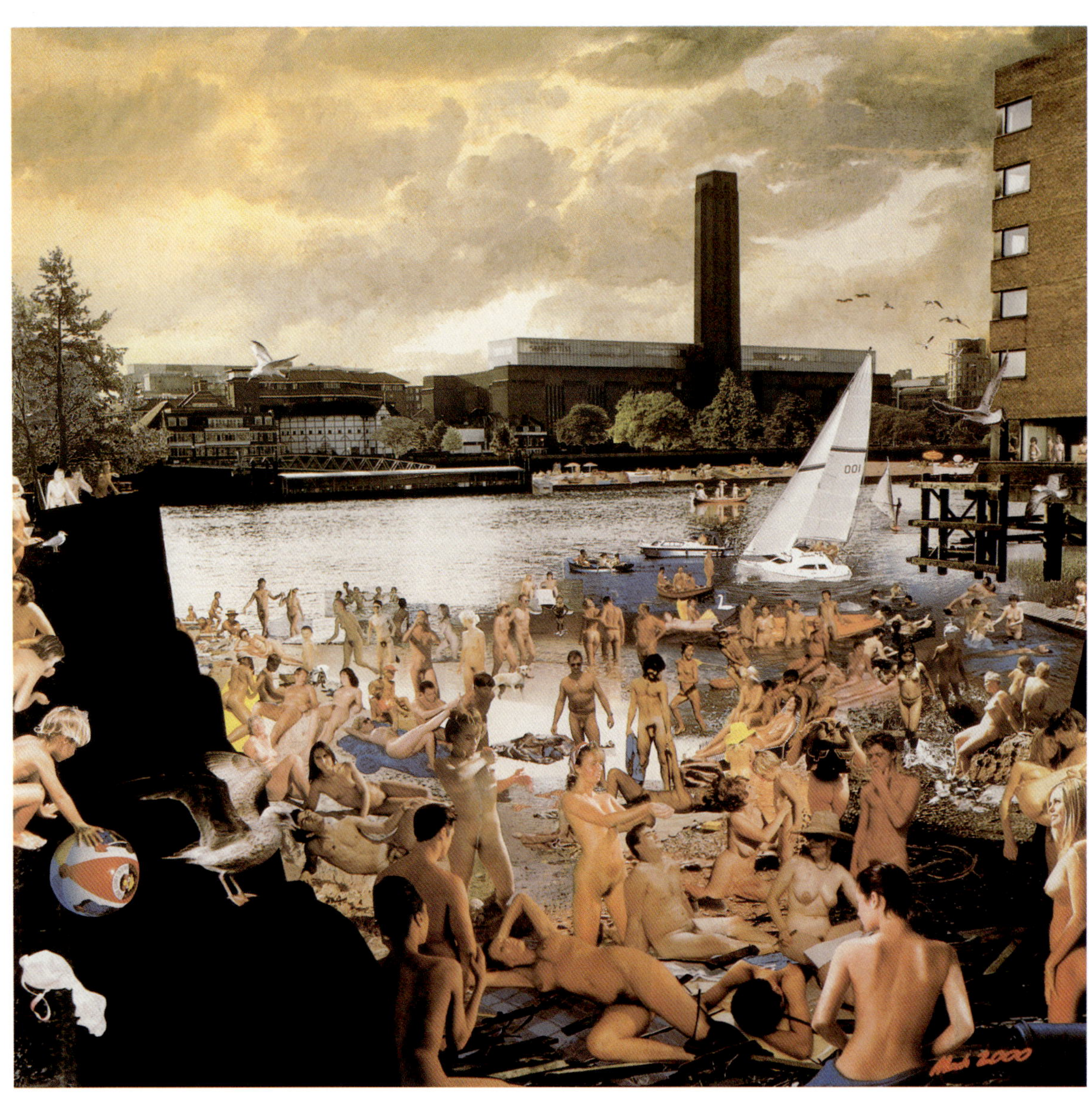

David Mach RA
Buff
Screenprint
75 × 75 cm

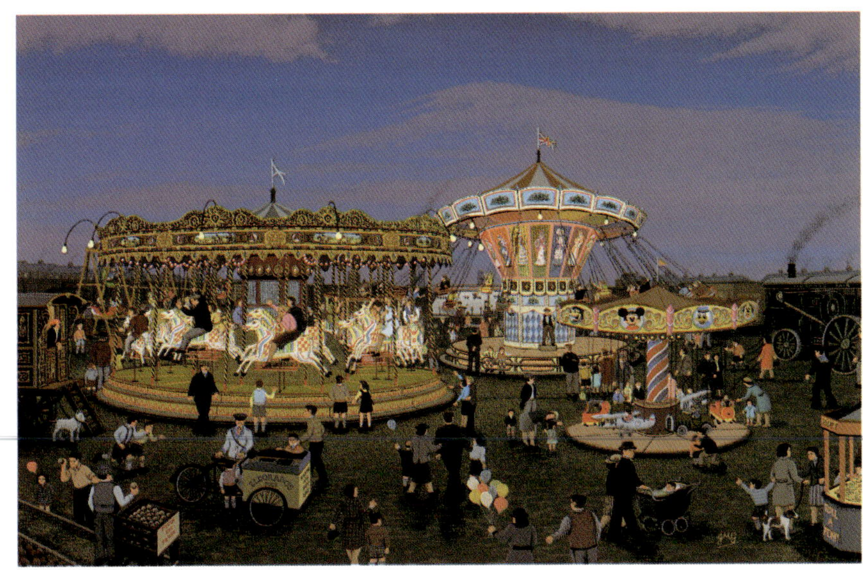

Joseph McGinn
The Shows
Oil
55 × 82 cm

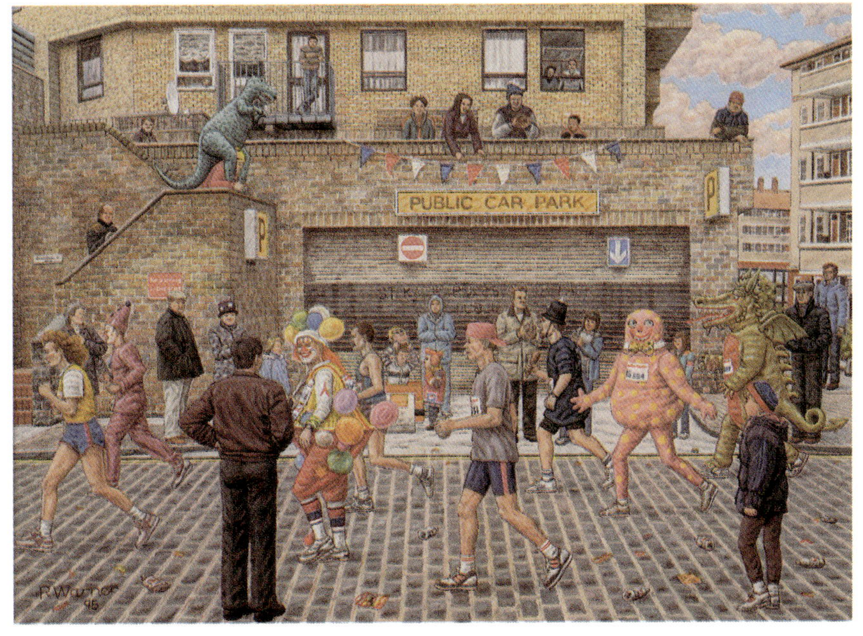

Robert Warner
Fun Runners
Oil
29 × 40 cm

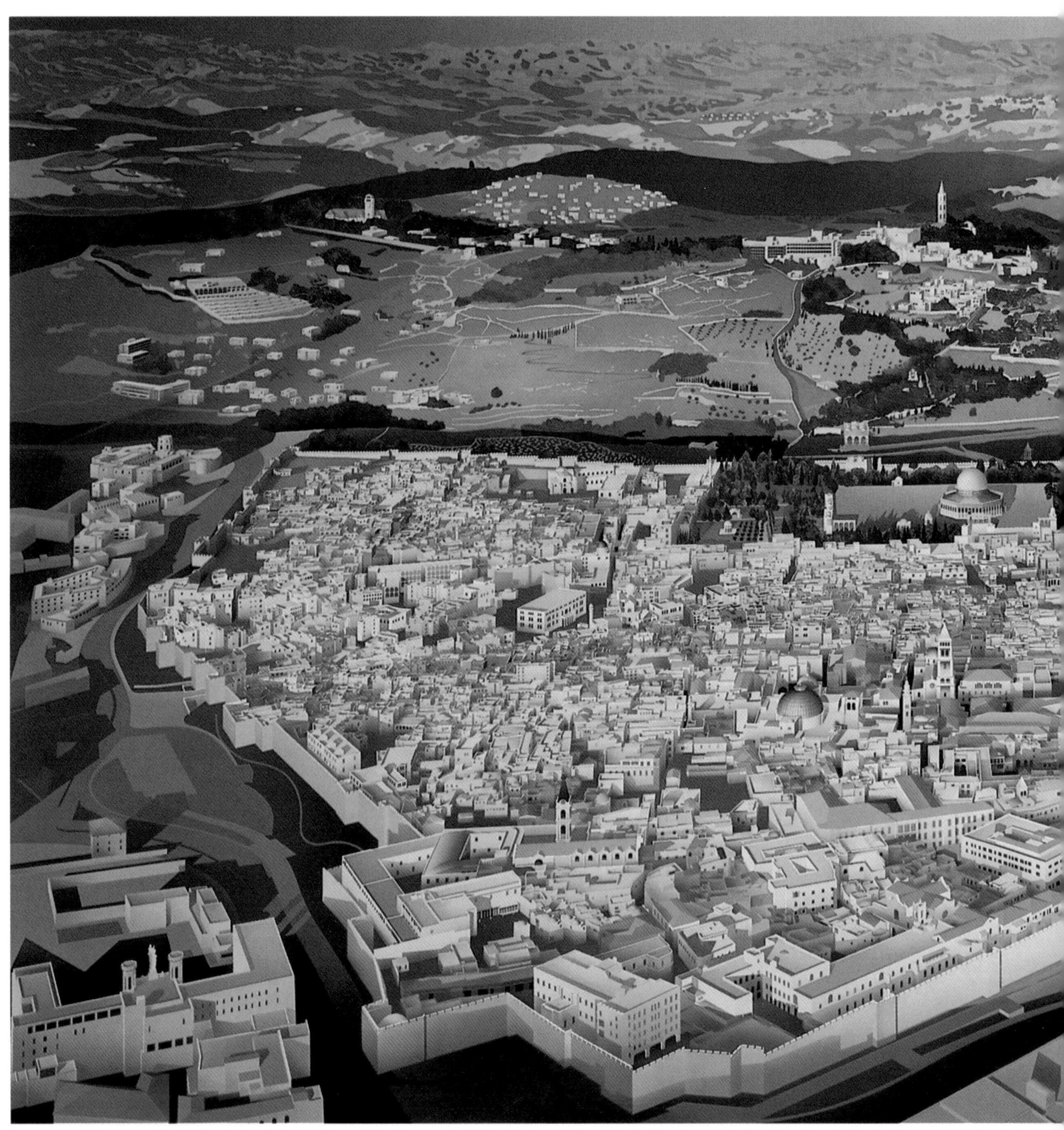

Ben Johnson
Jerusalem, The Eternal City
Acrylic
229 × 457 cm

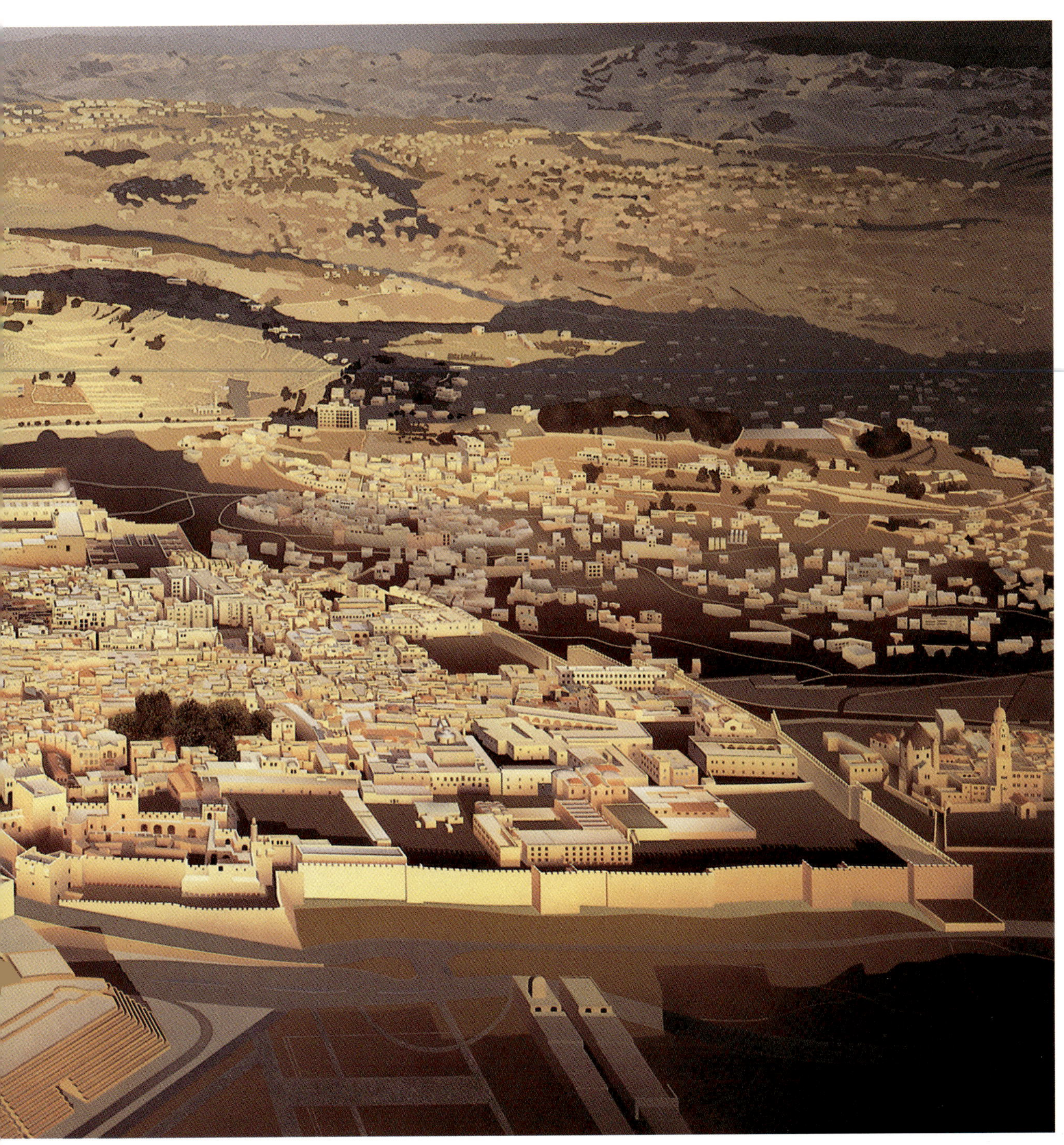

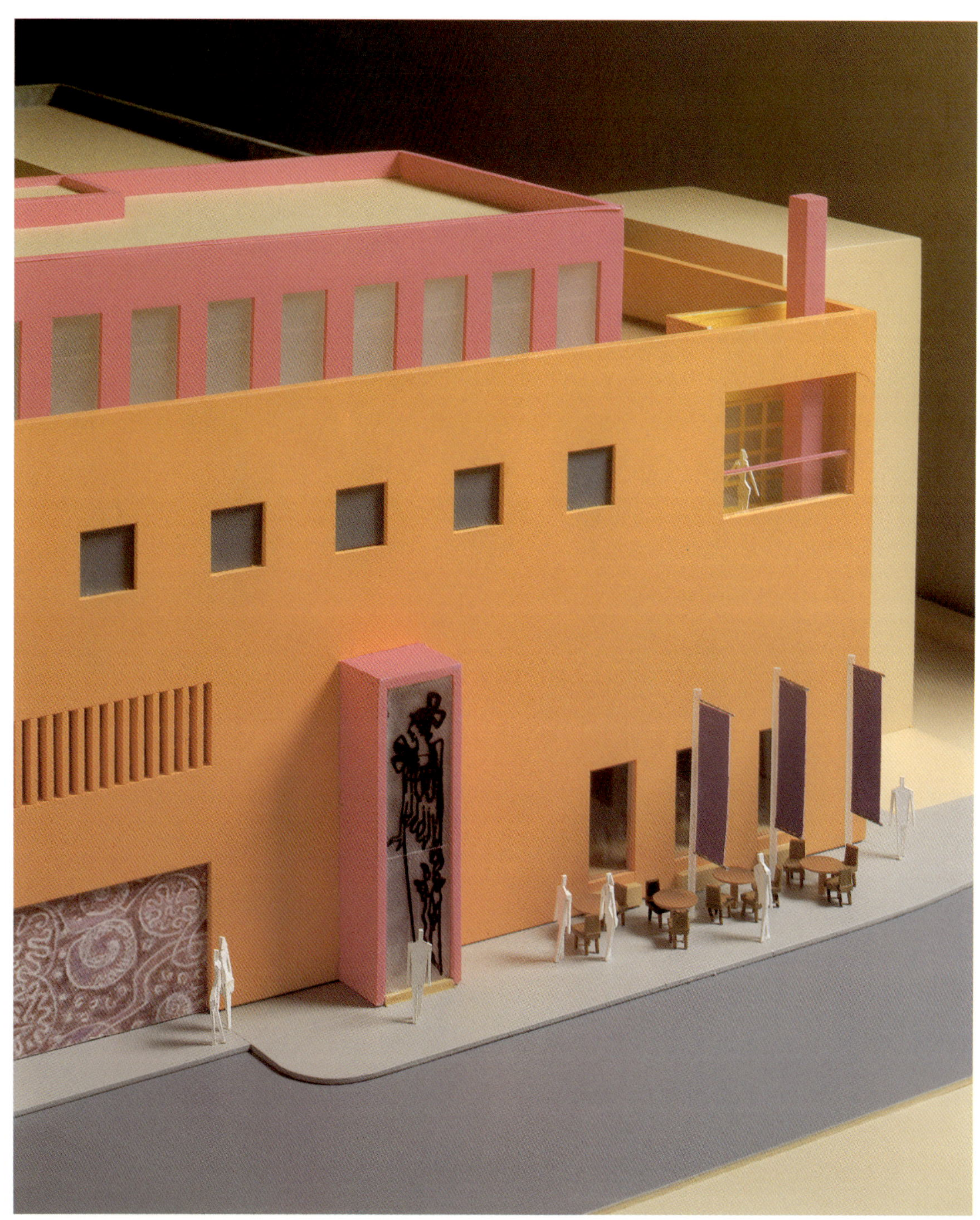

Ricardo Legorreta
The Fashion and Textile Museum and The Zandra Rhodes Foundation (detail)
Model
h 41 cm

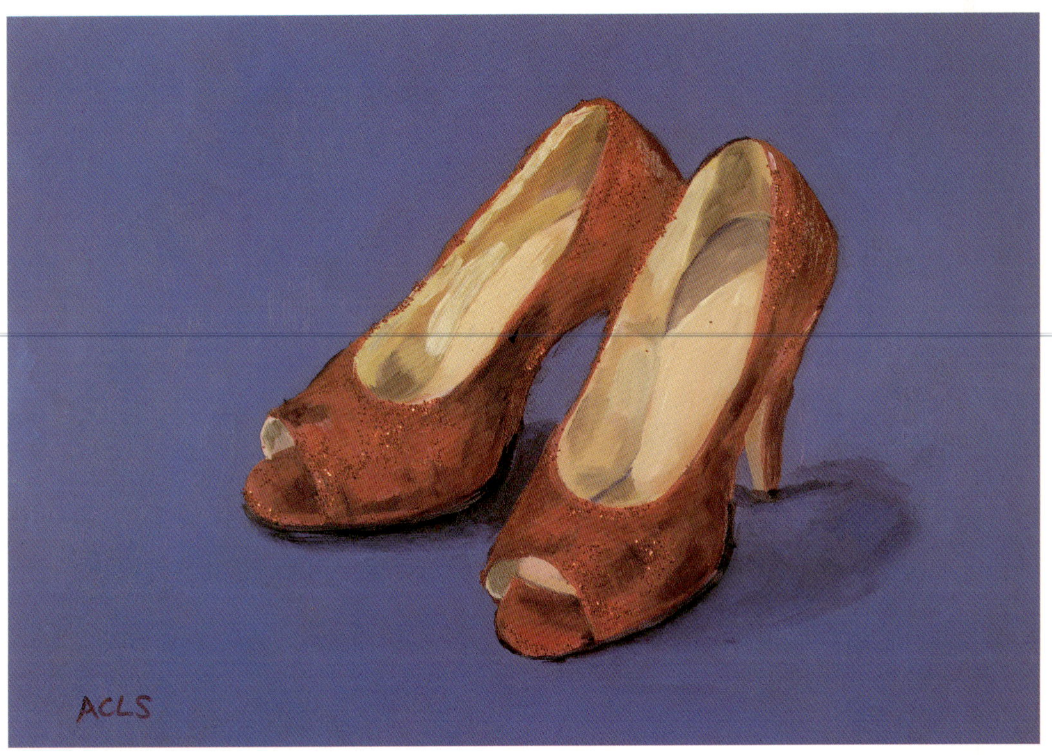

Amy Shuckburgh
Shoes I
Oil and glitter
32 × 43 cm

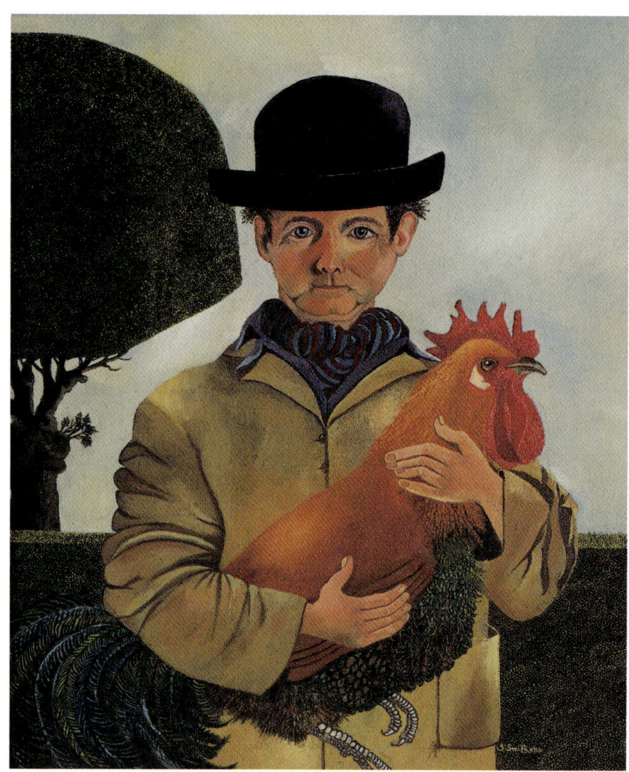

Shirley Smithers
Prized Possession
Oil
29 × 24 cm

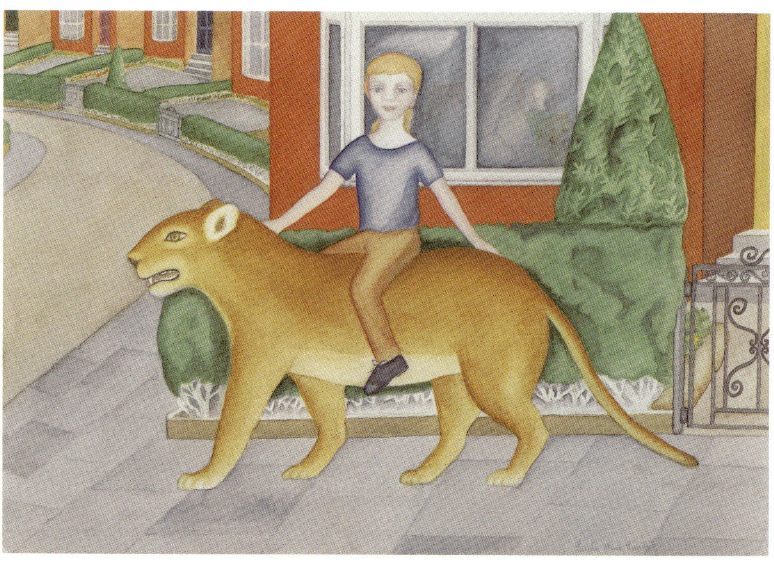

Linda Landers
Child on a Lioness
Watercolour
50 × 69 cm

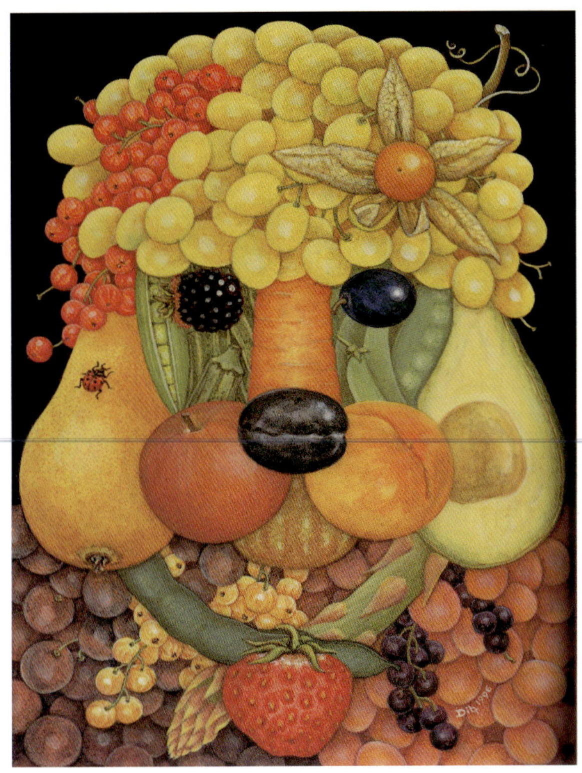

Ditz
The Greengrocer's Wife's Poodle
Acrylic
17 × 12 cm

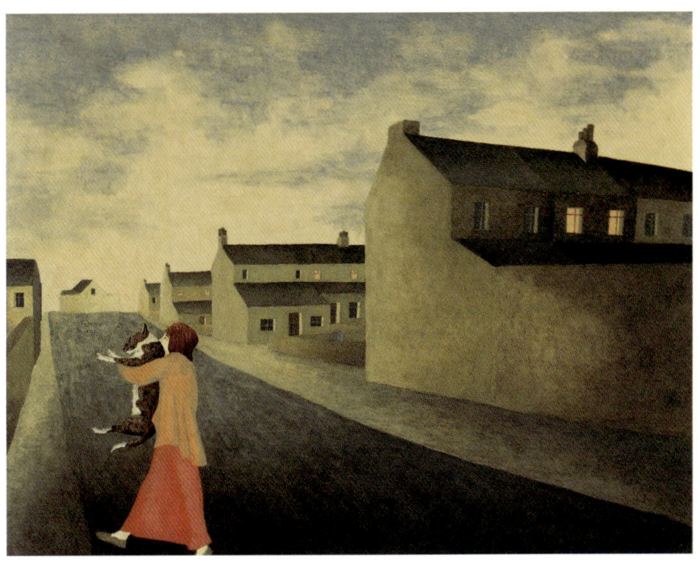

Kate Montgomery
Dog Baby
Casein
50 × 62 cm

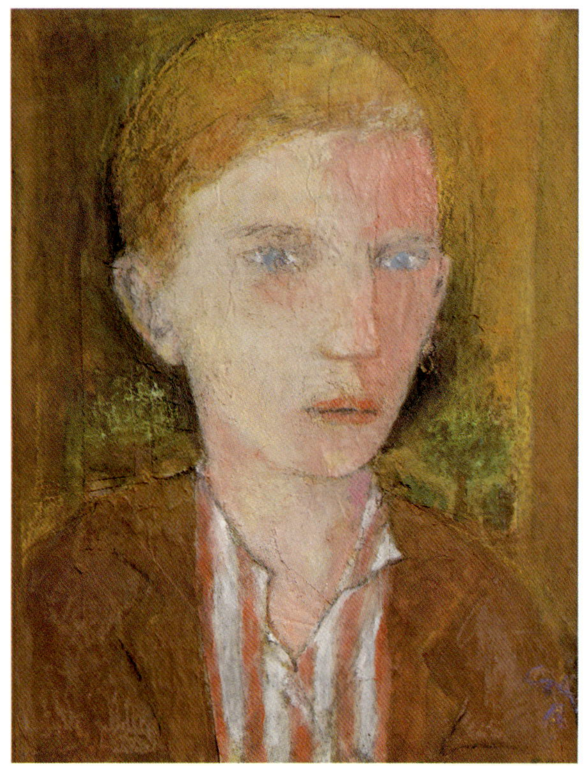

Colin Bellwood
Portrait of Hans O.
Oil and mixed media
30 × 23 cm

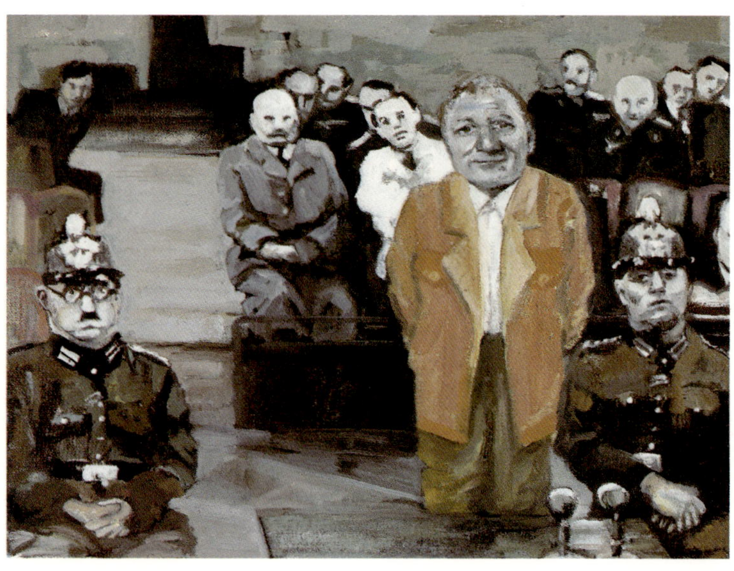

Jane Kelly
Ken before the People's Court
Oil
29 × 38 cm

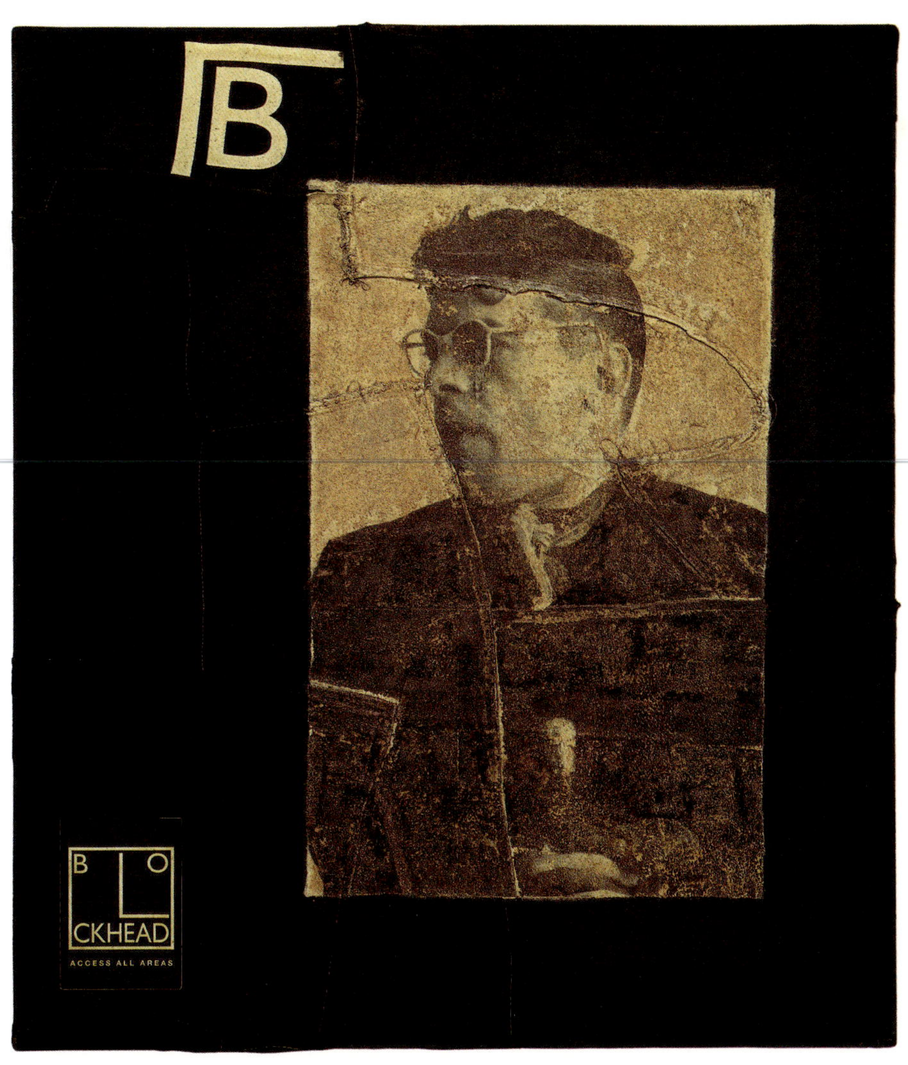

Ceri House
A Favourite T-Shirt for Ian
Mixed media
61 × 51 cm

GALLERY VIII

In stark contrast to Peter Blake's busy room is the airy sculpture hang of Tony Cragg and Ann Christopher. This is a gallery with a mission. As Cragg explains: 'In the Summer Show sculpture is traditionally seen in front of paintings, and too densely packed. It's my opinion that you can't put sculptures very close to one another because they start to fight and you get a cacophonic reaction amongst them. That's very often been the case at the Summer show. This is not exactly a minimal hang, there are still fifteen artists in one room, including Mach, Deacon, Flanagan, Chillida, Tàpies and Wilding. These works respect each other and they're each given an appropriate amount of space.'

Do they see this as establishing a precedent for future hangs? 'It's a start,' replies Ann Christopher, 'a move in the right direction. Each sculpture gives off an invisible demand for a certain amount of space around it. We've deliberately chosen to make this kind of statement about the need for space.' And Cragg concludes: 'The old Summer Show idea is of giving a certain group of amateur artists a chance, colleagues that one would like to succeed, students that one likes to support. This room is devoid of any of those concerns.'

GALLERY VIII

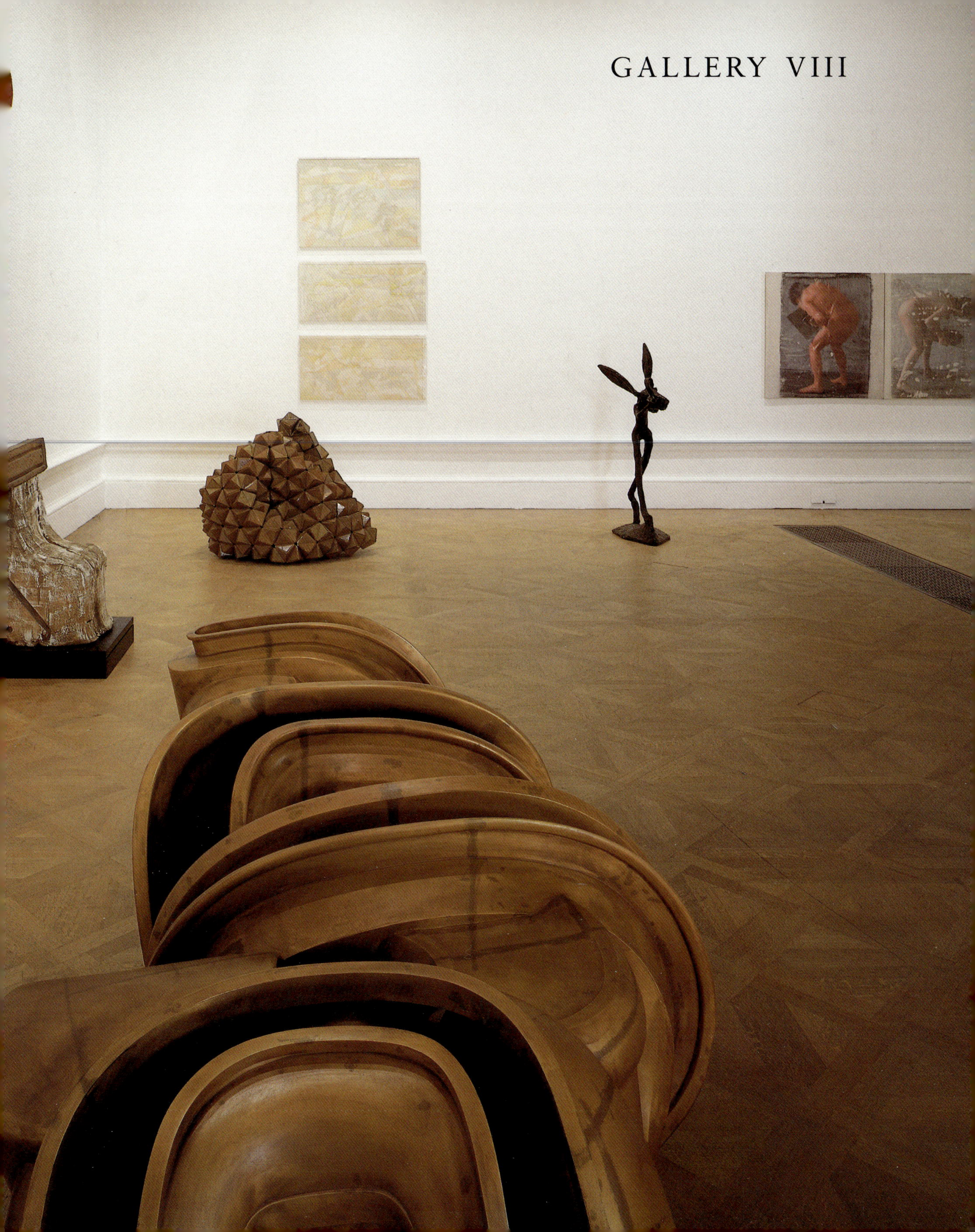

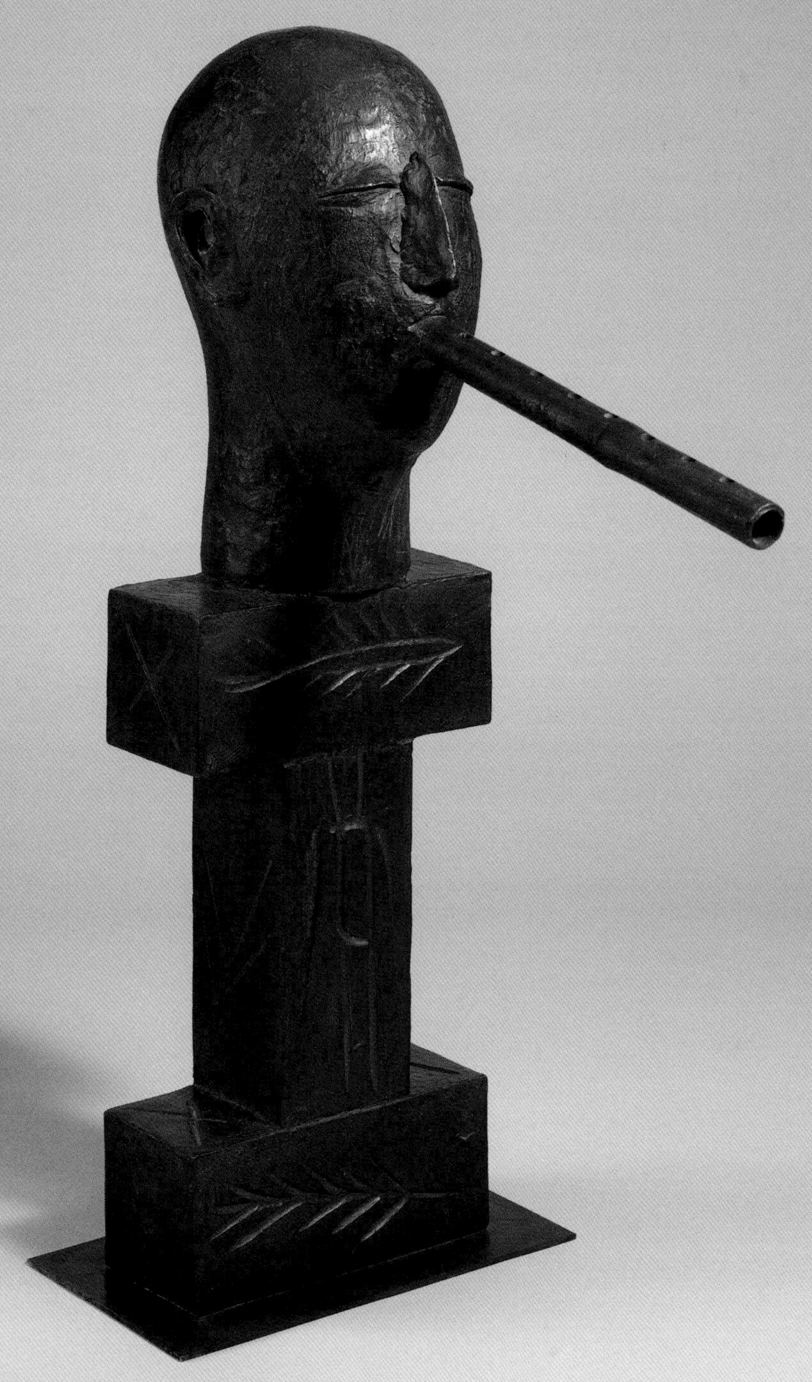

Mimmo Paladino Hon RA
Busto con Flauto
Bronze
h 67 cm

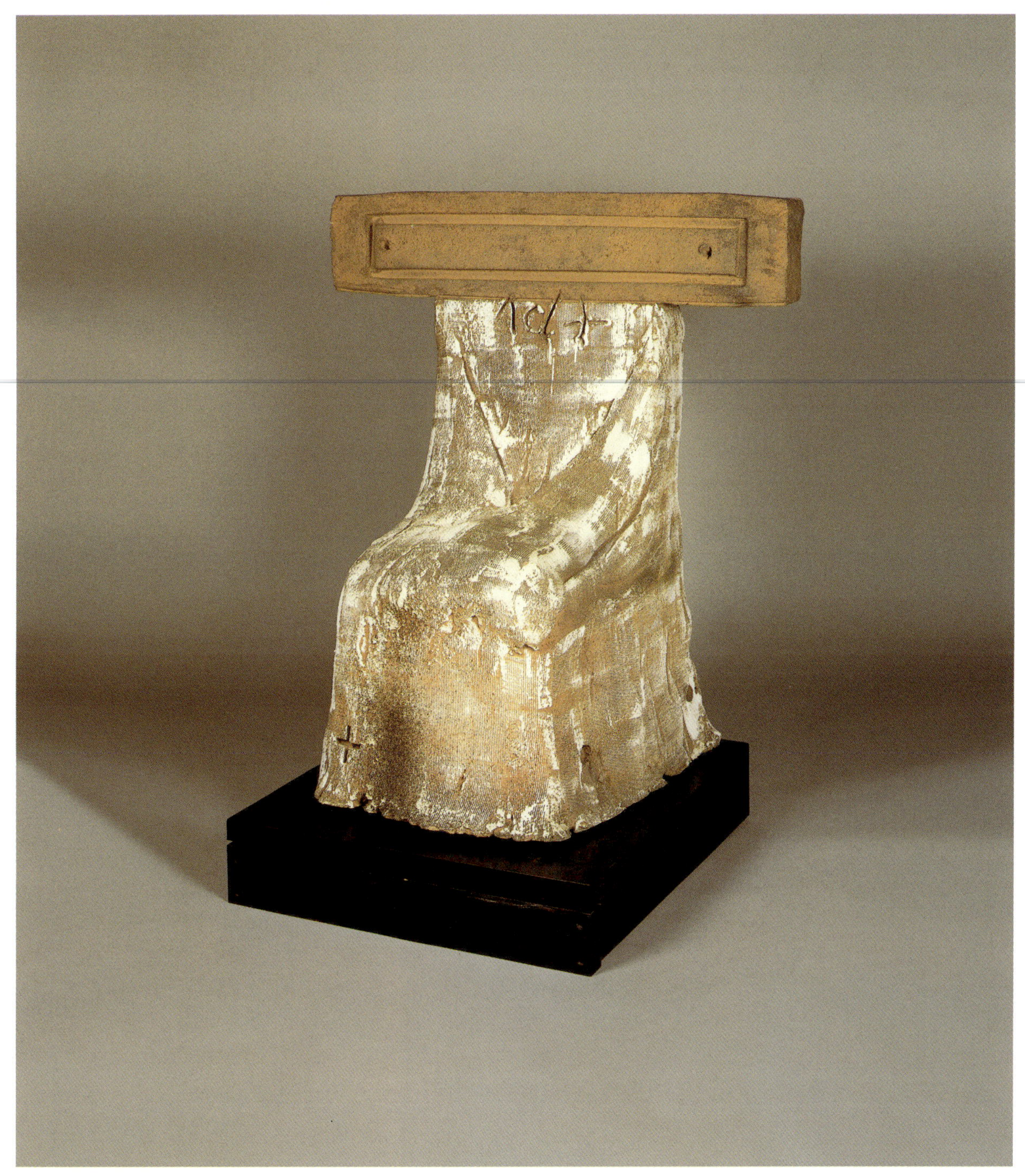

Antoni Tàpies Hon RA
Chaise avec Barre
Terracotta
h 104 cm

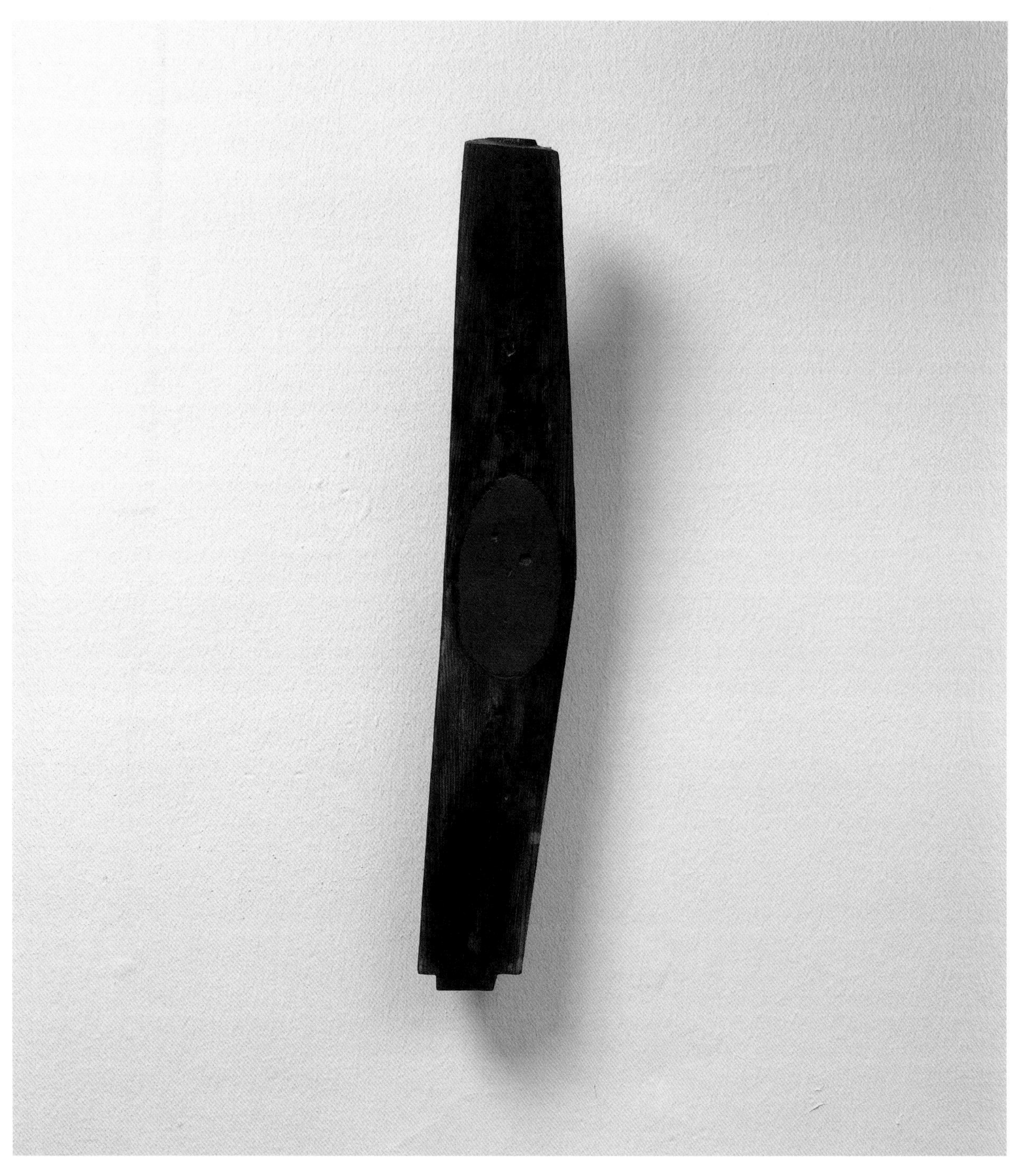

Alison Wilding RA
Hemlock 4
Hemlock, lead, pigment
h 56 cm

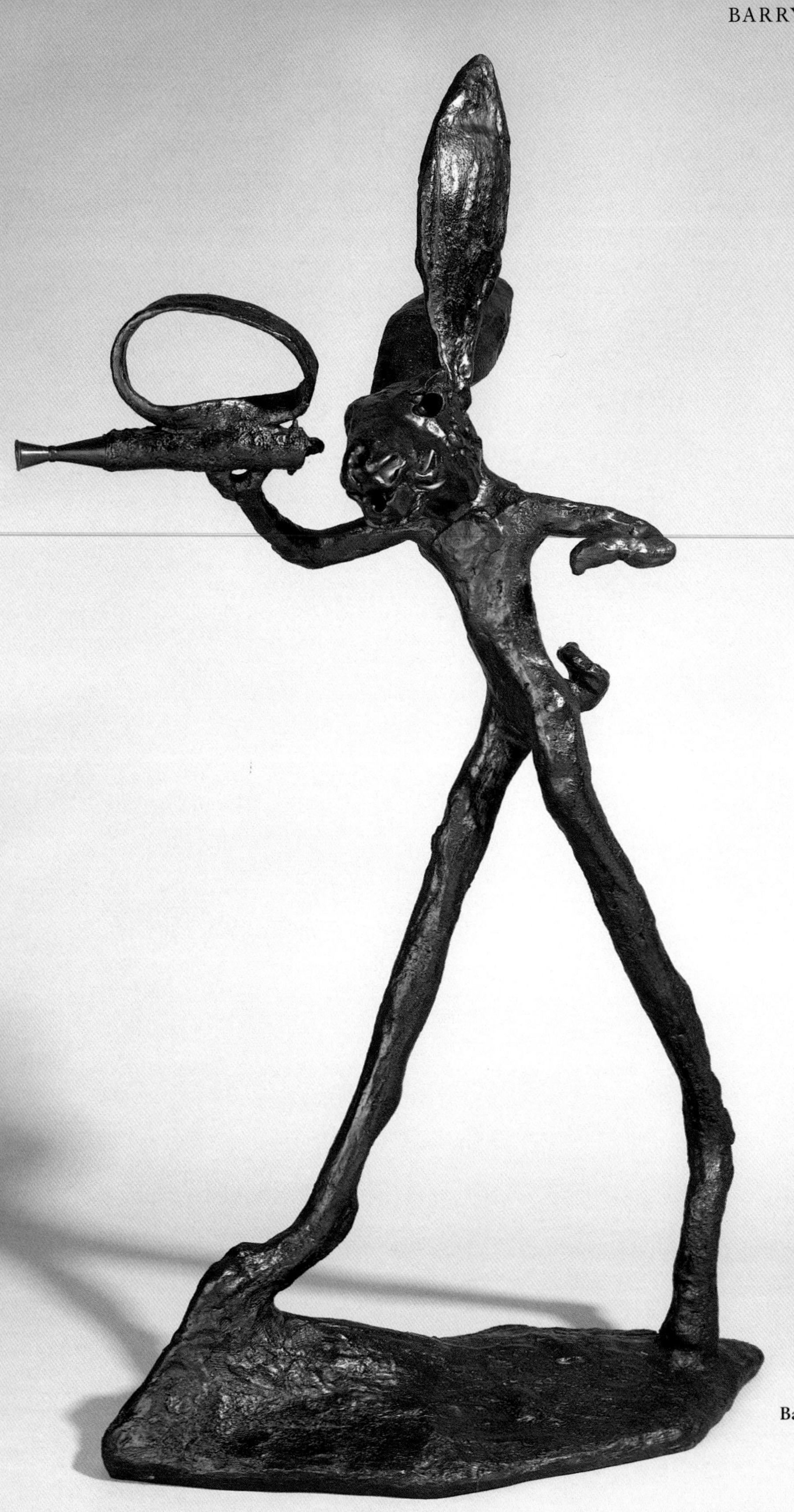

Barry Flanagan OBE, RA
Record 1994
Bronze
h 175 cm

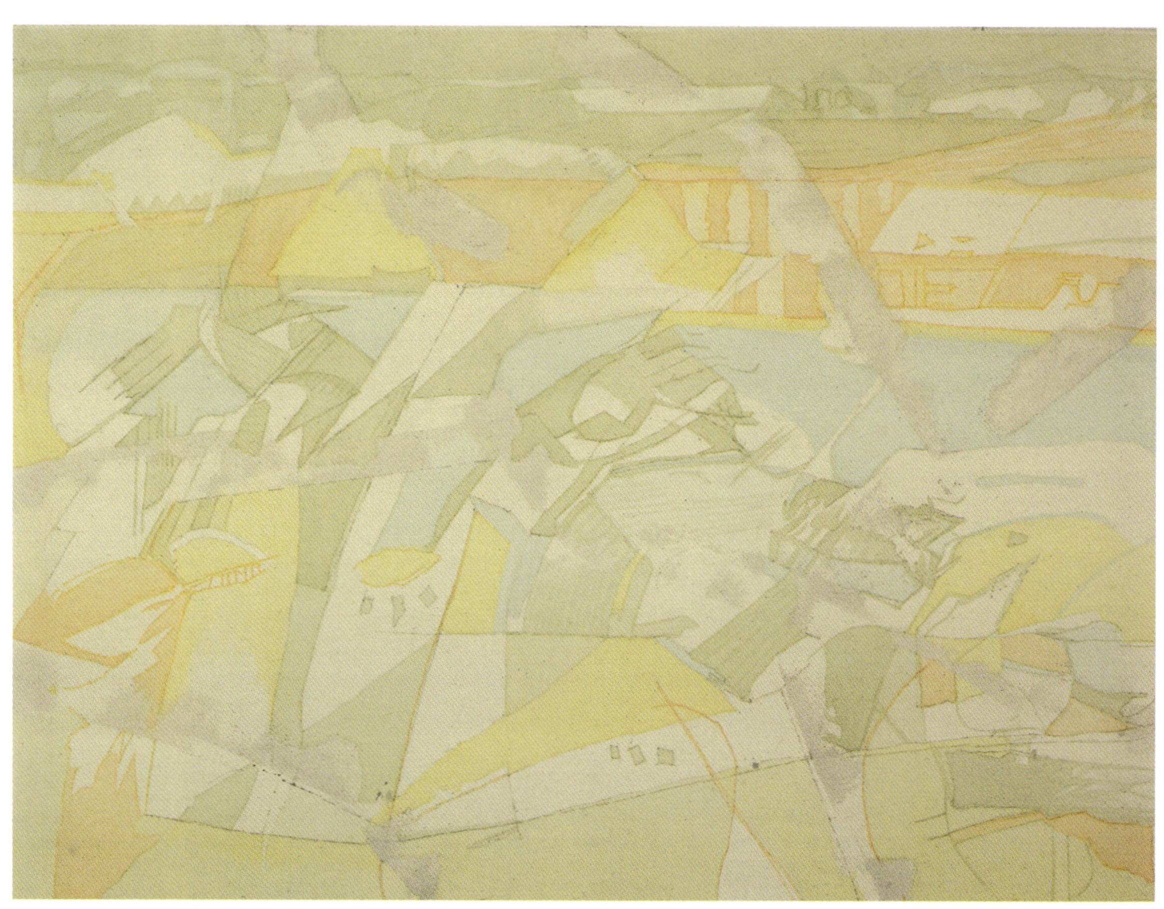

Flavia Irwin RA
Light Definition 21
Acrylic
93 × 123 cm

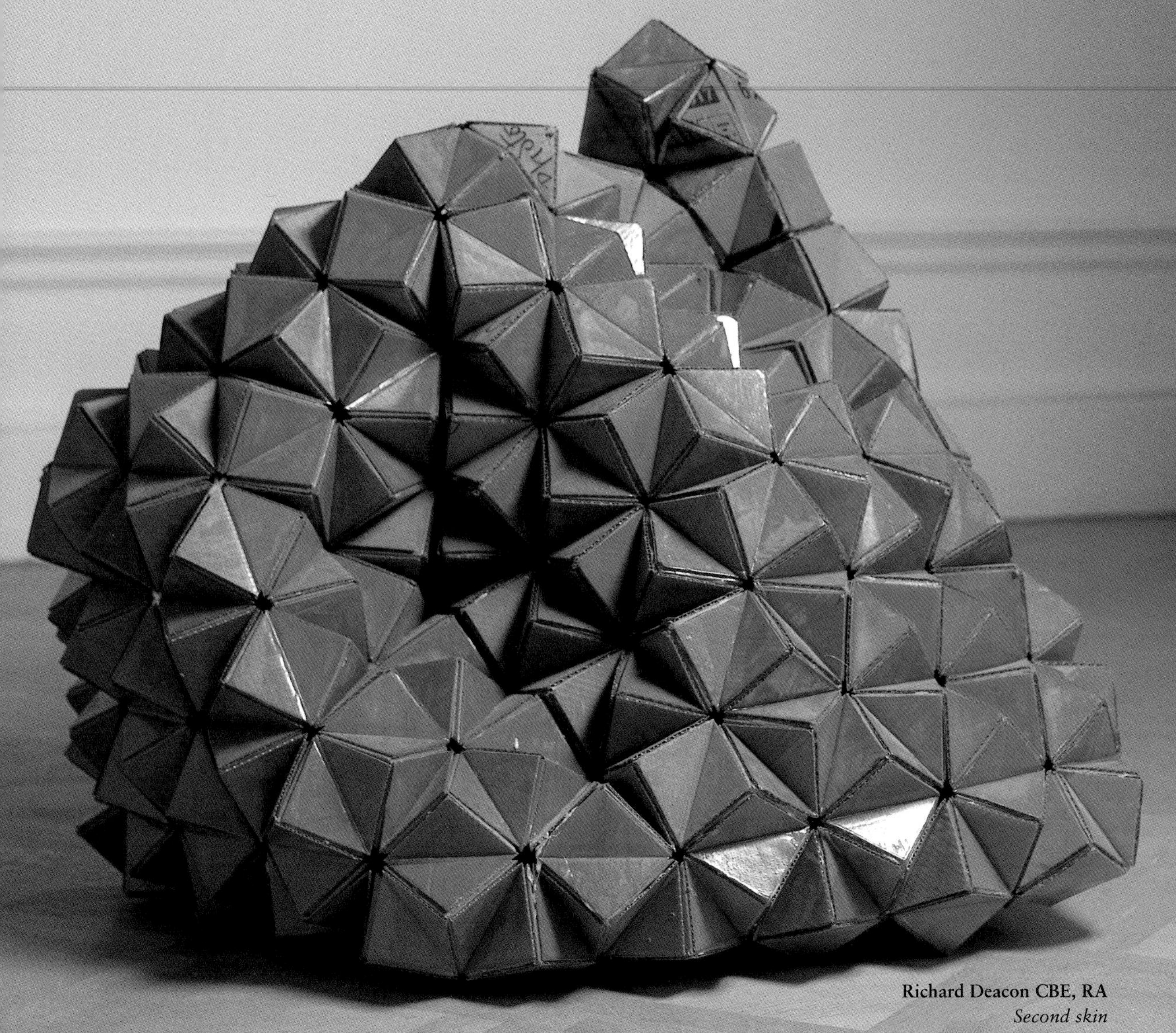

Richard Deacon CBE, RA
Second skin
Cardboard
h 115 cm

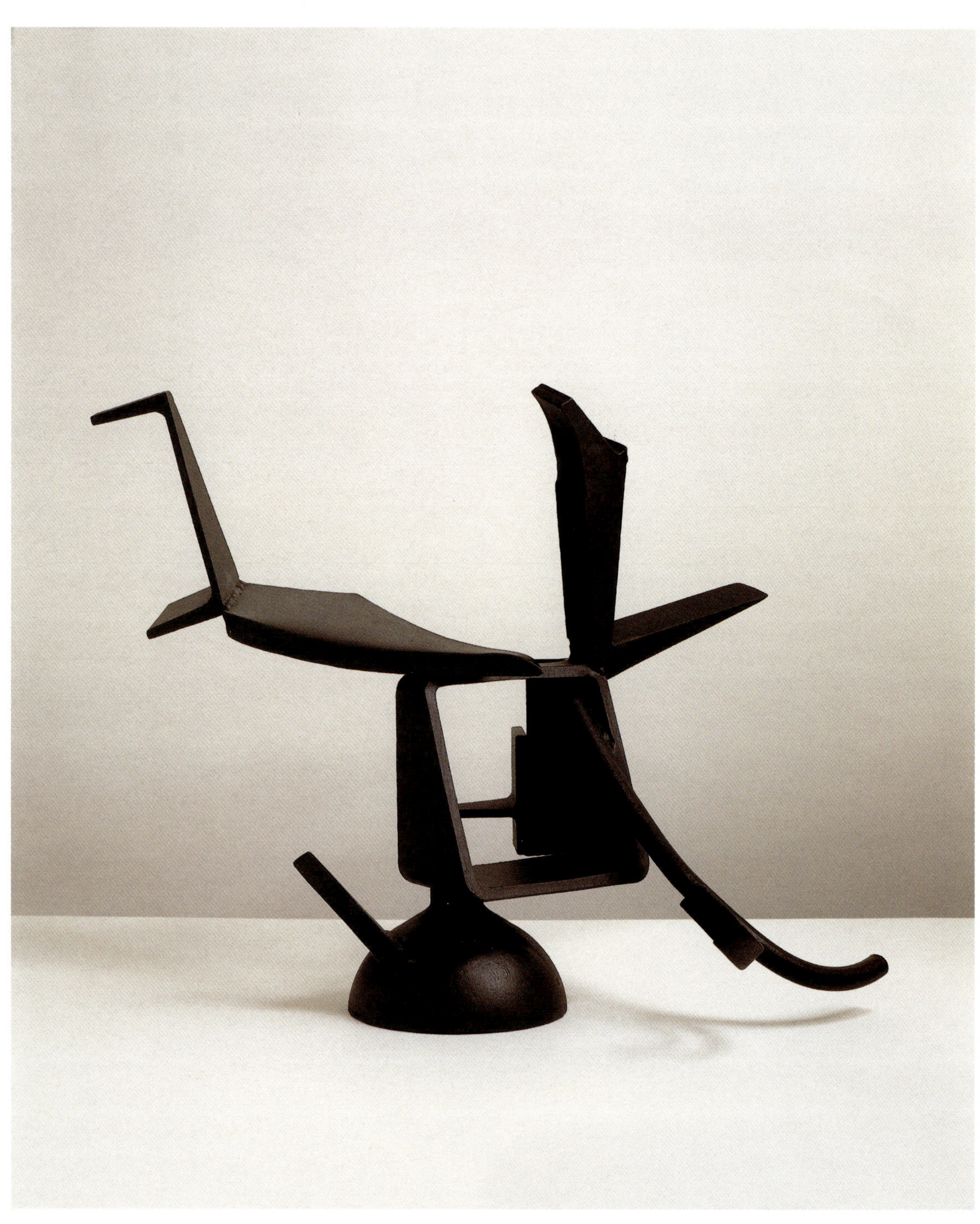

David Annesley
Dawn Chorus
Steel
h 58 cm

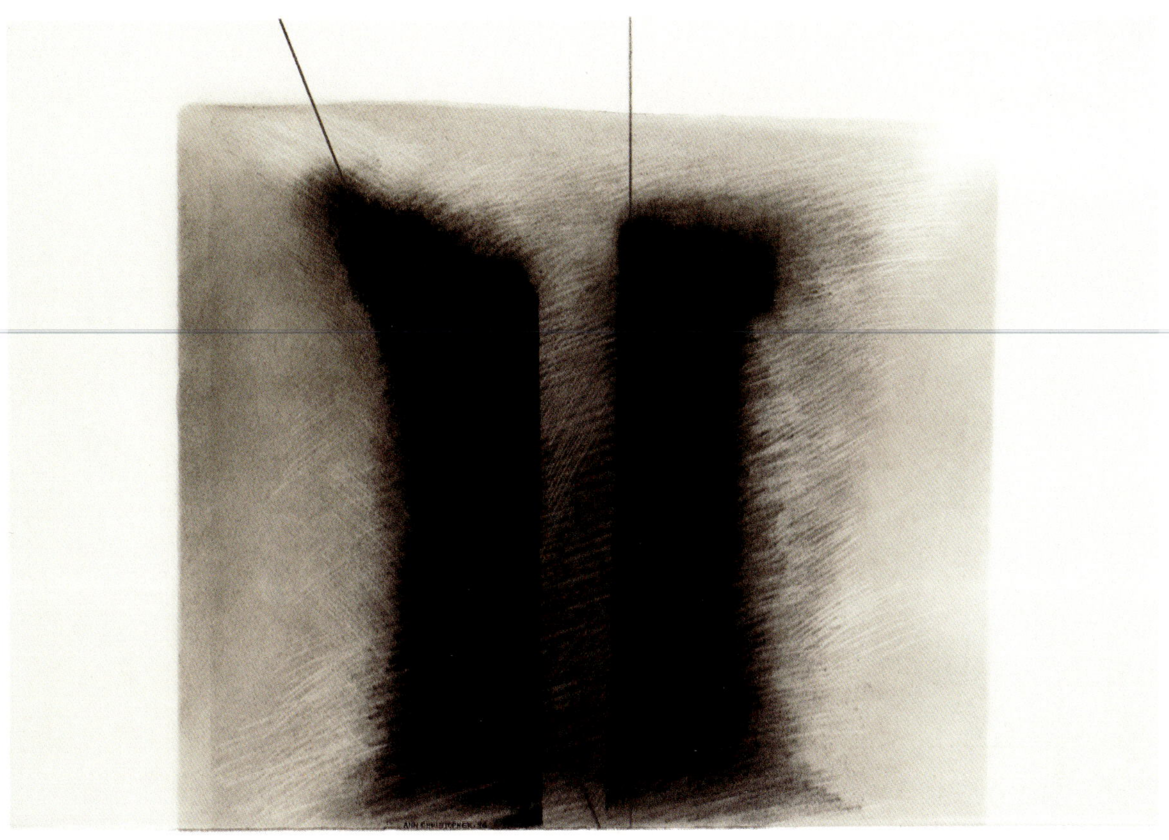

Ann Christopher RA
Shadow Line – II
Conte/Pastel/Graphite
37 × 50 cm

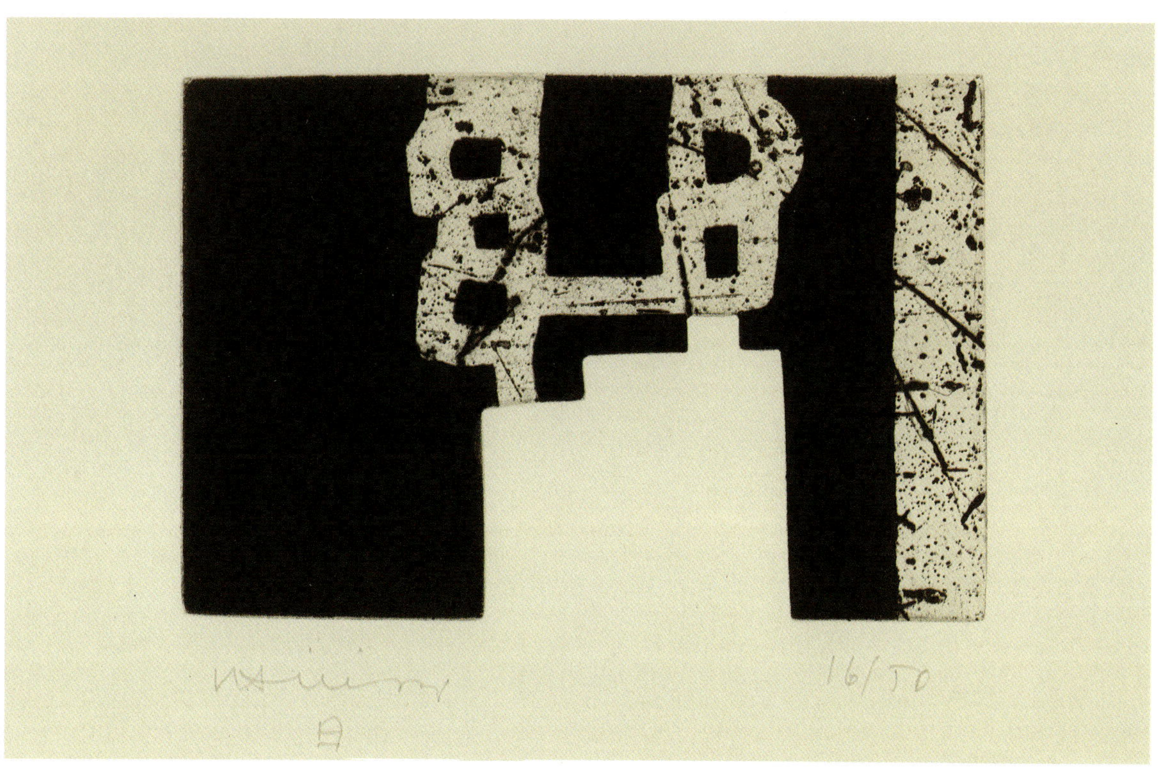

Eduardo Chillida Hon RA
Bikuistasun, 1996
Etching and aquatint
10 × 15 cm

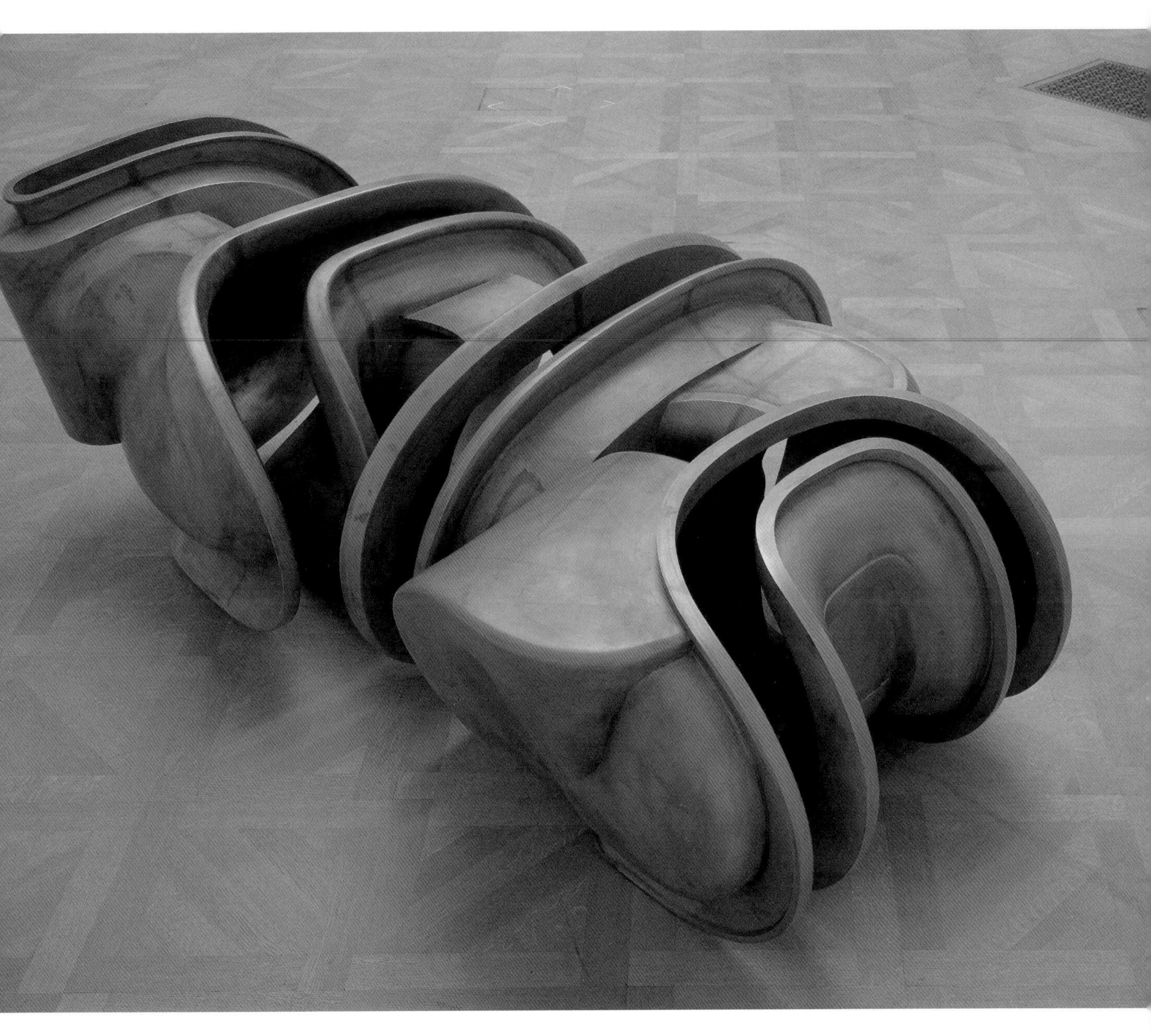

Prof. Tony Cragg RA
Can-Can
Bronze
h 93 cm

GALLERY IX

This room is also hung by Anthony Green. He is typically forthright: 'Gallery Nine is devoted to all those artists who can actually paint electric fires, gasometers, Grand Central Station, trees, sunsets, Welsh mountains, beautiful clouds over Selsey Bill. All the things which are now non-PC in avant-garde terms, but which are still of consuming interest to thousands and thousands of artists – artists such as Ken Howard and Fred Cuming and Kyffin Williams and Freddie Gore and Tony Eyton. These are artists you don't ignore but you can take for granted. They're as cosy as warm woollen vests that keep you artistically warm, spiritually warm, right the way through the British winter. They're wonderful paintings. You don't deny them, you simply want to lie back and revel in their warmth, their humanity.'

And how are these paintings to be presented? 'It'll be quite a traditional Academy hang though it won't be anywhere near as close and tight-fitting as in previous years. I decided early last year that it was necessary to put a gallery aside for the Senior Members so that they could have a little bit of space around them.

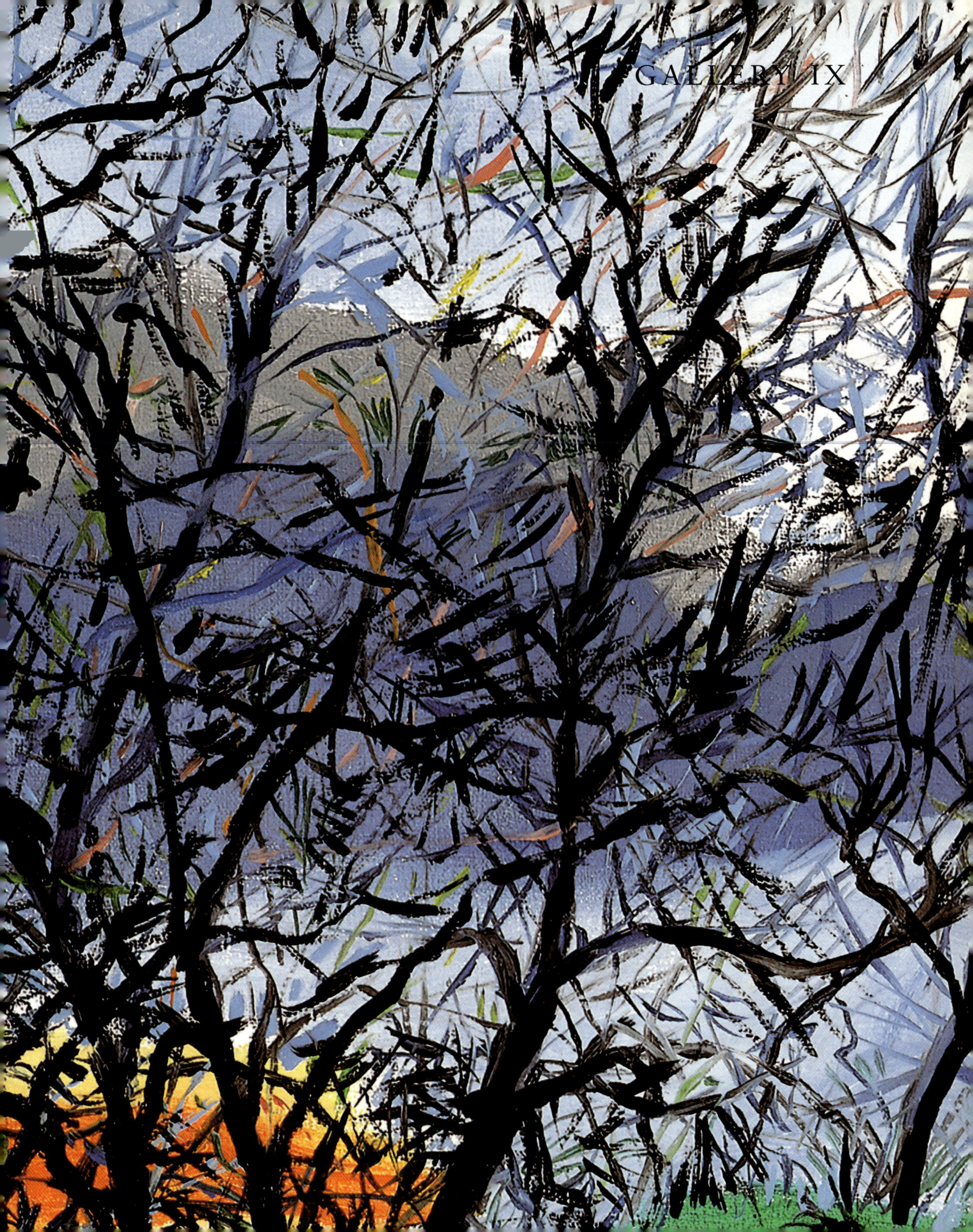
GALLERY IX

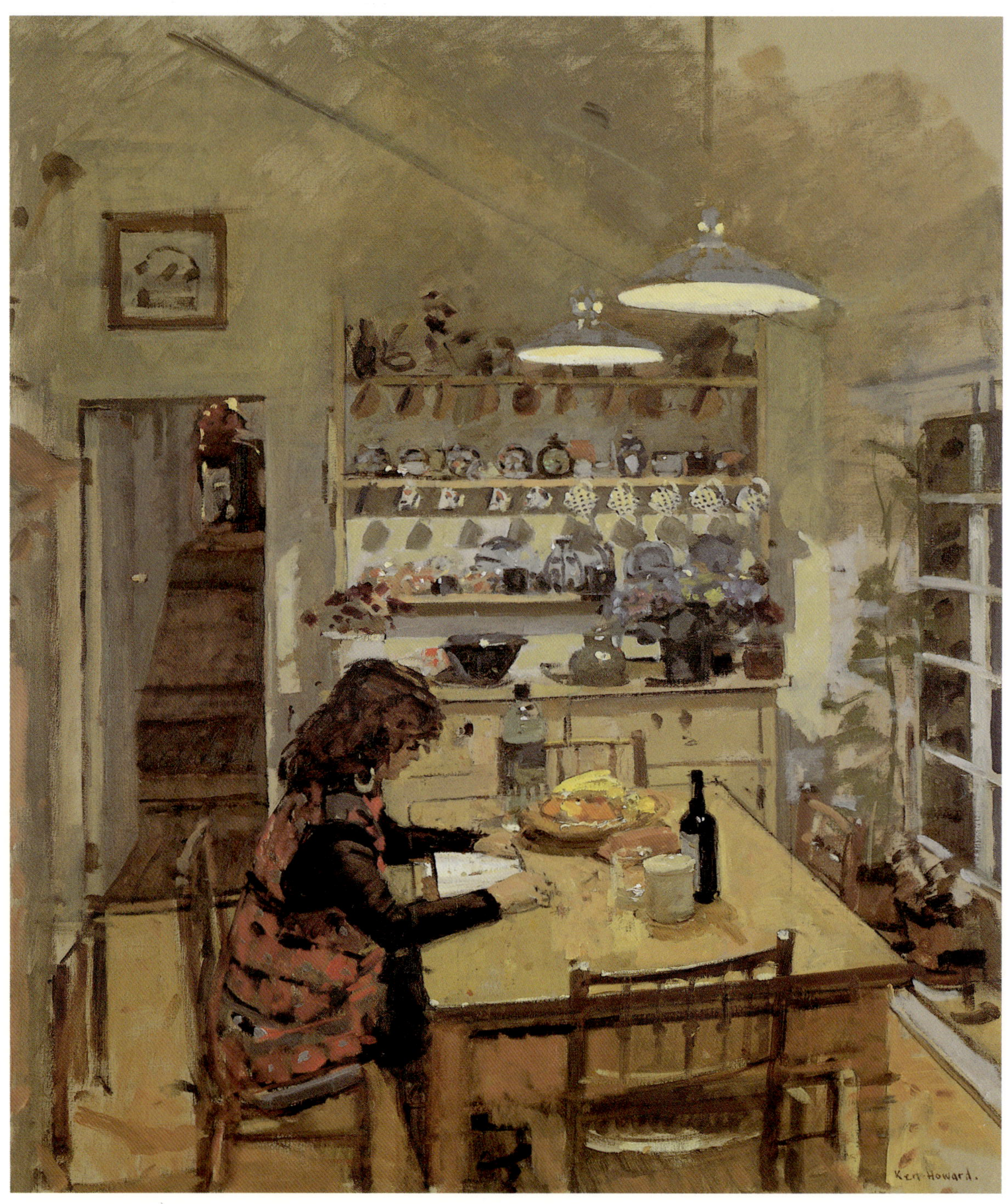

Ken Howard RA
Interior at Oriel
Oil
120 × 100 cm

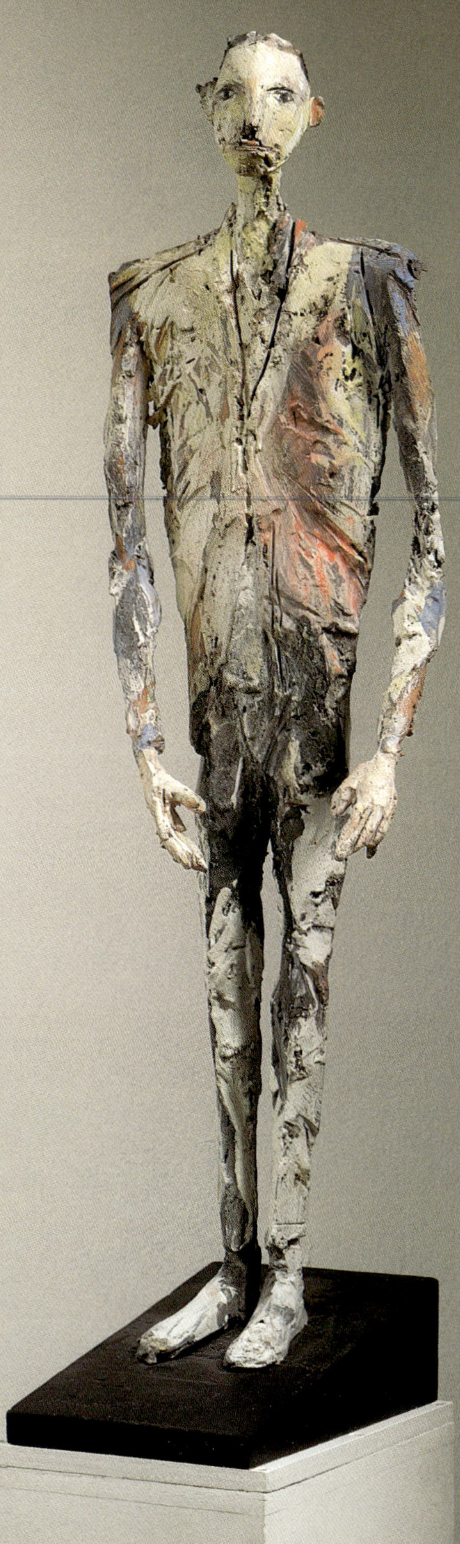

John Wragg RA
Prodigal
Resin
h 82 cm

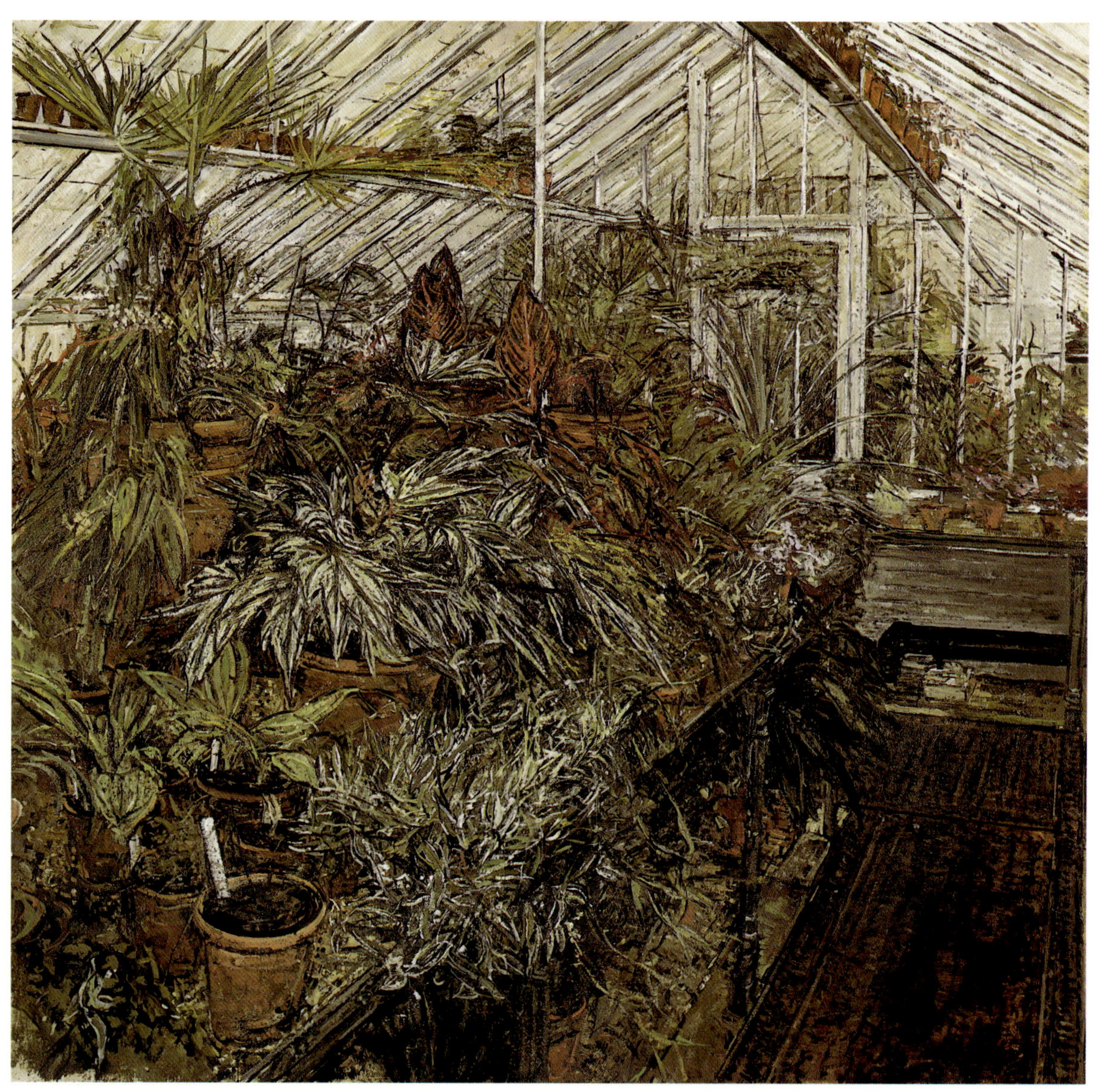

Olwyn Bowey RA
The Temperate House
Oil
92 × 91 cm

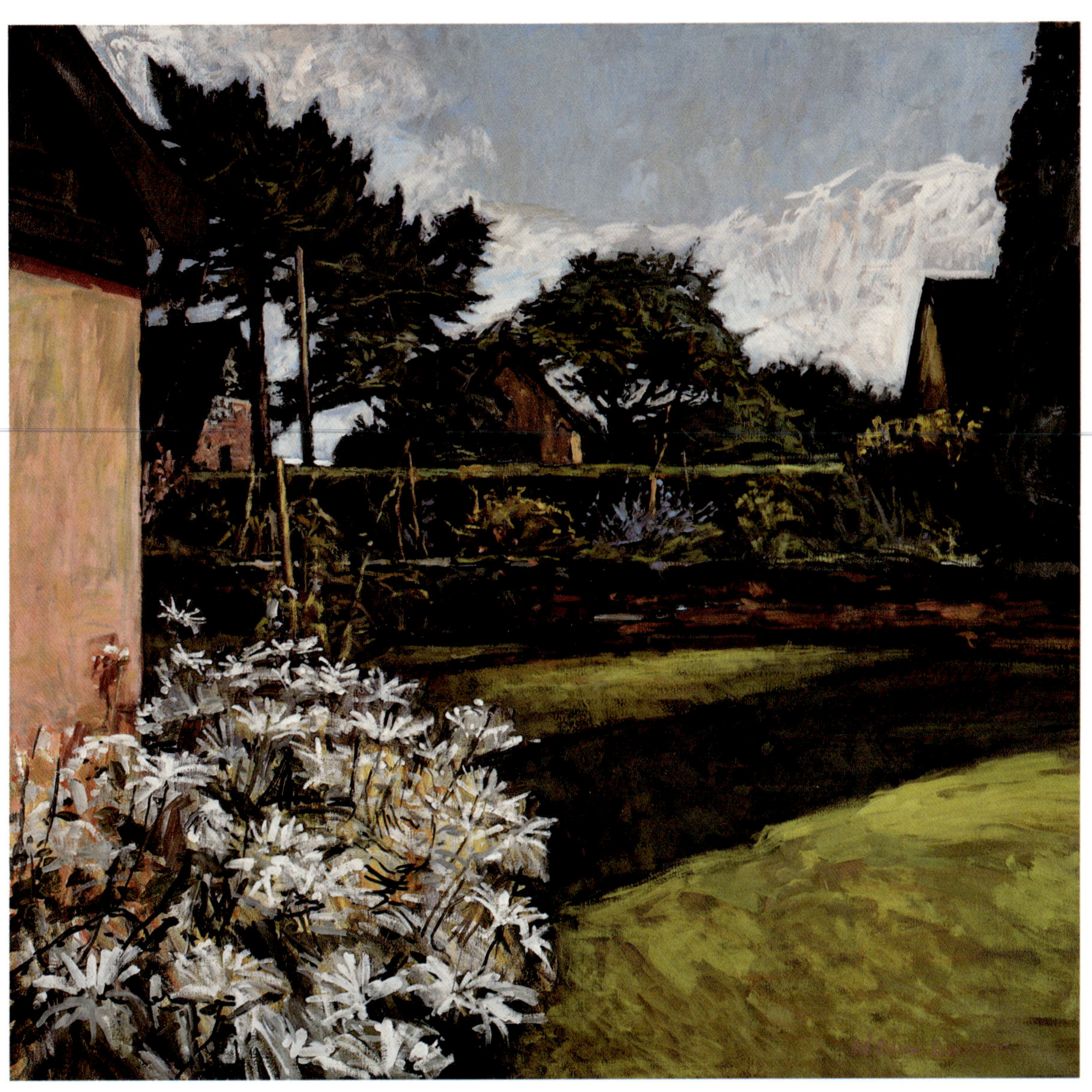

William Bowyer RA
Suffolk Garden
Oil
91 × 91 cm

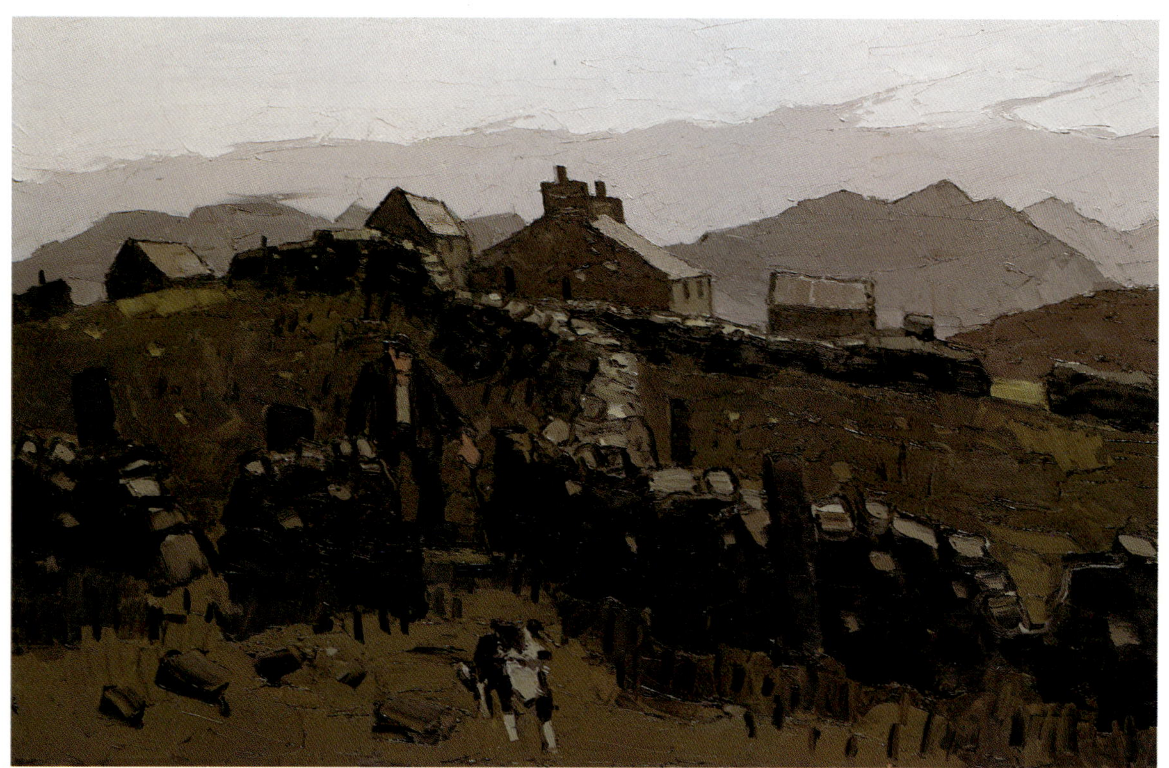

Sir Kyffin Williams OBE, RA
Buarth, Y Fron
Oil
76 × 127 cm

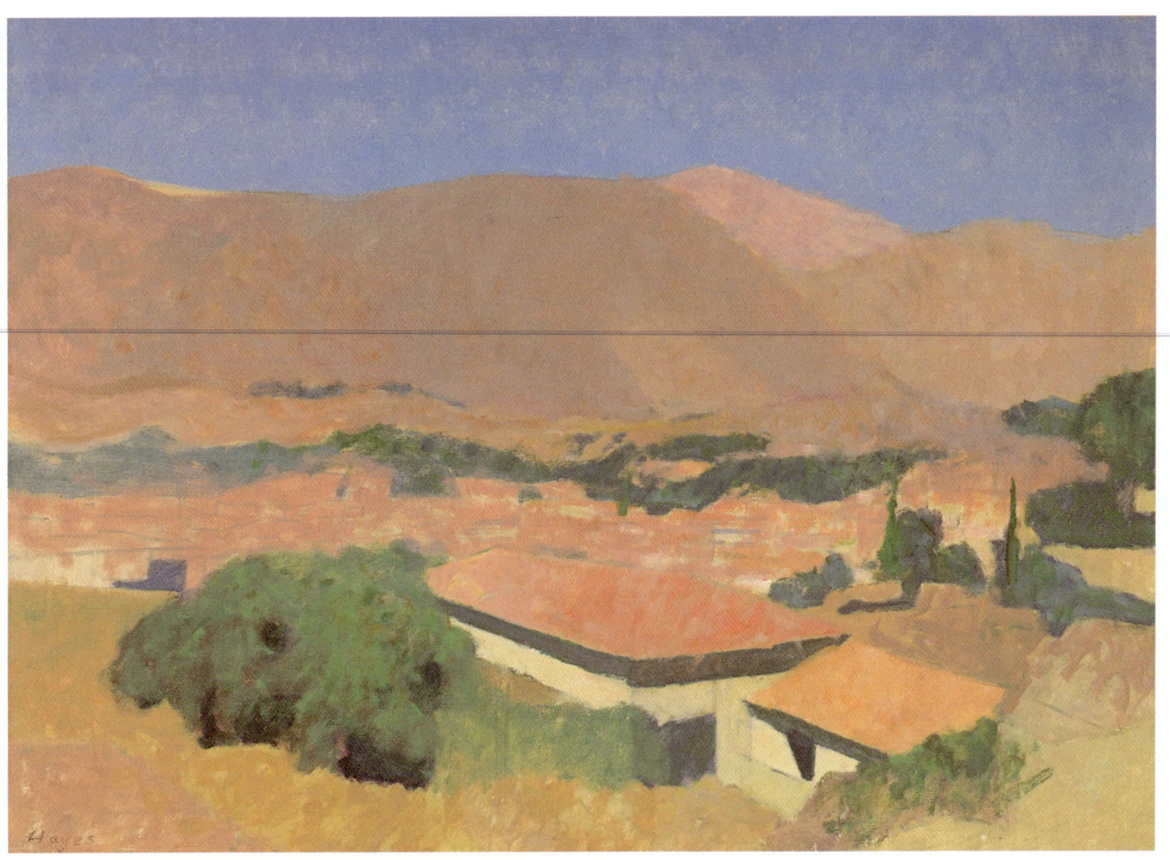

Colin Hayes RA
Cretan Village
Oil
77 × 101 cm

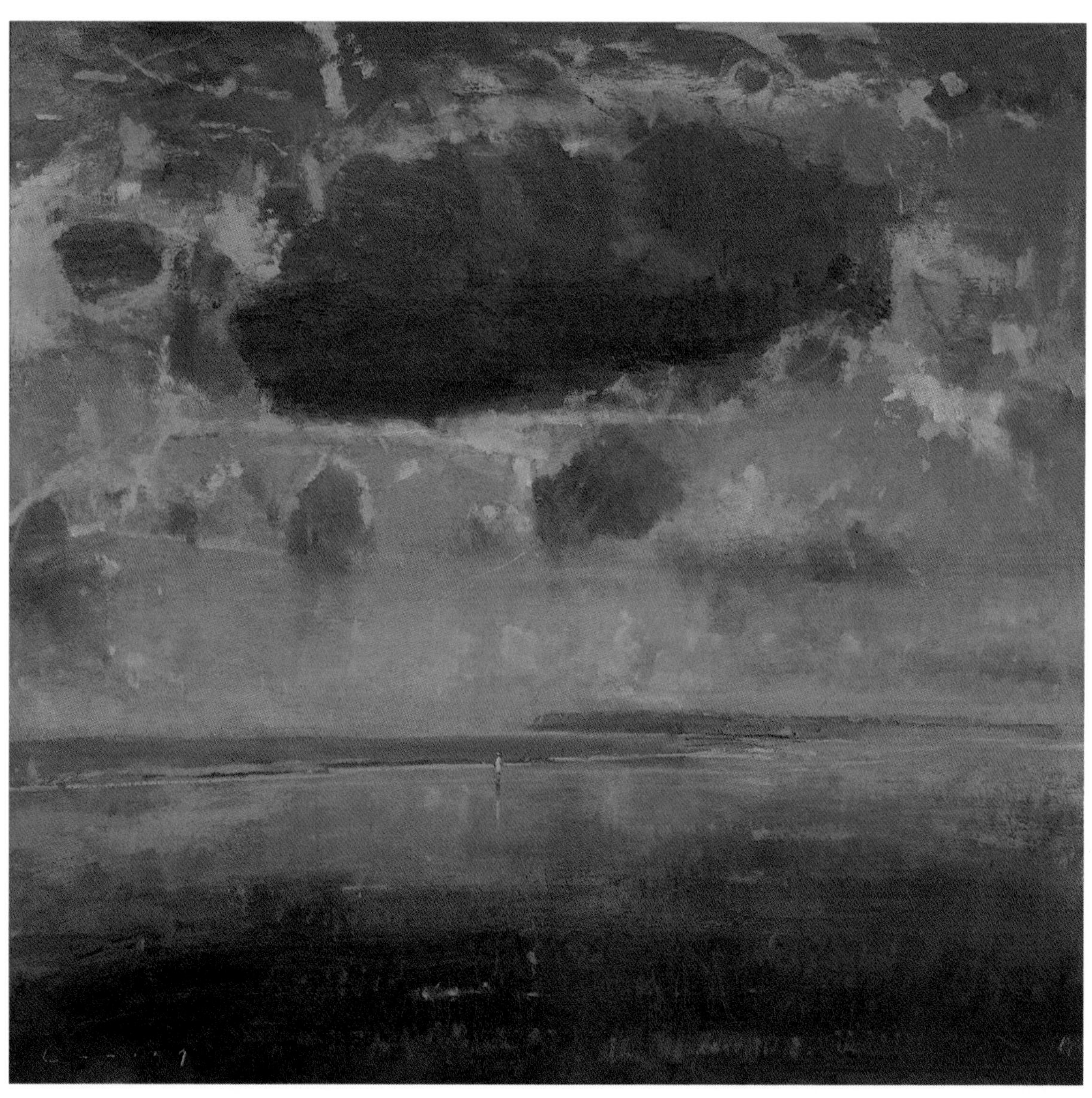

Frederick Cuming RA
Low Tide
Oil
90 × 90 cm

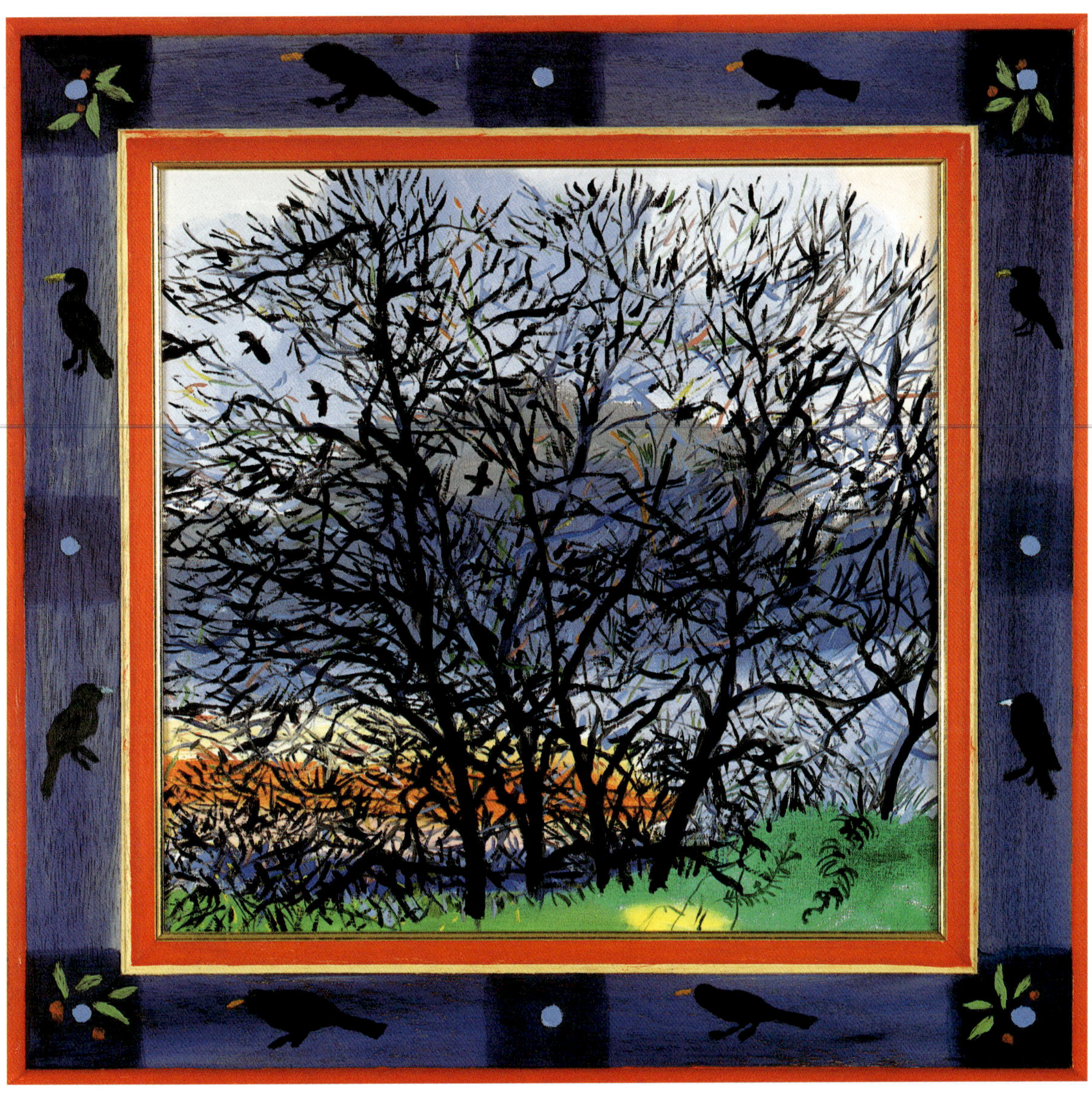

Philip Sutton RA
Mahorbier! Good Night
Oil
68 × 68 cm

GALLERY X

This year the Architecture room has moved to Gallery X, at the end of the Summer Exhibition. Hung by Ian Ritchie with Nicholas Grimshaw, it has a very different feel from the painting galleries.

What characterises the hang? 'There's a need for three-dimensionality and there's a need for colour. Very often the only colour you see in architectural exhibitions is in the photographs of built buildings. I think there's a new period of boldness coming, and something like Richard Rogers' group of a dozen fluorescent perspex models, of buildings he's already designed and built, such as the Dome, are like sweets in a shop. There are several models that light up, such as Eva Jiricna's, so it's actually a bit Christmassy. That's OK. It's quite a nice move for the architecture gallery to have a life of light, when the light comes into play in models. This year they will take pride of place, and the drawings will be hung above them, raised higher than usual, to give the models more space.

Grimshaw comments: 'The problem you're faced with always is of architecture being on the one hand practical and understandable, and on the other looking for something that has a real visual quality as art. If you wanted just to describe a building, you'd probably put up a dozen drawings – plans, elevations and everything else. We never select on that basis. We look for a quality of art within the frame or within the model case. They should always have a certain beauty. We don't want to put anything in just because it's an interesting building. But we wouldn't put it in if it wasn't a beautiful model. Equally we wouldn't accept a beautiful model of a horrible building. This is an Academy of Art, and we're trying to unite the idea of art and architecture.'

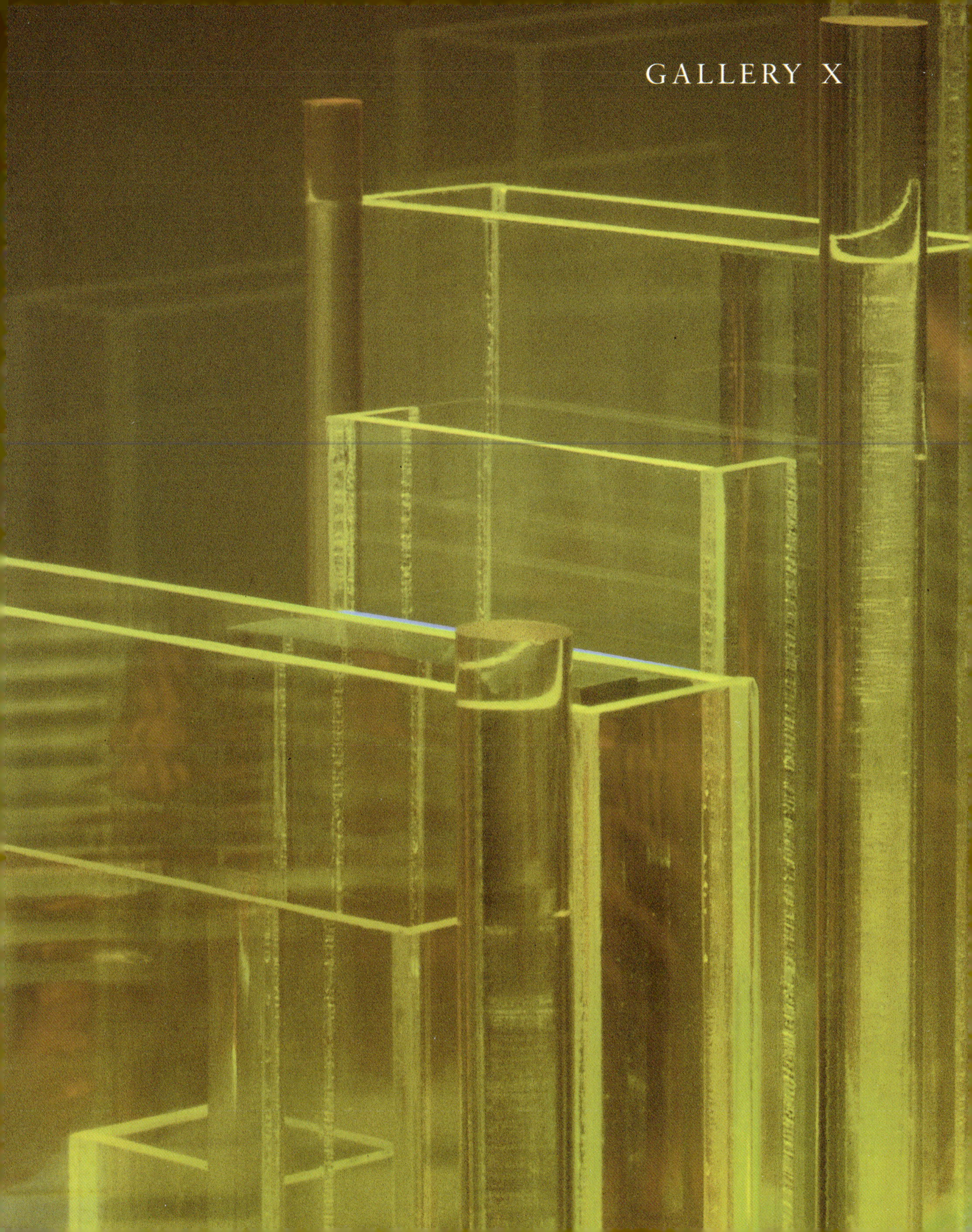

GALLERY X

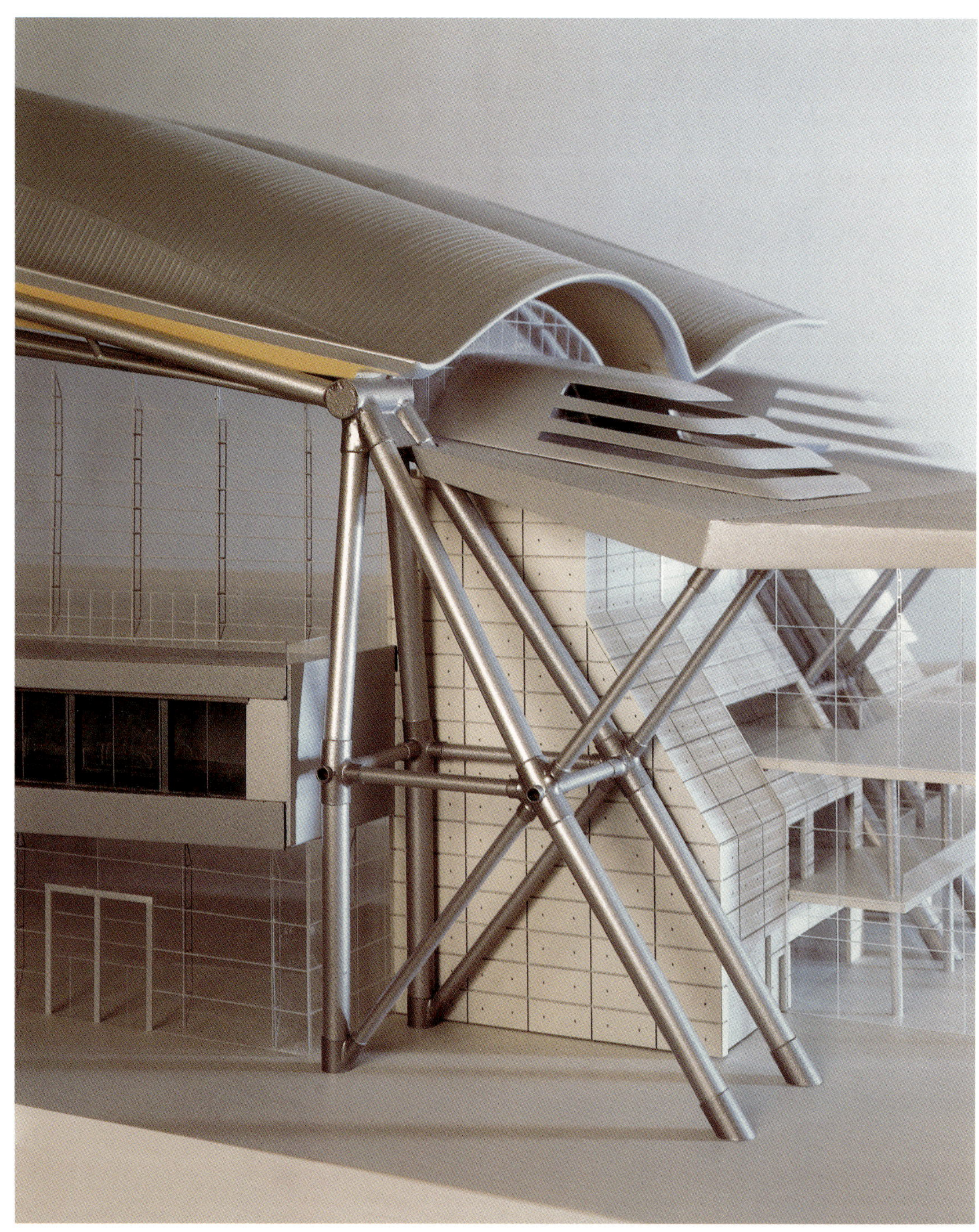

Nicholas Grimshaw CBE, RA (Nicholas Grimshaw & Partners Limited)
Sectional model: Messehalle 3, Frankfurt/Germany (detail)
Model
h 45 cm

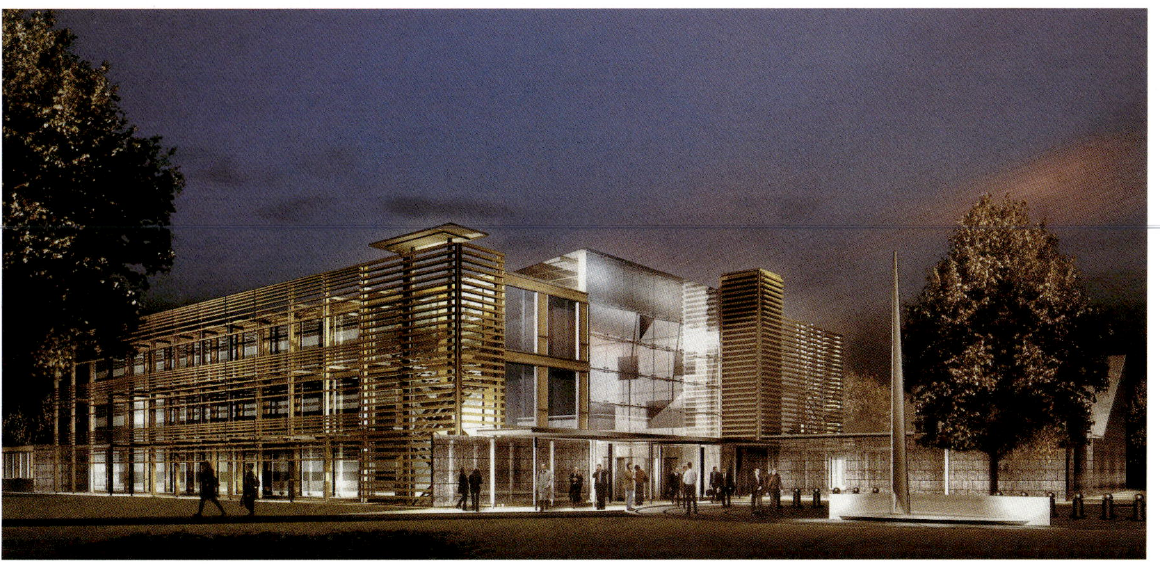

Paul Koralek CBE, RA (Ahrends, Burton and Koralek Architects)
New Headquarter for Offaly County Council (detail)
Computer Generated Image
40 × 82 cm

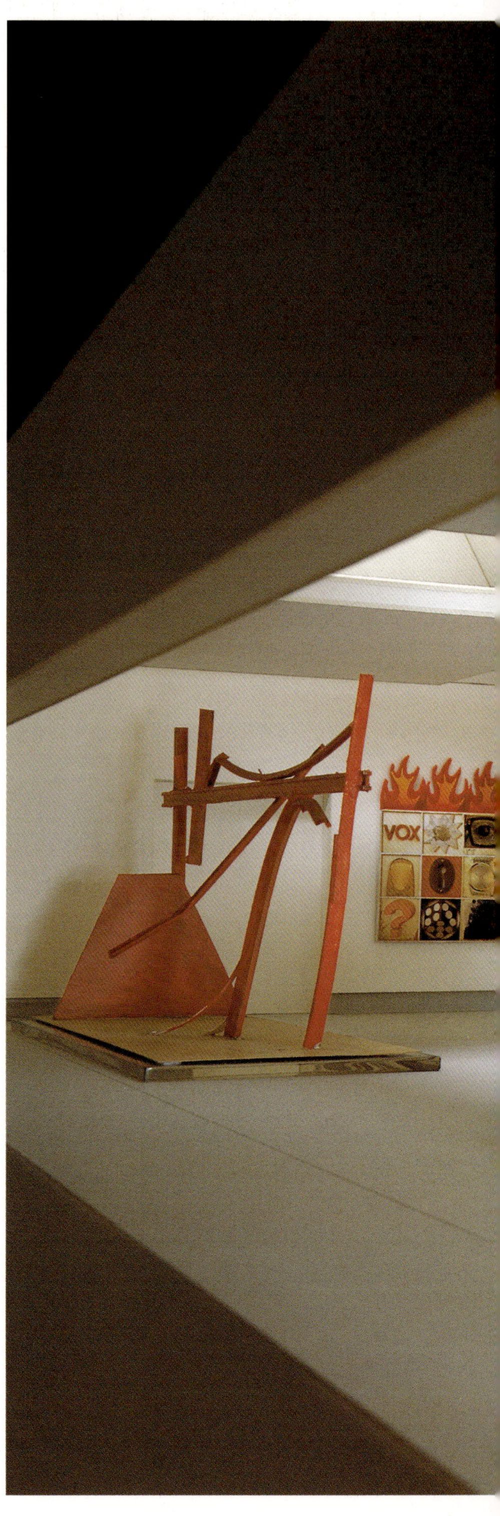

Prof. Sir Colin St John Wilson RA
in association with Long + Kentish Architects
Design for Pallant House Gallery (detail of South Gallery).
From left works by Anthony Caro, Joe Tilson, Patrick Caulfield, William Tucker, Paul Huxley and Peter Blake.
Model
h 54 cm

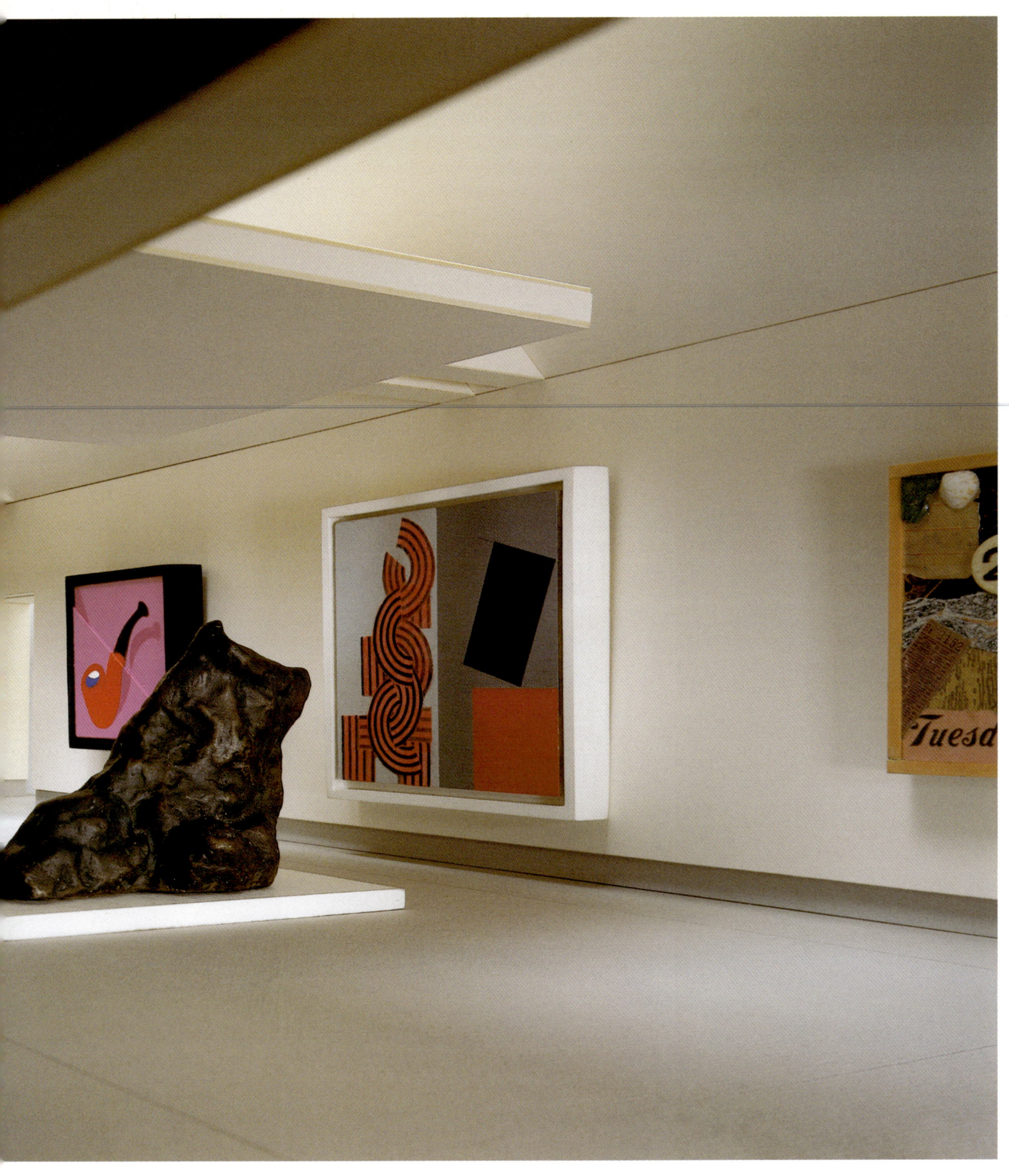

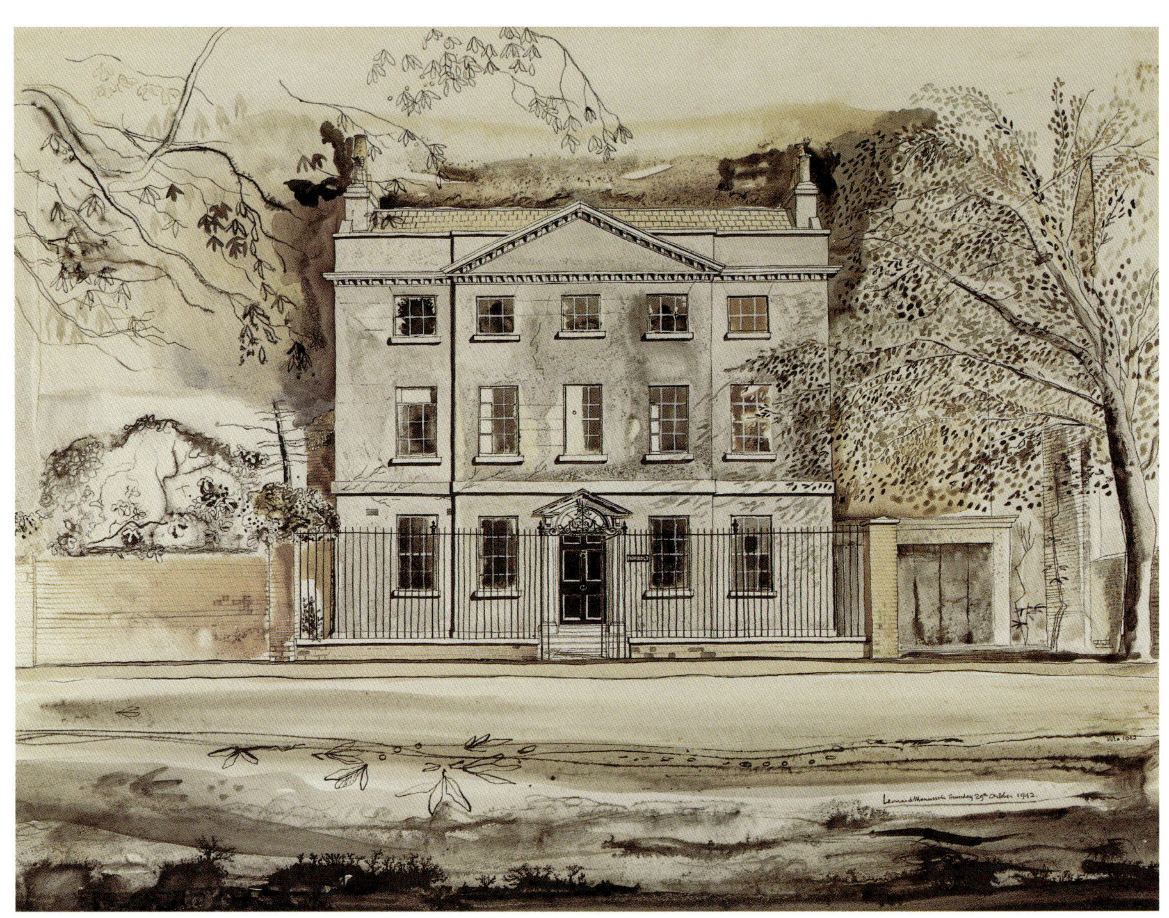

Leonard Manasseh OBE, RA
'Fairholt' Hadley Green
Ink
45 × 58 cm

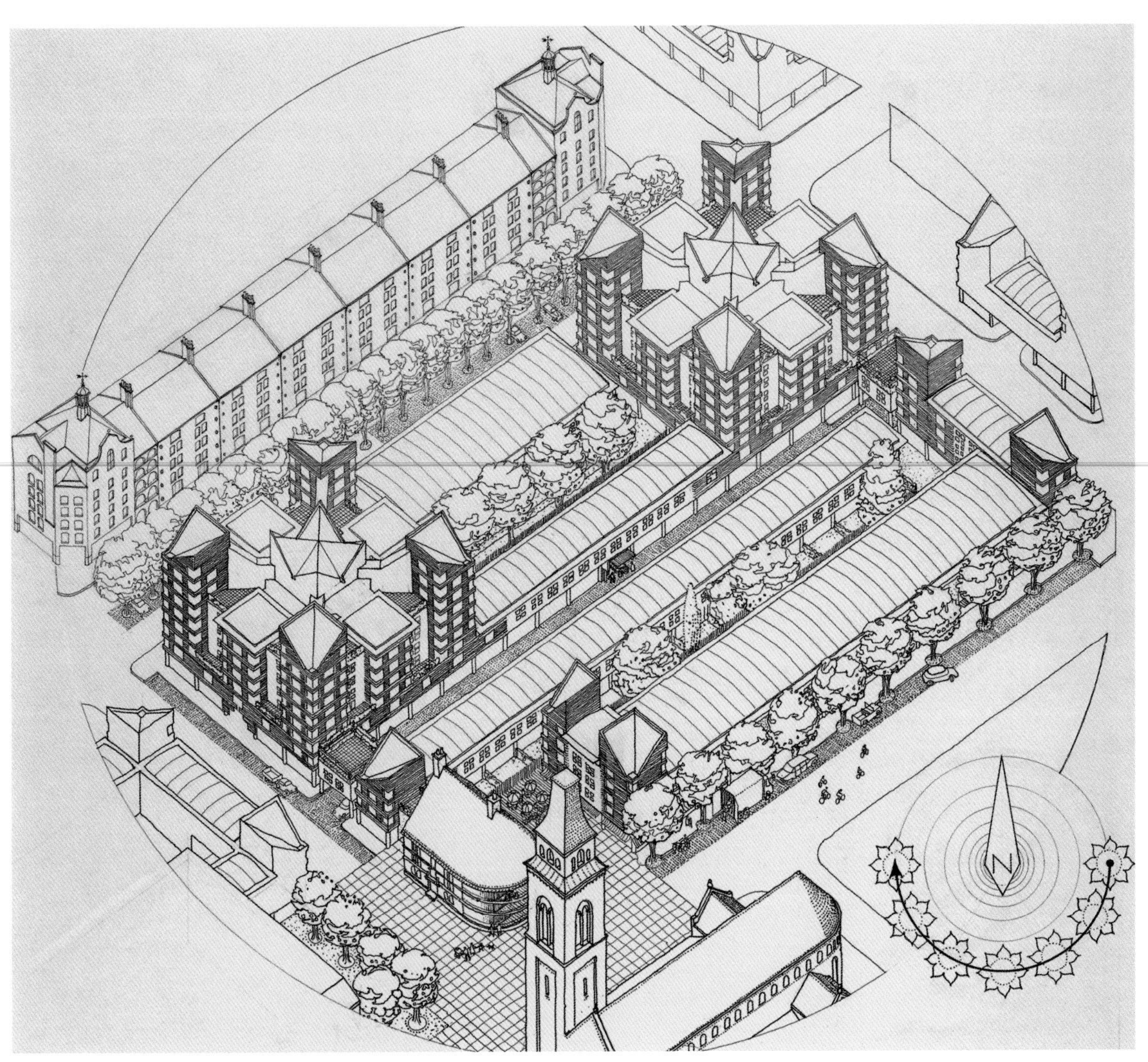

Edward Cullinan CBE, RA
Ancoats, Manchester
Ink
59 × 63 cm

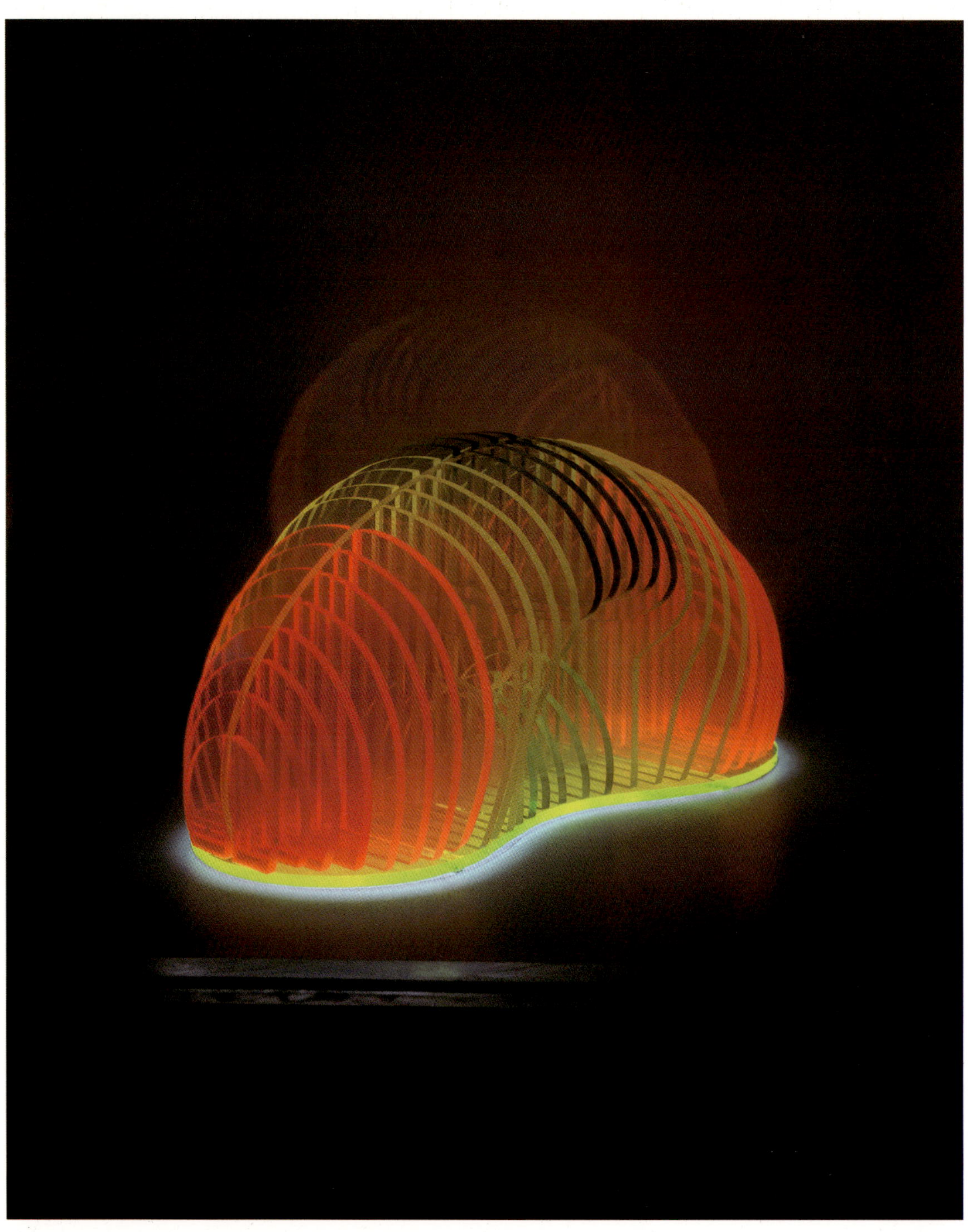

Lord Richard Rogers of Riverside RA (Richard Rogers Partnership)
12 mini models (detail: DAIWA, London)
Model
h 22 cm

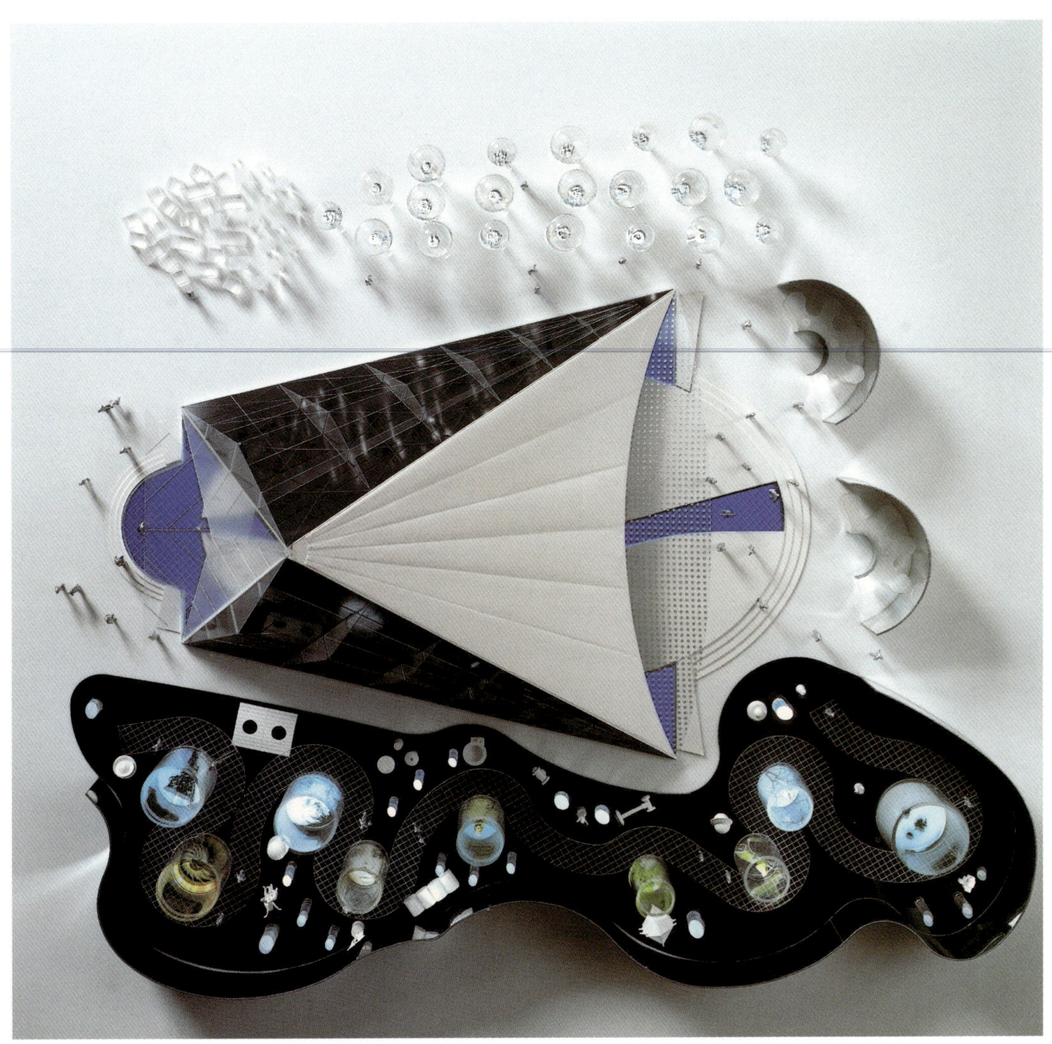

Eva Jiricna CBE, RA (Eva Jiricna Architects Limited)
Millennium Dome Exhibition, Soul Pavilion (Original Proposal)
Model
h 76 cm

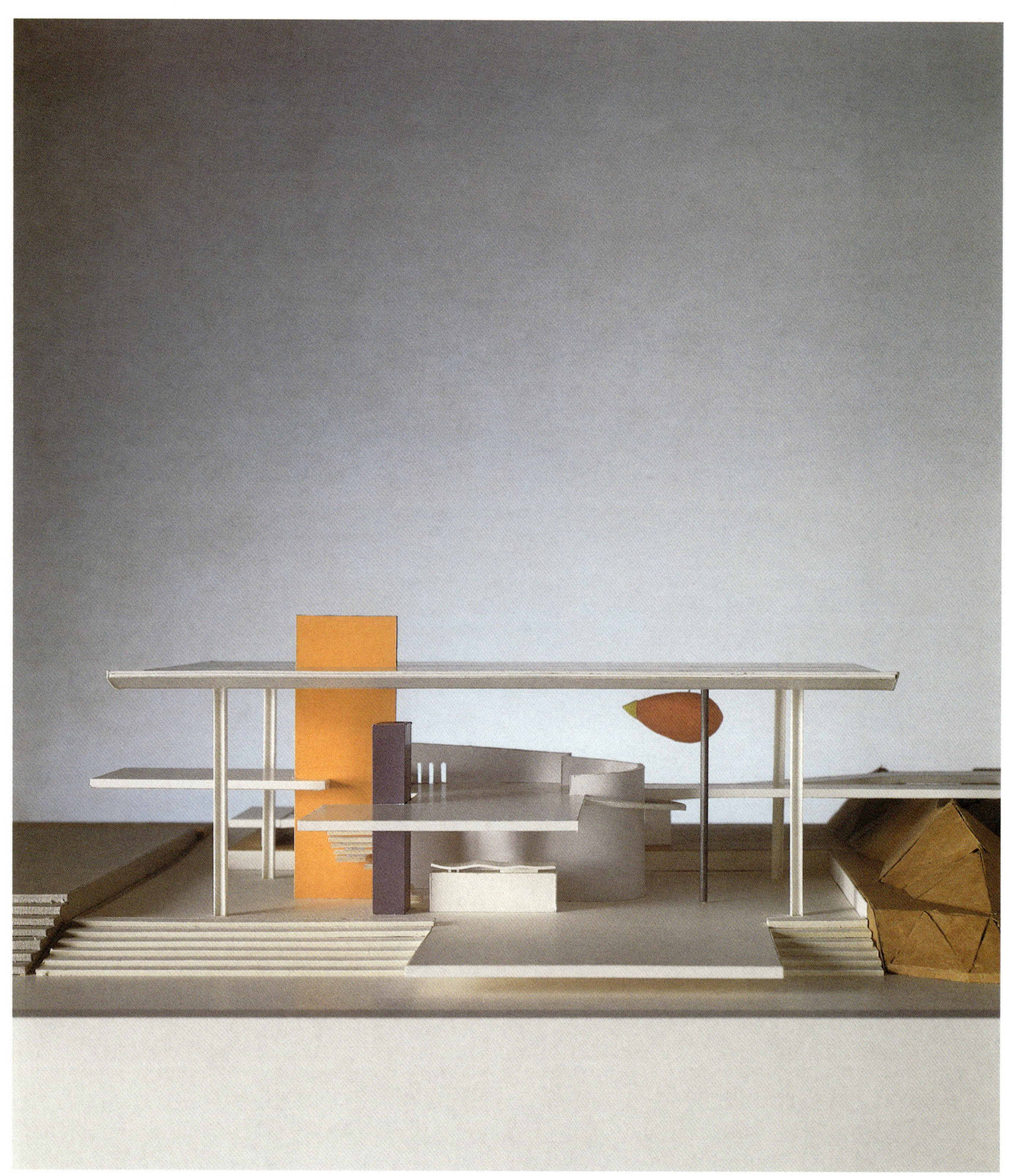

Gabriele Bramante
Tea Room and Leisure Pavilions at Pond, Worce, Weston-S-Mare
Model
h 17 cm

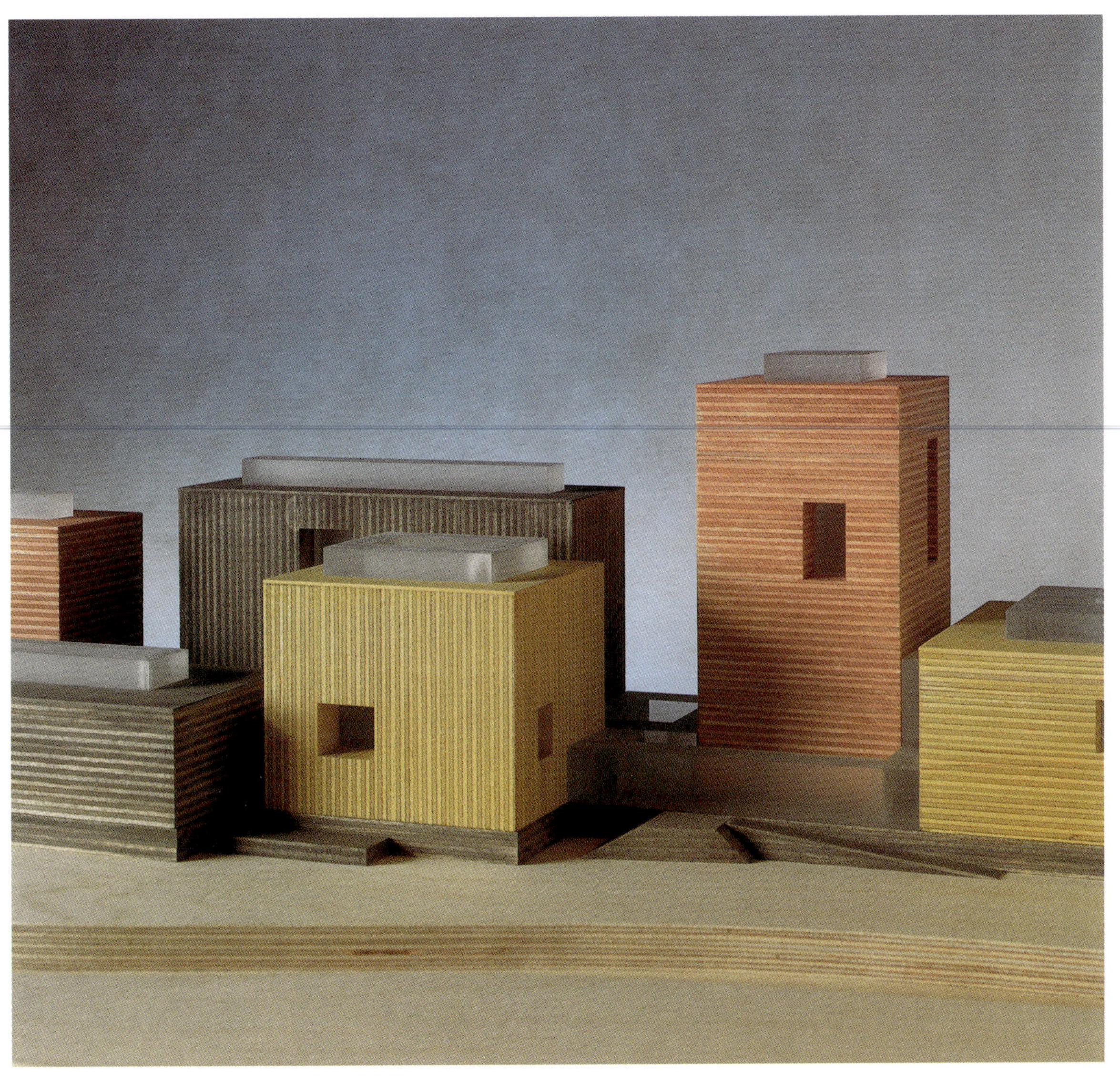

David Chipperfield Architects
Palace of Justice, Salerno, Italy (detail)
Model
h 33 cm

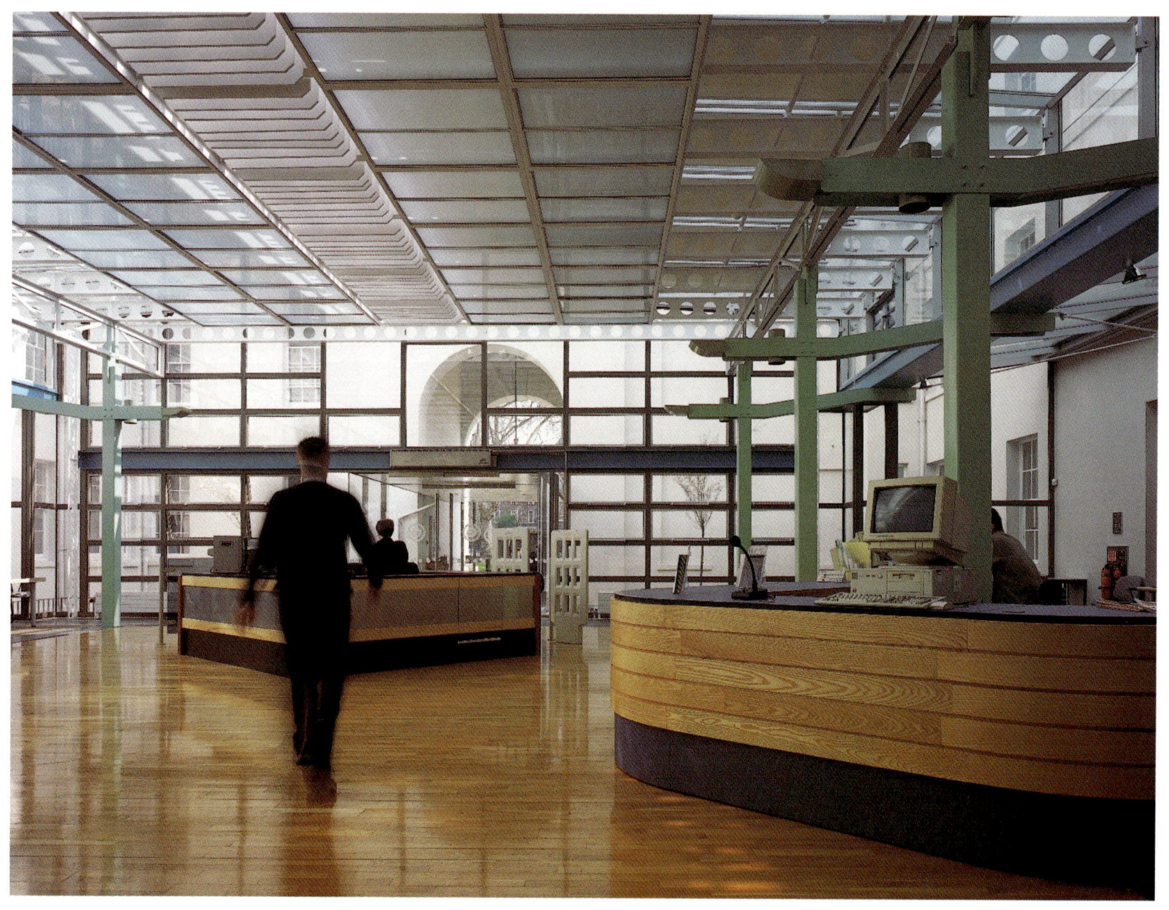

Prof. Trevor Dannatt RA (Dannatt, Johnson Architects)
University of Greenwich, Maritime Greenwich Campus, Regeneration of the Dreadnought Hospital as Library (detail)
Mixed media
84 × 73 cm

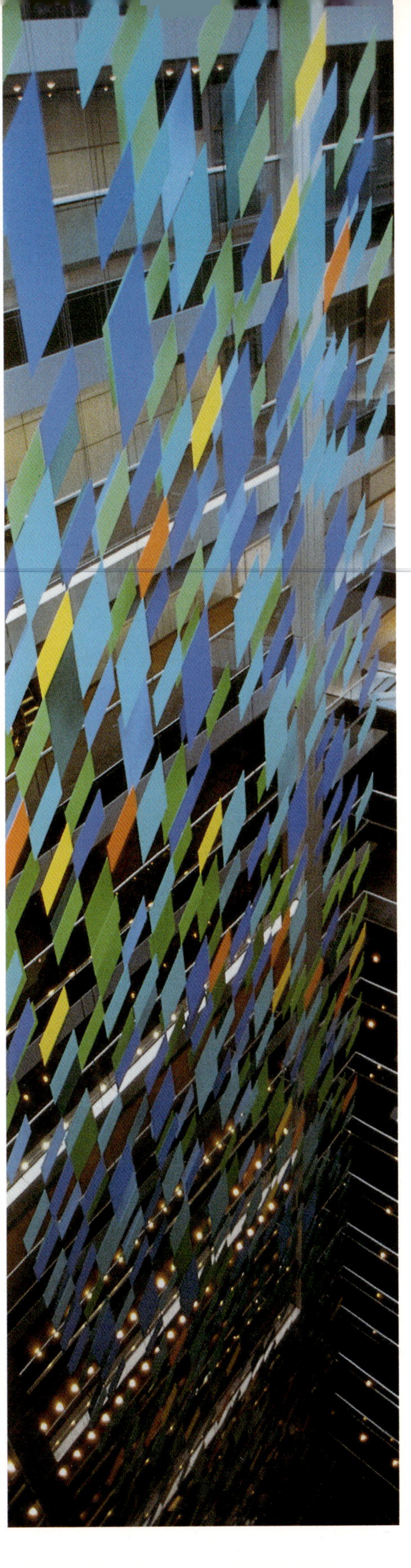

Lord Norman Foster of Thamesbank OM, RA
(Foster and Partners)
Citibank Headquarters, Canary Wharf, London; artwork by Bridget Riley (detail)
Acrylic and digital print
130 × 70 cm

LECTURE ROOM

The idea to ask the leading American abstract artist and Honorary RA Frank Stella to exhibit in the Lecture Room came initially at Tony Cragg's suggestion. 'It was very lucky for us that Stella said yes and had the time to do it', emphasises Cragg. 'These are major pieces of work and they will benefit the Summer Exhibition hugely.' Phillip King is likewise delighted, having known Stella and his work for many years. The installation consists of two canvases, together with enormous free-standing sculptures, which initially had caused the Hanging Committee some concern about the sheer mass of these works in the gallery. Stella's reply was quite emphatic: 'I believe people go to art galleries to see art, not white walls. I spent a lot of time working the arrangement out on a computer mock-up. We tried every possible configuration, taking into consideration the load bearing of the floor. I was able to walk through it virtually and I've got a good idea what it will be like. I thought the pieces looked good when I showed them in Miami, but I'm overwhelmed by how they look here in this beautiful gallery. I realise that the location of the sculptures will mean people will only get two oblique long views of the paintings and if they want to be in front they will have to be up very close but that's alright by me. I'm very pleased with the result.'

The works exhibited in this gallery by Frank Stella were brought here by the kind support of A.T. Kearney, in addition to their existing three year sponsorship of the Summer Exhibition

LECTURE ROOM

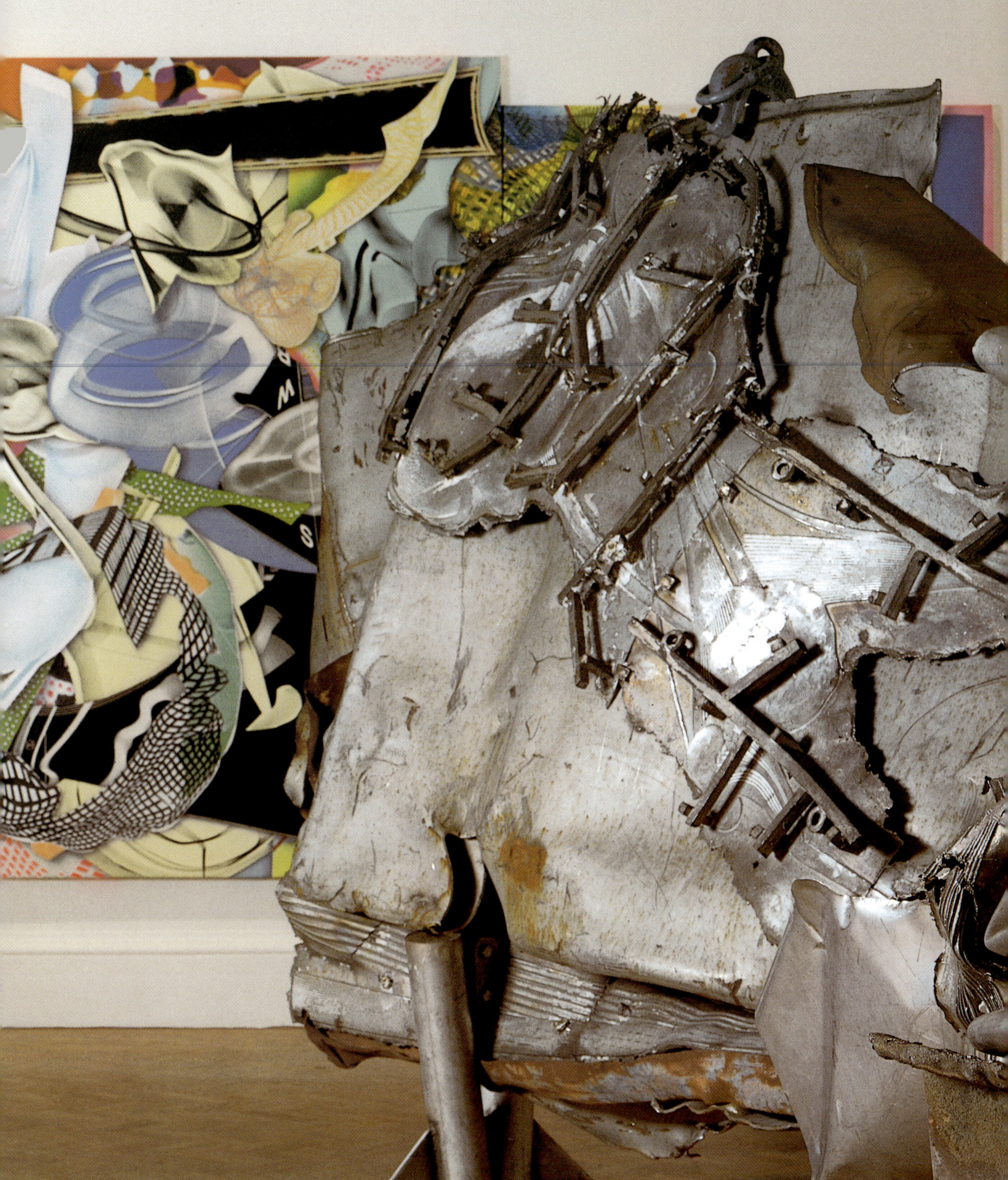

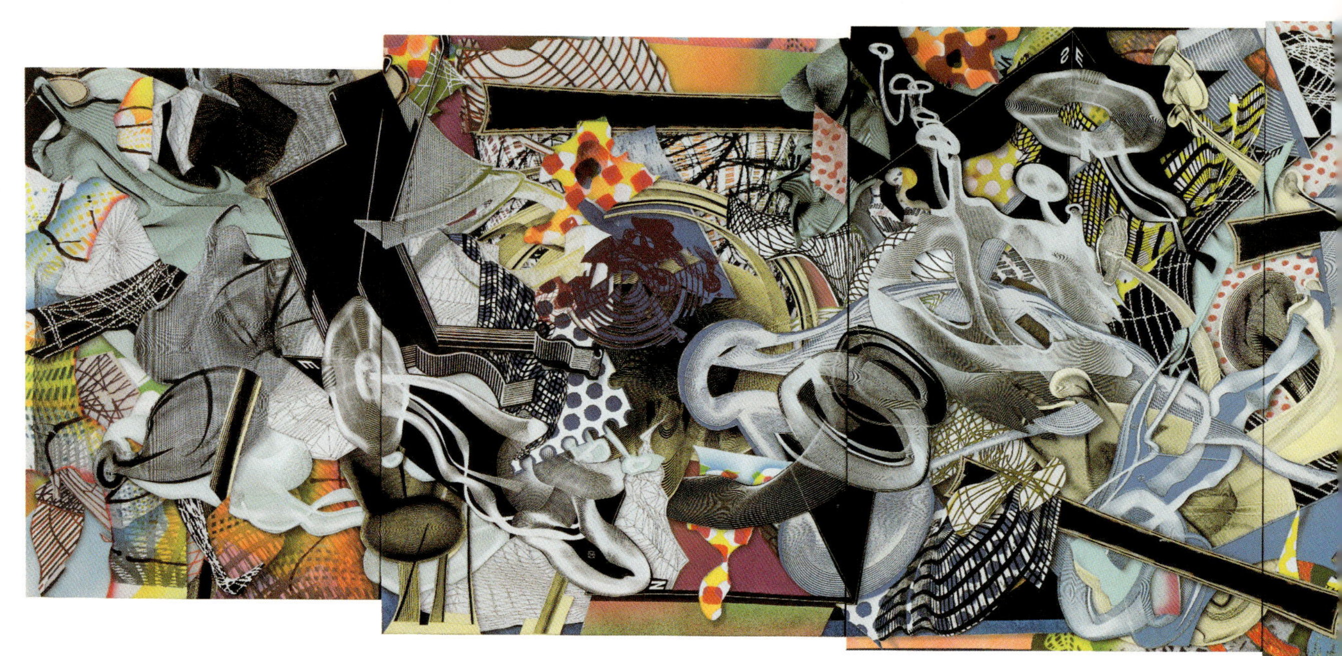

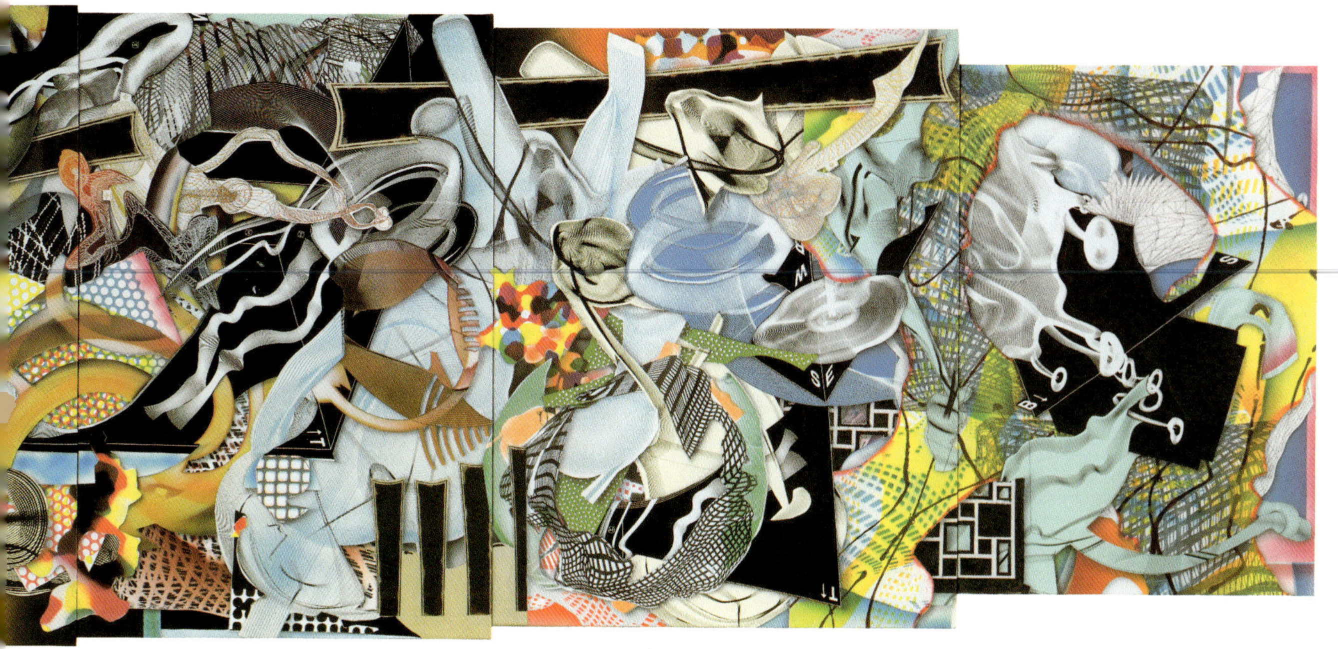

Frank Stella Hon RA
Die Marquise von O.
Acrylic
300× 1300 cm

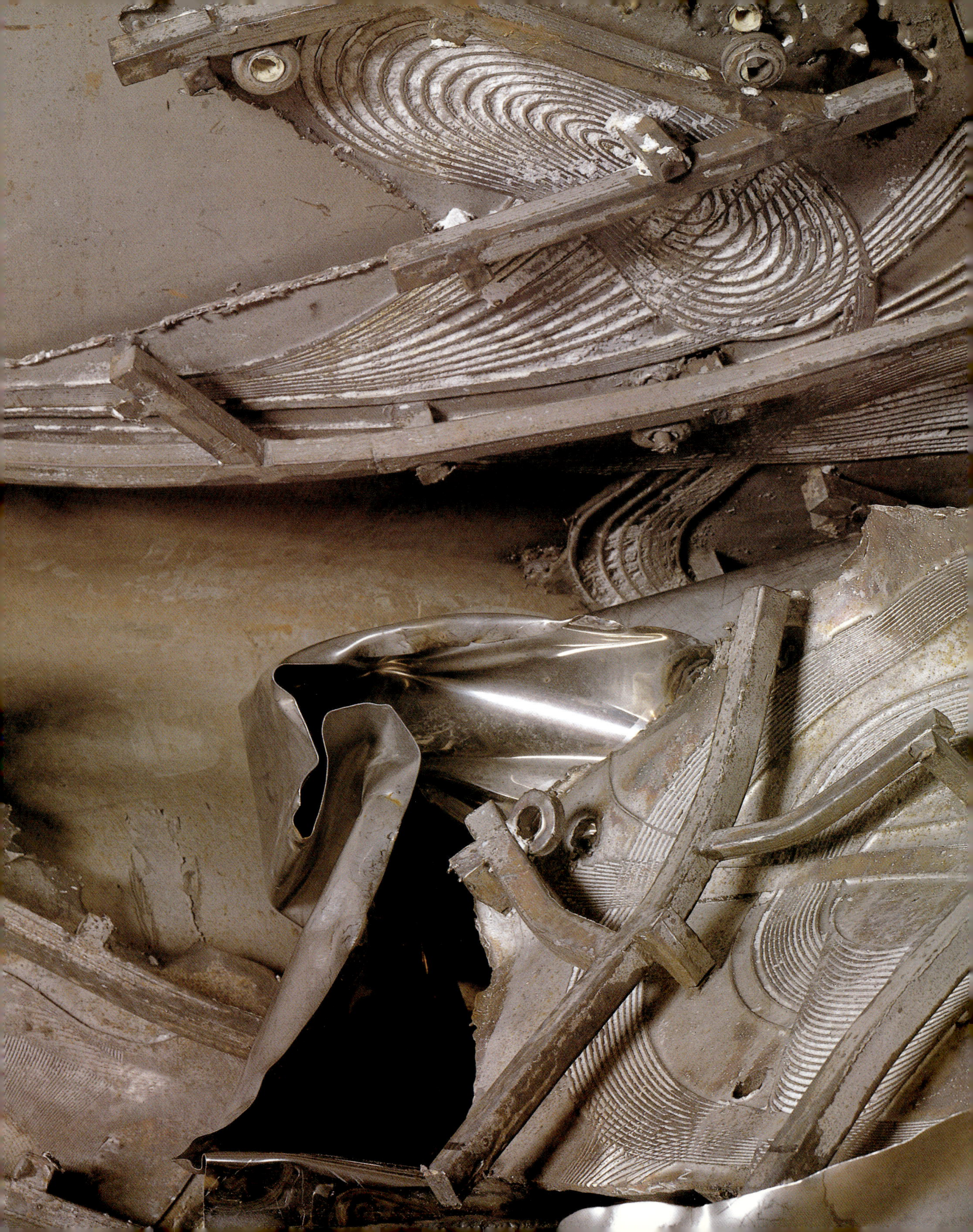

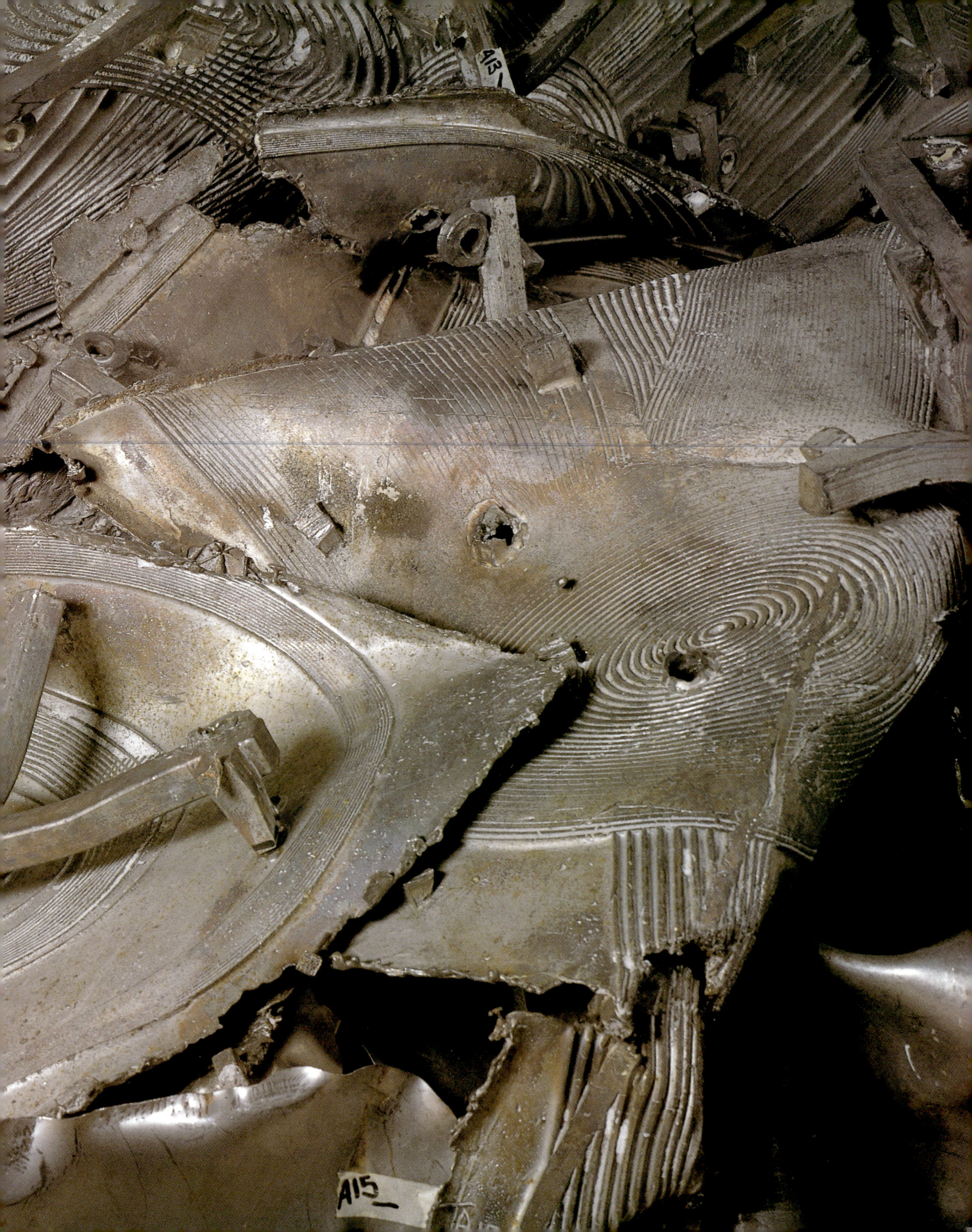
A13
A15

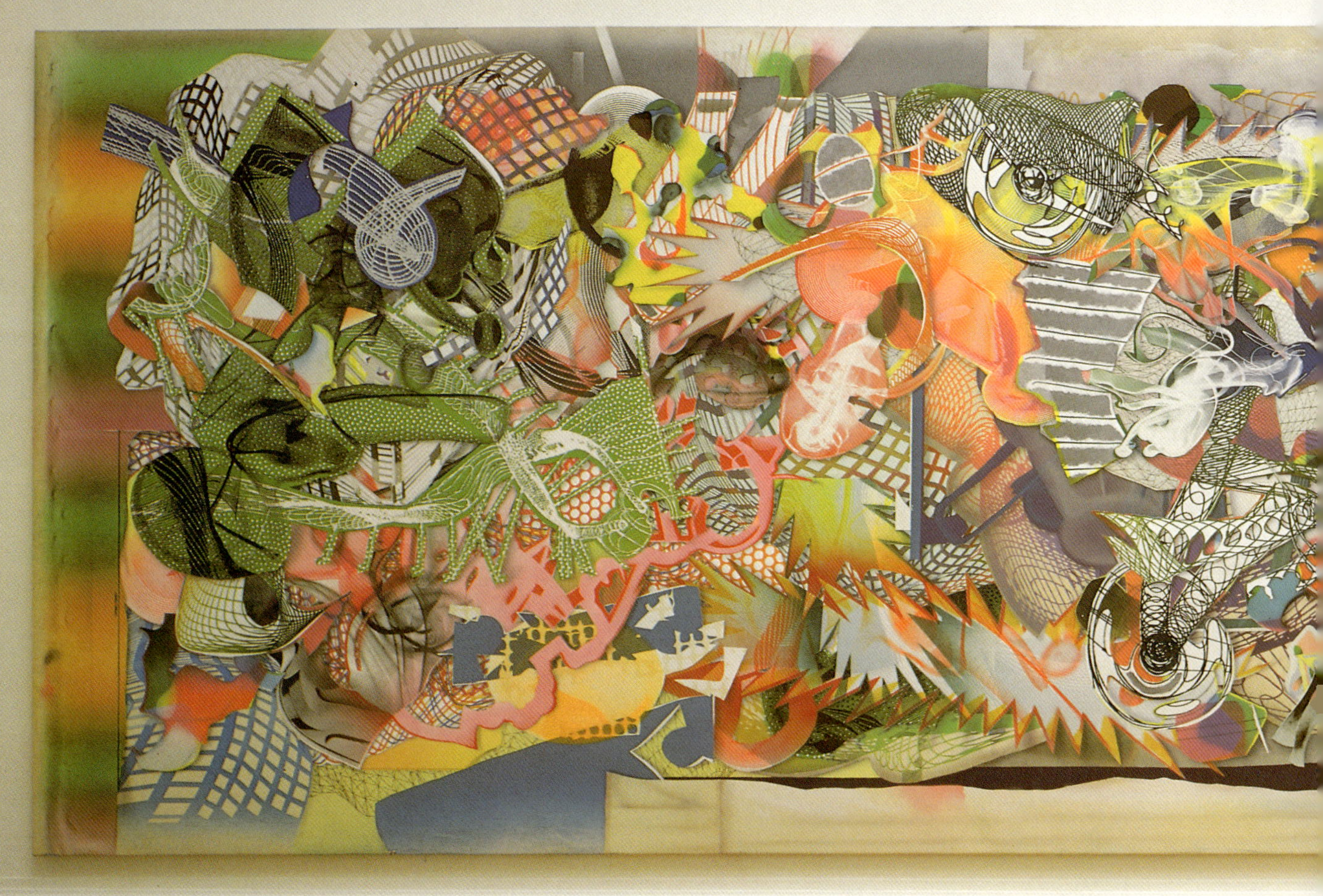

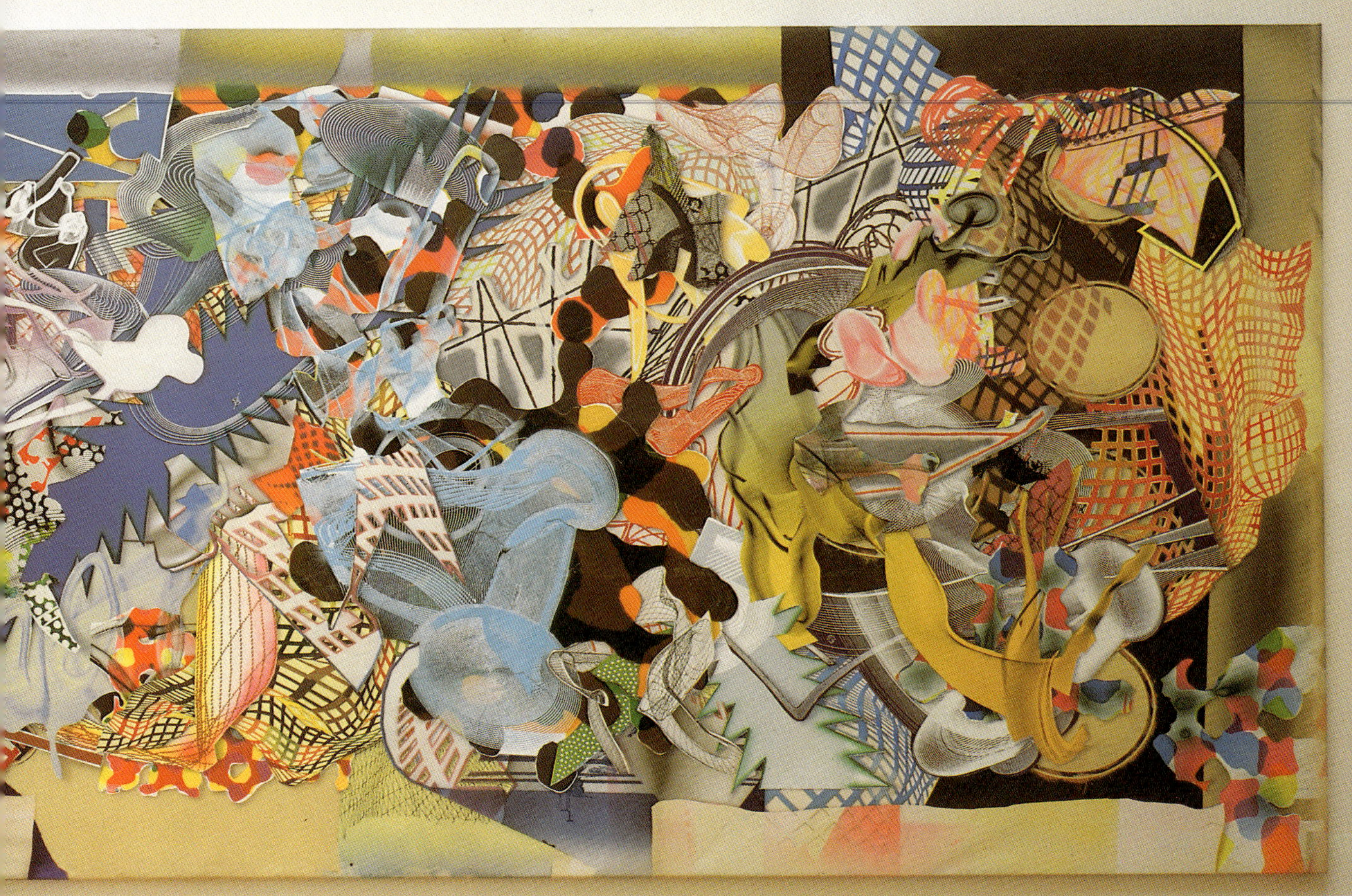

Frank Stella Hon RA
Das Erdbeden in Chile
Acrylic
300 x 1300 cm

CENTRAL HALL

The Octagon this year is hung by the two Anthonys, Green and Whishaw. 'We wanted it cool and hot, we wanted it sassy and extended', intones Green. 'And we've done it! Here we've got Hoyland, maestro of the colour statement, a whole wall of Adrian Bergs – who everybody thought was figurative but in fact whose abstract qualities are so dominant – and a new member Maurice Cockrill coming on strong here in very large reds.' ('Epistemologically correct', interposes Whishaw.) 'They are all colour dominant', says Anthony Green, 'going for your gonads with the colour'.

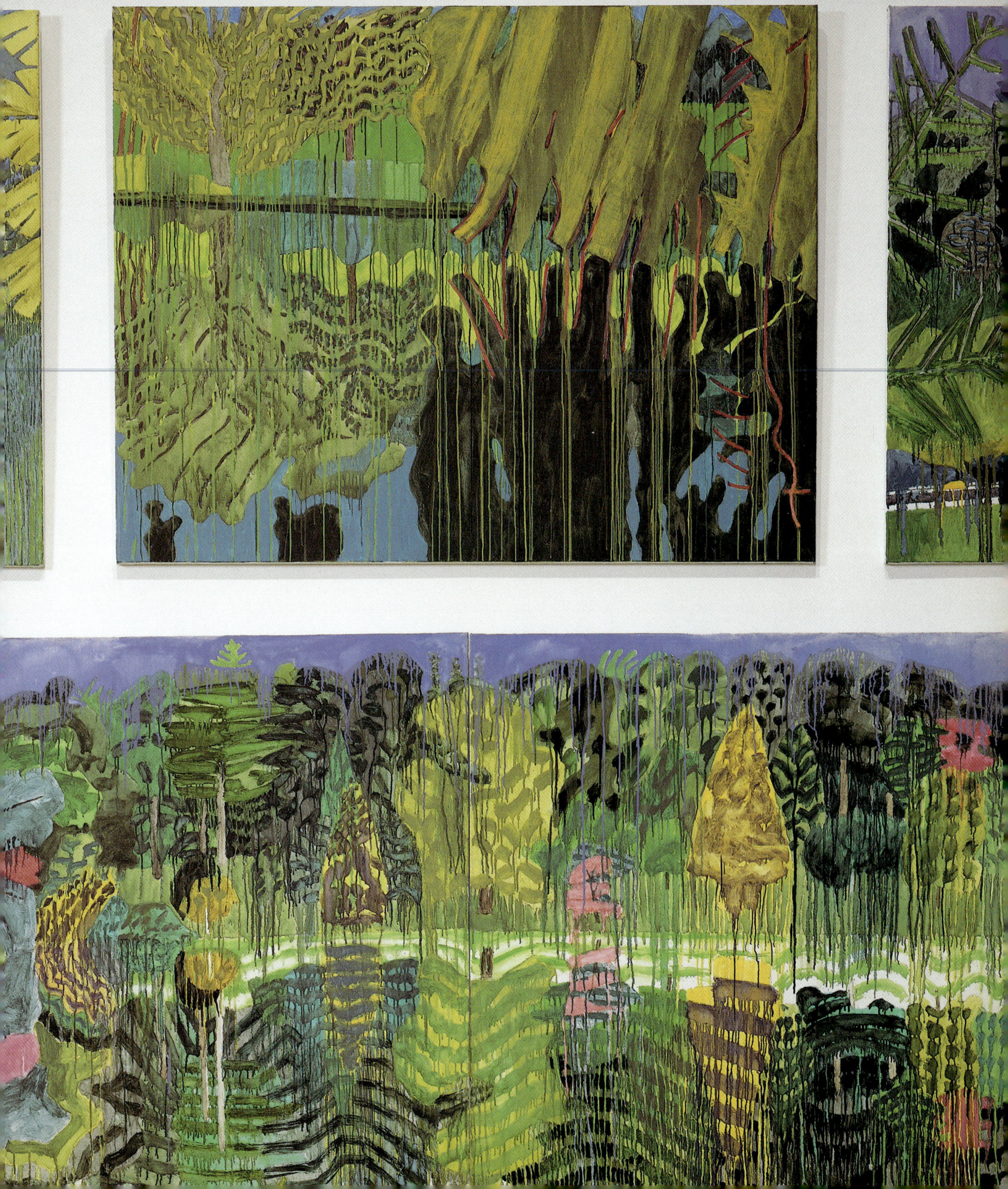

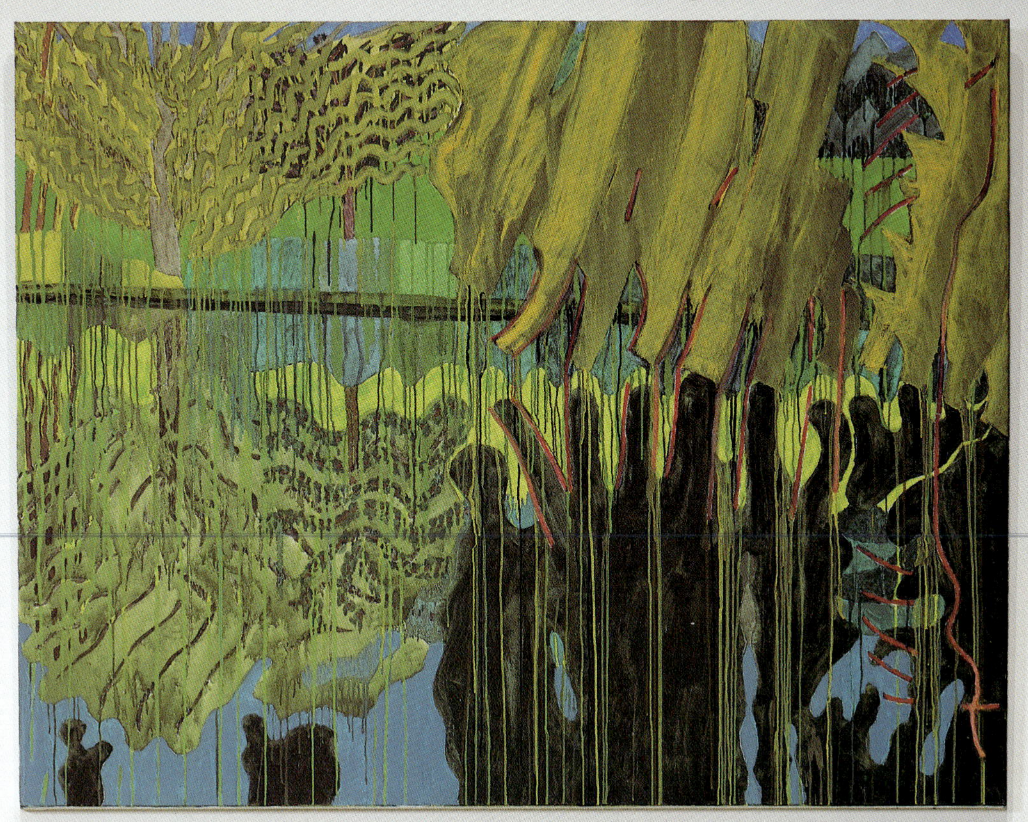

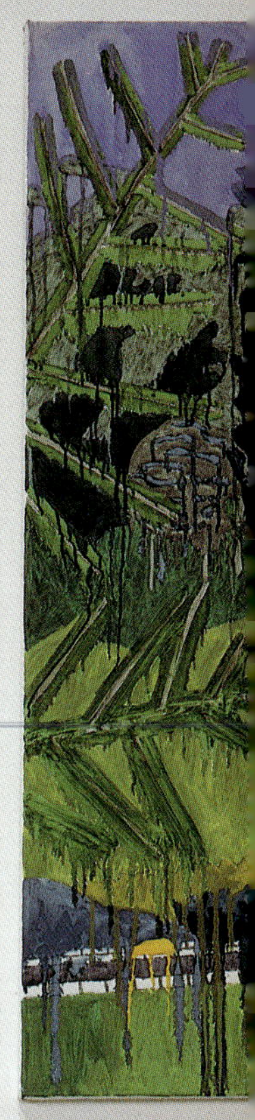

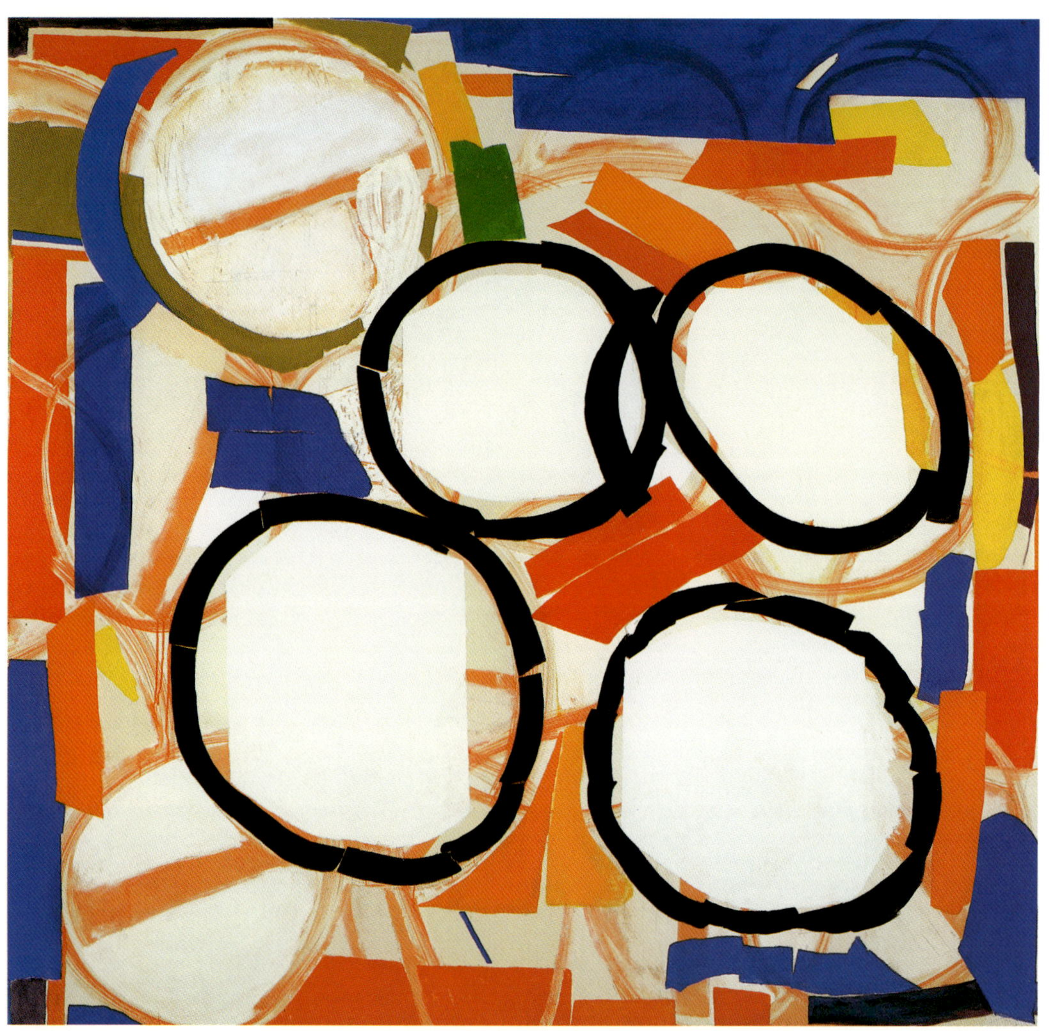

Sandra Blow RA
Circle Series (Interaction)
Acrylic
244 × 244 cm

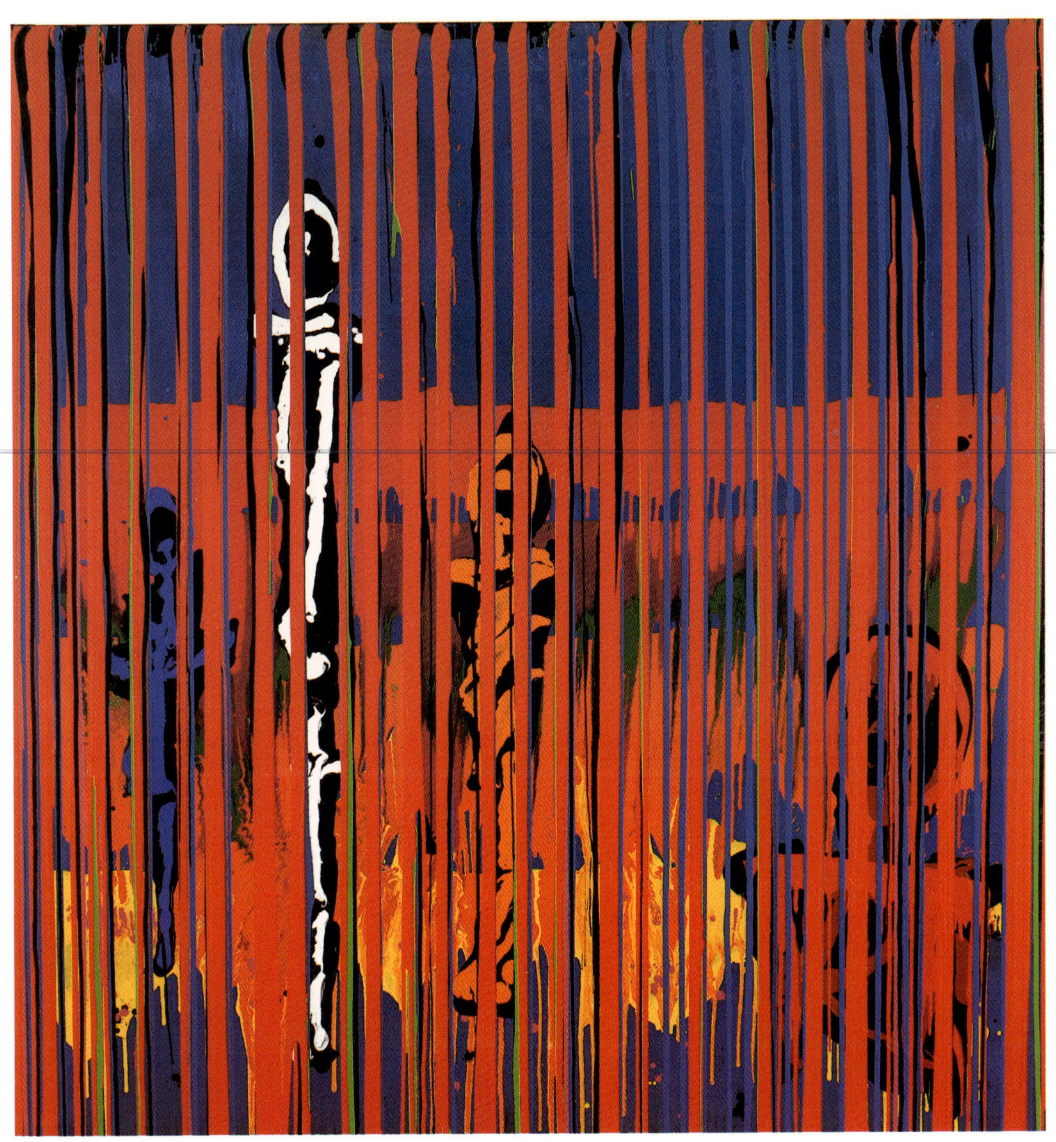

John Hoyland RA
Life of Man (Jac mel) 14.4.2000
Acrylic
254 × 236 cm

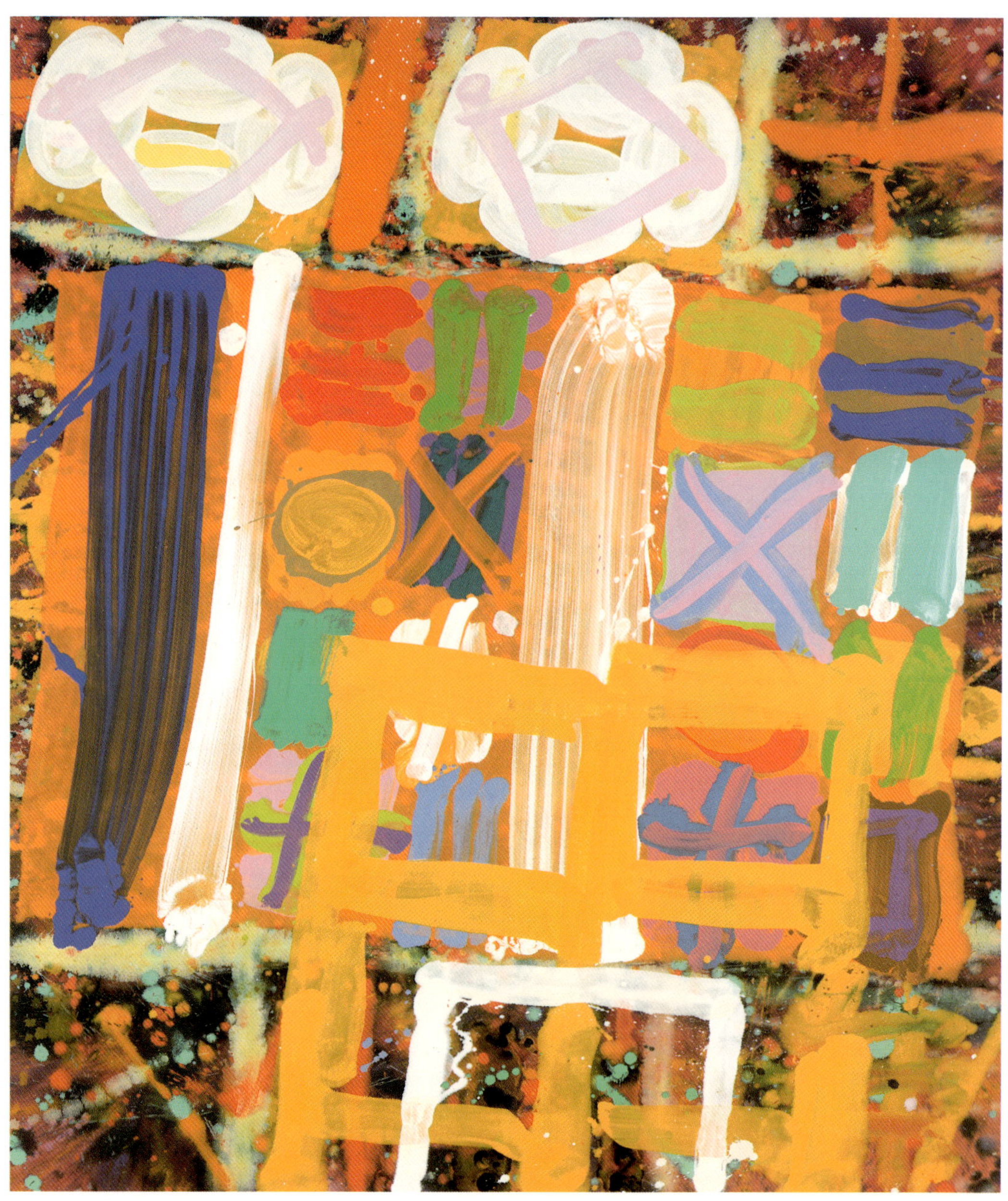

Albert Irvin RA
Redcliffe
Acrylic
183 × 153 cm

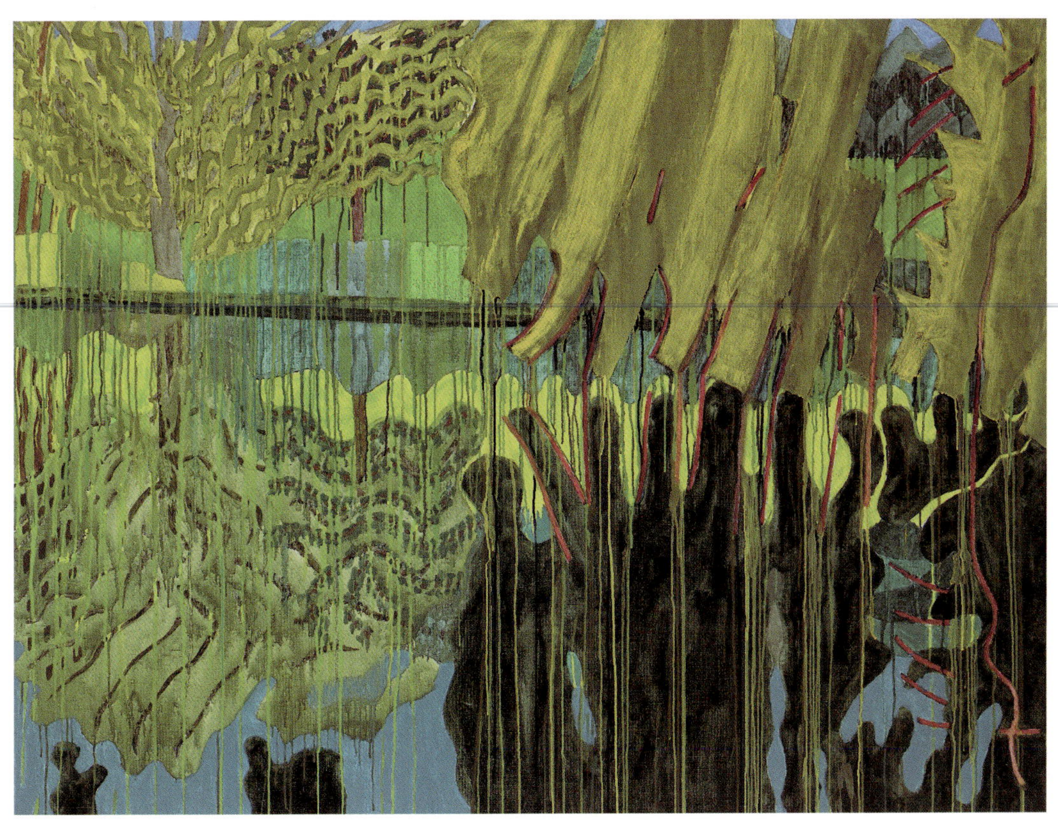

Adrian Berg RA
Abbey Grounds, Cirencester, 17 July
Oil
121 × 152 cm

Index

Royal Academy of Arts in London, 2000

Registered Charity No. 212798

The Royal Academy of Arts, Registered Charity number 212798, is Britain's founding society for promoting the creation and appreciation of the visual arts through exhibitions, education and debate. Independently led by eminent artists and architects, the Royal Academy receives no annual funding via the government, and is entirely reliant on self-generated income and charitable support.

You and/or your company can support the Royal Academy of Arts in a number of different ways

Through The Royal Academy Trust

Registered Charity No. 1067270

- The Trust was founded in 1981 to 'receive, invest and disburse funds given in support of the Royal Academy of Arts'.
- Separately, £20 million has been raised for capital projects, including the Jill and Arthur M Sackler Wing, the restoration of the Main Galleries and the re-design of the courtyard.
- Future projects include the restoration of the Fine Rooms, and the provision of better facilities for the display and enjoyment of the Academy's own Collection of important works of art and documents charting the history of British art.
- Donations from individuals, trusts, companies and foundations also help support the Academy's internationally renowned exhibition programme, the conservation of the Collection and educational projects for schools, families and people with special needs; as well as providing scholarships and bursaries for post-graduate art students in the RA Schools.
- Companies invest in the Royal Academy through arts sponsorship, corporate membership and corporate entertaining, with specific opportunities that relate to your budgets and marketing/entertaining objectives.
- A legacy is perhaps the most personal way to make a lasting contribution, through the Trust endowment fund, ensuring that the enjoyment you have derived is guaranteed for future generations to come.

☎ To find out ways in which individuals, trusts and foundations can support this work (or a specific aspect), please telephone Paul Hobson on 020 7300 5698 to discuss your personal interests and wishes.

☎ To explore ways in which companies can become involved in the work of the Academy to mutual benefit, please telephone Pamela Carswell on 020 7300 5705.

☎ To discuss leaving a legacy to the Royal Academy of Arts, please telephone Paul Hobson on 020 7300 5698.

Through Membership of the Friends

Registered Charity No. 272926

The Friends of the Royal Academy was founded in 1977 to support and promote the work of the Academy. It is now one of the largest such organisations in the world, with over 80,000 individual members. Friends' donations contribute around 20% of the Academy's total annual income.

Membership of the Friends means:

- free, flexible access to all Royal Academy exhibitions, a free quarterly colour magazine (including the extensive programme of lectures and events), the use of the popular Friends Room, the opportunity to attend previews for each exhibition and many other benefits.
- the opportunity to discover art from different countries, cultures and periods without the hassle of buying a ticket each time you visit.
- sharing the experience with your friends and family at no extra cost (one adult guest and up to four young people aged under 16 are admitted free with the Friend).
- the chance to increase your contribution as a Contributing Supporting or Patron Friend – and receive in return an invitation to exclusive evening Private Views, extra guest passes, complimentary catalogues and priority booking for the Academy's programme of lectures and events.

☎ To arrange for further details and a Friends' enrolment form to be sent to you, or to enrol immediately by credit card, please telephone 020 7300 5664/5668. (Please note that you save £5 on single membership and £10 on Joint membership by arranging to pay by Direct Debit.) You can also join on the spot at the Friends Desk in the Front Hall and begin to use your membership card immediately.

☎ To discuss the options to increase your contribution as a Contributing, Supporting or Patron Friend, please telephone Katherine Watson on 020 7300 5708.

Cover:
Die Marquise von O. (detail) by Frank Stella Hon RA

Frontispiece:
Study for a Mother Goddess by William Tucker CBE, RA

Page 6:
Sun Roots (detail) by Prof. Phillip King CBE, PRA

Page 11:
London to Paris (maquette) by Prof. Sir Eduardo Paolozzi CBE, RA

Page 13–15:
London to Paris (details) by Prof. Sir Eduardo Paolozzi CBE, RA

Page 41:
After Rubens II (detail) by John Hubbard

Page 63:
Flowers for Mary by Philip Medley

Page 109:
Circus: (Study) (detail) by Gus Cummins RA

Page 121:
Pyramid, Sphere, Cube (detail) by David Nash RA

Page 129:
Jerusalem, the Eternal City (detail) by Ben Johnson

Pages 130–131:
Wall in gallery VII showing the paintings with their labels ready for cataloguing

Page 157:
Mahorbier! Good Night (detail) by Philip Sutton RA

Page 167:
12 mini models (detail) by Richard Rogers Partnership

Pages 181, 184–185:
Chatal Huyuk Level VII, 1999 (detail) by Frank Stella Hon RA

Published by the Royal Academy of Arts

British Library Cataloguing-in-Publication Data.
A catalogue record for this book is available from the British Library

ISBN 0 900 946 903

Editorial co-ordinators Nick Tite and Carola Krueger
Catalogue designed by Herman Lelie
Colour reproduction Dawkins Colour
Photography FXP Photography and John Riddy
Photographs on pages 13–15 by Phil Sayer

The making of the Pallant House model was generously supported by John Jones Art Centre, London.

Typeset by Stefania Bonelli
Production co-ordinator Uwe Kraus
Printed in Italy